NGATI DREAD

Volume Two
No Dreadlocks No Cry

ANGUS GILLIES

Rogue Monster Books

ISBN 978-0-473-15164-5

Dedication

For my wife Tui,
my sons Rogie, Pele
and Cassius and my
daughter Aroha

Acknowledgements

The author would like to thank everyone who was willing to be interviewed, all the family and friends who supported him during this project, particularly his wife Tui for the cover art and his father Iain for accompanying him on some of the interviews and the staff and management of The Gisborne Herald newspaper, which allowed the use of its photos and archives.

**SOME OF THE CHARACTERS & INTERVIEWEES
IN VOLUMES ONE & TWO**

Danny Batchelor: Police Photographer
Sonny Brown: Rasta Hamana Brown's dad
Chris Bunyan: Policeman and former schoolmate of Chris Campbell
Barney (Pani) Campbell: Former Ruatoria policeman and Chris's brother
Chris Campbell: Rasta leader
Ike Campbell: Chris's brother
Joe "Boots" Campbell: Chris's brother
Gary Condon: Former police officer
David Conway: Gisborne Herald reporter
Luke Donnelly: Shot Chris Campbell dead
Russell Fairbrother: Napier lawyer
Pop Gage (Hori Keeti): Late tohunga, who prophesied the coming of a great spiritual leader on the East Coast
Jimbo Grace (Maku Turei): One of three men convicted of burning down Robbie Grace's house
Robbie Grace: Ruatoria man who was jailed for murder
Norm Gray: Former head cop in Ruatoria
Rex Harrison: Former Gisborne CIB detective with family ties to the Rastas
Cody Haua: Rasta, kidnapped Laurie Naden
John (Hone) Heeney: Campbell's right hand man in the Rastas
Tom Heeney: Ruatoria deputy fire chief and John's dad
Hemi Hikawai: Former CIB detective who investigated most of the Ruatoria crimes
Lyn Hillock: Former Gisborne deputy fire chief
Tiger (Tika) Hongara: Rasta
Gallace Hongara: Rasta
Alex Hope: Former head cop in Ruatoria
Hughie Hughes: Pakeha electrician in Ruatoria
Dion Hutana: Rasta convicted of burning down Ngati Porou Marae
Bob Kaa: Neighbourhood Support Group ("The Vigilantes")
Hone Kaa: Priest and expert witness on Maori culture in Joe Nepe's murder trial
Brett Kane: Policeman accused of assault against a Rasta
Sammy Keelan: Rasta

Hori Keeti (Pop Gage): Late tohunga, who prophesied the coming of a great spiritual leader on the East Coast
Cyrus Kennedy: Rasta accused of arson
Denis Kohn: Gisborne lawyer
Eddie Kotuhi: Escaped from jail with Dion Hutana, was there when the marae was burned
Lance Kupenga: Was beheaded by Joe Nepe
Paetene Kupenga: Lance's dad
Bruce Laing: Former Ruatoria traffic officer
Jonathan McClutchie: Rasta accused of arson, also accused police of assault
Stu McEwen: Former head of New Zealand CIB
Ken McKinnon: Ruatoria Fire Chief
Bob Marley: Late Rastafarian singer/songwriter
David Mataira: Accused of arson, along with John Heeney
Graeme Mathieson: "Vigilante" accused of burning down John Heeney's house
Dick Maxwell: Rastafarian who claimed he was kidnapped and assaulted by police
Eruera Ranfurly "Tuck" Morice: Rasta who was accused of arson
Laurie Naden: Former CIB detective kidnapped by Rastas
Dave Neilson: Policeman accused in Dick Maxwell case
Joe Nepe: Rasta who beheaded fellow Rasta Lance Kupenga
Eric Newman: Policeman accused of assault against a Rasta
Sue Nikora: Early influence on the Rastas
Junior Paul: Friend of the Rastas, who became their victim
Whiro Ratahi: Former Deputy Commander in Gisborne police
Raewyn Rickard: Beau Tuhura's sister
John Robinson: Former policeman respected by Rastas and colleagues
Haile Selassie: Late Emperor of Ethiopia, considered the Second Coming by Rastafarians
Gordon Sutton: Childhood friend of Chris Campbell
Sarah Sykes: Secretary of Te Poho-Te-Aowera Marae, south of Ruatoria
Victor Takarangi: One of the main "vigilantes"
Te Kooti Arikirangi Te Turuki: 19th century rebel prophet, founder of Ringatu church
Ed Te Rauna: Former Rasta

Malcolm Thomas: Policeman accused in the Dick Maxwell case
Chris Thompson: Hata's brother
Hata Thompson: Rasta, kidnapped Laurie Naden
Laura Thompson: Hata's mum (Aunty Ga-ga)
Steve Tresidder: Former Ruatoria policeman
Tony Tuhou: Rasta accused of arson, also accused police of assault
Beau Tuhura: One of the early Rasta leaders
Brett Waihi: Rasta accused of arson
Hurae Wairau: Rasta convicted of burning down Ngati Porou Marae
Kate Walker: Aunty of Rasta John Heeney (victim of arson)
Glynn Walker Findlay: Policeman who helped interview Joe Nepe before his arrest
Genevieve Westcott: TV current affairs reporter
Mike Wilkinson: Policeman accused in the Dick Maxwell case
Colin Williams: Pakeha farmer, member of pioneer family
Jeremy Williams: Pakeha farmer, member of pioneer family
Peter Williams: Auckland defence lawyer for Joe Nepe
Stuart Williams: Pakeha farmer, member of pioneer family
Paul Wiseman: Former Gisborne Police Commander

WELCOME

Beau Tuhura, former Ruatoria Rastafarian: All the Rastas are connected to Te Aowera Marae. Te Aowera means The World of Fire.

Sarah Sykes, secretary of the marae: Everyone keeps calling it Te Aowera. But it's not. It's actually Te Poho o Te Aowera. That means the bosom - or the heart - of the world of fire.

Lyn Hillock, former Gisborne Deputy Fire Chief: My boss back then Ian Clark and I used to read a magazine called Fire International. It's an American magazine and it gave us a real insight into events like the Watts riots and the contingency plans for the brigades. But we never, ever, in our wildest dreams thought we'd have to implement those procedures used by the Los Angeles Fire Department in New Zealand, let alone in a little place like Ruatoria. But we did. I always wanted to visit this other fire station that dealt with a notoriously tough area of the Bronx in New York. But I didn't need to. It came to me in the guise of the Ruatoria Rastafarians.

THE STORY SO FAR

From 1985 to 1990 the small town of Ruatoria on the East Coast of New Zealand was terrorised by a sect calling itself the Rastafarians.

The group was made up of ex-Black Power and Mongrel Mob members who belonged to an extended family based in the Whareponga/Hiruharama area just south of the township.

The Rastas mixed Rastafarianism from Jamaica with local beliefs and prophecies and the Ringatu religion started by the 19th century Maori warrior prophet Te Kooti and came up with something totally radical and unique. It was predicted locally that a spiritual leader would arise in Ruatoria and I believe that some of the Rastas, including Chris Campbell, John Heeney and Beau Tuhura, believed it might be them.

The Rastas started out cutting the fences of farms belonging to the Williams family, who were descended from early Anglican missionaries and who, over time, had acquired large tracts of land on the East Coast. The Rastas had been led to believe that one hundred-year leases had expired on this land and they wanted the Williams family out.

The Rastas' mission was to clear the area of all Pakeha farmers and to have the land returned to its original Ngati Porou owners.

Soon, as well as cutting fences, they were burning down buildings. Haysheds, houses, and the police station cum courthouse were burnt down. The townsfolk, the fire fighters and the police wondered what would be next. The Rastas were also busy thieves and cannabis growers.

But the police struggled to get any convictions. The Rastas, led by Campbell and Heeney, were far too crafty and clever.

But there were problems within the group. One Rasta beheaded another. A young man who befriended the Rastas had the "devil beaten out of him". A horse, which the Rastas claimed they were trying to break in, died after being dragged behind their car. Chris Campbell, Hata Thompson and Cody Haua were jailed for kidnapping Detective Sergeant Laurie Naden.

By now the Rastas weren't just targeting Pakeha farmers, but everyone who represented the establishment and even Maori they believed had slighted them. The locals had just about had enough. A

PART 4
RUATORIA BURNING

CHAPTER 1

A RASTA'S HOUSE IS HIT

On the night of Saturday, February 22, 1986, hours after the forestry fire and Chris Campbell's arrest for kidnapping Laurie Naden, there's another arson, a house fire. But this one's different to all the others: there are people inside.

Interestingly, those people are Rastafarians: John and Donna Heeney and their small son. Luckily, they manage to get away before the flames really take hold.

The fire brigade is called to the house in the Crossroads area of Ruatoria at about midnight. John Heeney is arrested on a warrant relating to another matter.

The fifty to sixty-year-old house is destroyed in the fire.
So why was John Heeney targeted? In an interview in November, 2000, Rasta Joe Nepe said that John Heeney, David "Scooby" Mataira and "Diesel" Dick Maxwell were the Rastas' main fire-starters. Joe wasn't dobbing his mates in. He just mentioned it in passing. The people behind the burning of Heeney's house had probably heard those names bandied around, too.

John Heeney: When Chris took Laurie Naden hostage on the hill the Senior Sergeant John Robinson, Robbie Robinson, come down. (To Donna): Remember that one that busted us two o'clock in the morning one day at the shed, one night at the shanty. Him and all his hoods pulled in and I told them to fuck off, ay. (To me): They were wanting to come and search our place. I don't know what they were looking for but just to put pressure on. And he come up to me and he

said they were gonna clear the area and shoot through. That was the
order.

Q: When was this?

This was the same time Chris took Laurie Naden hostage on the
hill.

Aw yeah.

See they burnt our house down the same time.

They burnt your house?

This one over here, me and Donna were in. Same time.

So who do you reckon would-a burnt that down?

Aw, this white man, young fulla. They caught him, took him to
court, found him not guilty, reckoned he was illiterate, didn't know what
he was doing.

Was he a local guy, or?

Yeah, yeah.

So he took it in his own hands to...

He'd had all his prize Arabs stolen, ay.

Horses?

The boys had stolen their horses, ay. Yeah.

Donna Heeney, John's wife: He was really just a runner, cos he
was only seventeen, eighteen, ay, that boy. He was more or less the
bum-boy. The vigilantes dropped him off. His mum and dad are called
Mathieson.

**Genevieve Westcott, the Close Up current affairs
programme, March 1986:** It's a Wild West way of life that's horrified
local farmers. They say the trouble all began with fence-cutting and
horse rustling. For city people that might not sound like much, but for
country folk like the Mathiesons, it's driving them off the land.

The Mathiesons say they've lost a lot of horses to the Rastas.
Only one has ever been recovered. This family is now facing financial
ruin.

Genevieve: When's it all going to end?

Margaret Mathieson: One doesn't know.

Allan Mathieson: One doesn't know.

Margaret: The mare we got back just about wasn't worth owning
when we got her back. She was blinded. Her four feet were bleeding
when we got her back. There were rope burns all round her feet and
legs, leg cuts from where she'd been running through the manuka, a big

long raw patch on her back where the saddle had been sitting incorrectly, scars all round the face and the head, and both eyes were blind.

Genevieve: To you, a horse is not just another animal is it?

Allan: No.

Margaret: No, they're your mate. You look at a man who goes on the hill mustering stock. He's got no one to talk to. All he's got is his dogs and his horses. And they become his mates. And no one wants to see anything that you love get hurt.

John Heeney: The Takarangi was the dude that dropped the young Mathieson fulla off. V.J. Takarangi… fuck 'e's another arsehole over here. He's a teacher, V.J., but you don't forget these things, ay. They set our house on fire, midnight.

They did?

Me, my missus and our baby were inside.

Donna: Well, he was the one that drove the vehicle, but that boy was the one that got in the car and did the deed. And he picked the boy up in his vehicle.

John: Pakeha fulla. Mathieson.

Victor Takarangi, Neighbourhood Support Group, on the Close Up programme: It's really frustrating. We see the cops grab these scum of the town – and I mean that – drag'm away to the courts only to see the cop van coming back and these young fullas are just in the car ahead of them all the way into town. That brasses us right off.

Donna Heeney: But they deny it to this day, you know, after they got away with it back then. They still think the same.

John Heeney: The young guy Mathieson denies it but he made a statement that he did it.

To the cops?

And he said in his statement that I offended his girlfriend. I don't even know the dude's girlfriend. Haven't seen her in my life. What's her name? Plews, or something. Aw fuck I don't even know the girl. Never heard of her in my life. Anyway, they burnt this down. Come in, phht.

Burnt it?

Burnt it to the ground.

Donna: After the arsons on the hay barns and all that.

John: They locked me away. I was watching the house burning down and the cops came and dragged me away and I didn't come back until eighteen months later.

Donna: It was after that old courthouse got burnt down. Then they came and did the deed on this.

Far out.

John: So we went and did the deed on that.

Ha, ha.

And that, and that, and that, and that. We were wanting to do it on *him* but he wasn't there when the brothers turned up.

Tuesday, February 25: *Graeme Mathieson is arrested in Ruatoria at midday, and charged with the arson of Rastafarian John Heeney's house at the Crossroads. Mathieson appears in Gisborne District Court at 4pm. He's remanded on bail and is given name suppression.*

Genevieve Westcott on the Close Up programme: Within forty-eight hours police make a dramatic arrest. Charged with arson, an eighteen-year-old shepherd officially on duty with night patrol at the time of the torching. His parents are stunned.

Allan Mathieson: I don't think he done it.

Genevieve: You don't think he did it?

Allan: No.

Genevieve: What if it's proven though in court that he did do it?

Margaret Mathieson: I still have reservations.

Genevieve: Can you understand why he might do something like that though? Could you explain it to me?

Allan: Well if they drove him to it by pinching his horses like they did well perhaps he did.

Margaret: They constantly hassled him.

Genevieve: Now when you went to see your son today at the police station, what did you say to him?

Margaret: That his mother still loves him.

Allan: There's not much else you can say.

Margaret: Irrespective of what has happened, I still love him.

Q: Is there any sort of background of fires and all that, like old stories...

John Heeney: In Ruatoria?

In Ruatoria, or old stories that you guys have heard about fires?

Yeah. The last township of Ruatoria burnt down. Down Tuparoa. Burnt to the ground. Whole township. Phht.

What was that?

Ruatoria used to be at Tuparoa before here.

Is that at the beach or something?

Yeah. That's where the town was, down there. Then it burnt to the ground. And they built it over here.

Donna: First Ruatoria was down on the coast, for the shipping.

John: I'll tell you this, Angus: you know what Ruatoria means?

What?

The murderous pit of Toria.

Murderous pit of Toria?

Yeah. Rua: that's where you store your kai in.

Yeah.

And a murder went down. And along came the slave called Toria. She was the slave girl of the kuia down here in Mangahanea, Hine Tapora. And then this warrior, Tamahae, came through and BANG! He killed Hine Tapora. But when he found out that Hine Tapora was the big kuia, he put her in Toria's rua. Tamahae hid her body in there and then he carried on doing his killing all the way back around to Te Kaha.

So that's what the name of Ruatoria means?

Yeah.

A Dictionary of Maori Place Names, by A. W. Reed: Ruatoria: Correctly Ruaatoria, kumara pit belonging to Toria.

Angus: So how did Ruatoria actually get burned down that first time?

John Heeney: Must-a been some arsonist in the whanau, I suppose.

Ha, ha, ha.

Drunk, ay, lighting a cigarette out the back.

100 Years of Waiapu, by Charles Rau: In the early 1900s a small business area consisting of two small shops, a post office, a smithy, a billiards parlour and a bakery developed. The area was known as the Crossroads.

The buildings in the little town were close together and this helped and contributed to the town's complete demise. Fire broke out and swept quickly through the wooden buildings, destroying or damaging them beyond repair. The town was reconstructed a mile and a half further south and was eventually called Ruatoria.

Superintendent Paul Wiseman, quoted in The Gisborne Herald on Tuesday, February 25: "The situation there in the future can't be any worse than it has been. It has stretched our resources and we have had problems in Gisborne.

"Our staff in Ruatoria have worked extremely long hours, in extremely difficult conditions. They have been away from their wives and families. Their wives and families have been worried about them and it has caused concern all round.

"I have total admiration for all the police staff who have been involved in the operation in Ruatoria and also for all the police staff back here in Gisborne, who have held the fort. While the others have been away those back in Gisborne have had a heavy workload.

"We have still quite a bit to do up there. We have the arson in the forestry. We have to tie up the arson of the house. Inquiries are still continuing into the arson of the police house and of the hut at the airport, together with all the inquiries involved in the alleged offences committed by Campbell, Thompson and Haua. We find the result is very satisfying. It belies what other people said, to go in and shoot it out and so forth. That is a ridiculous concept. This is New Zealand."

More details are revealed about Graeme Mathieson's alleged arson of the house at the Crossroads occupied by Rastafarian John Heeney and his partner Donna Moses. The Crown alleges in the High Court in Gisborne that Mathieson, a member of the Neighbourhood Watch Group, set up to guard against arson attempts, burned the house to "get even" with the Rastas.

For a prosecutor, Terry Stapleton shows remarkable empathy toward the accused. He describes Mathieson as a hard and willing worker at a station near Ruatoria, and just as he worked hard as a shepherd, he worked willingly for the Neighbourhood Watch Group.

On February 17, Mathieson found that three of his horses were missing. They'd cost him $500 each, which he'd paid with his wages. He spent some time that week looking for them. He was upset and distressed *and became convinced that the Rastas were responsible for taking them. Mathieson believed the Rastas had stolen other horses and they had also threatened him, his mother, and his girlfriend.*

On the day of the fire Mathieson was on day patrol from 6am to 6pm with the surveillance group. He later arranged to go on night patrol as well.

Two days after the alleged arson, Detective Bob Flaus took a statement from Mathieson. He said he'd been dropped off at Manutahi School. He got some petrol in a container and matches, which he left in the grass opposite the house. He poured the petrol along the wall of the house and in a doorway and then lit it. After returning to the school he was picked up by car.

John Heeney and Donna Moses were sitting in the kitchen. They'd put their baby to bed at the front of the house, where the accused said he lit the fire.

Stapleton says that when Heeney and Moses saw the flames they took their baby outside, where they smelt petrol. Heeney was unable to beat out the flames with a mat and rang the fire brigade. Interestingly, the Ruatoria exchange said it was unable to contact the fire brigade. But it later contacted them through the police. The fire brigade and police arrived at 11.15pm and stayed until 2.30am, when it was concluded the fire had been deliberately lit.

Senior Sergeant John Robinson, interviewed in 2001:
Graeme Mathieson got acquitted, even though he admitted doing it. The jury still said not guilty.

Another thing there is that Tom Heeney was the deputy fire chief, while his son John was one of the main guys running around setting all the fires.

And when John's house got burnt his mother, Peg, jumped up and down and yelled and screamed and said they were trying to kill her boy and her grandchild. But she'd done nothing before to stop her boy. She knew what he was doing. But once someone done something to him…

Having said that the fire at John Heeney's house was the only one done with people in the building. That was silly of Mathieson.

FIRES IN THE MAIN STREET

Excerpt from an interview the author and his father, Iain, did with Bob Kaa, at Bob's house in Ruatoria in the early 2000s (I can't remember which year): I had a couple of visits from the Rastas. They come up my driveway early in the morning. I took'm out there by the barbecue, sat'm down. When I found out what they wanted I just told them, "No. End of conversation. On yer bike."

They wanted me to make a public apology and say that they were good boys and they were trying their best, that they were Maori and they wanted to be Maori.

I said, "Kia ora, that's good. But you're going about it the wrong way."

By this time it was patently obvious that Sue Nikora was the architect behind the boys. But it had got out of control. And these boys realised they do have a bit of mana, they do have a bit of power. They didn't need Sue. Sue only kick-started it. And by this stage they were doing their own bloody thing.

And I look back on what happened and, sure, this is a nice place to live. I wouldn't leave here. Where the fuck am I gonna go? I could go to Gisborne and live but I don't want to.

People say to me, "Why're you still staying here?"

I say, "What's wrong with it? Ruatoria's not the only township in this country that's been hit by arsons."

My family's here. I came home to die. And that's gonna happen one day. I'm sixty-one. And I know my family hasn't got far to take me to bury me back at my ancestral plot. I'm happy with what I got and I'm happy with my life.

When we bought this place we'd already sold our house in Bulls. We only paid $8000 for this place, the whole section. It's huge. And of course Kopua said to me, "You're fuckin' mad. That Pakeha only bought it for 4000."

I said, "So?"

That was in 1974. It's valuation now is 53,000. If I was gonna sell it, I'd sell it for 50,000. I'd be happy with 50,000. I wouldn't want any more. And I mean that. But I won't sell it. I'll give it to my kids. They've all got no fuckin' money. They're always asking their father for a few bob.

Friday, August 22, 1986: It's 9.45pm and Joe's Bookshop in the main street of Ruatoria is going up in flames. Some young people at the Kai Kart food outlet are the first to see the fire. And they raise the alarm immediately.

The Ruatoria Volunteer Fire Brigade manages to put out the fire. But not before it's caused extensive damage to the shop. They've just finished cleaning up and have gone home when a constable, stationed outside the charred building, notices another fire. It's at Ruatoria Motors, owned by surveillance group chairman Bob Kaa. The alarm is raised all over again. The firemen jump back into their vehicles and head back to the scene. But it's too late. The large wooden garage that's dominated Ruatoria's main street for years is consumed by flame. Tonight's fires are the first time main street businesses have been hit.

Ken McKinnon, Ruatoria Fire Chief (retired): There was the bookshop fire. We put that out and I came home. The cops were staying there looking after it. Next thing they radioed the fire brigade. There was a bit burning up the top. So I got up there, put that out. Then I said, "You like a cup of tea?" So I went and made a couple of flasks of coffee and tea and some sandwiches and took'm down for them.

I came home and had just got to bed. Up the siren went.

When I got down you couldn't drive across the street because Bob's garage was on fire and the flames were so hot.
There was only two of us firemen attended the fire, plus a young fire-girl. We took the Bedford machine up the street a bit further. I was driving the tanker and this girl was a bit small to hold the hose. So I ran the hose out, charged it up and then ran over to give her a hand. By this time the fire is raging up the top end. The next thing you know, the oxygen bottle blows up. BOOM! It blows the windows out of a house and a shop across the road and lifts the verandah off. It was terrific.

The explosion woke up the other firemen and they came down. When the fire was out we went looking for the bottle. We thought it might have been lying on the floor and shot out through a window and be lying half a mile away in a paddock.

But what happened was Bob's father's car was over the pit in the garage and it must have gone underneath and stayed there.

Bob Kaa: My brother said to me, "Look, isn't it about time you came home to the coast."

I said, "Fuck off. I've just built a new home. This is home, mate. This belongs to the wife and I."

He said, "No, no, no. Our parents have gone. It's time you came home."

I said, "I'll only go home on two conditions and these are actually my wife's conditions: the road's tar-sealed and there's power."

And so we came up for a visit. Aw yeah, they had bloody tarseal and they had power. So we had to come home.

The other thing was that when we came home we had to decolonise our thinking. We'd lost touch with our Maori side. The language was still stuck in the back of my mind. I knew it. But I had parked it, put it on hold for twenty-odd bloody years. So for the first two years when I got home I was going to tangi and just listening and taking notes. I'm not saying I'm a bloody expert today. But I think I've caught up.

I said to my brother, "Christ, I'm still bloody young." We were in our thirties. "We don't want to sit around." So we bought the garage together. It was the biggest service station, car sales, panel-beating shop, biggest one on the coast. Cost us a few bob but it was worth it. We were open seven days a week.

My brother left and I bought his half out. And we were just moving into the grocery thing that's happening now at service stations. We were negotiating with Shell and we were going to expand. We were just getting to that phase when we got burnt out. When I told my brother what had happened he couldn't believe it.

But I was glad to get out. I had a rethink and realised I'd had enough.

CRUEL TIMING

Saturday, August 23: The heat from the blaze at Bob Kaa's garage was in fact so intense that spouting on the other side of the road melted.

Gisborne Deputy Fire Chief Lyn Hillock is at the scene this morning, trying to find out how the fires started. Police are treating them as suspicious, and say an accelerant may have been used. A four-person CIB team, headed by Detective Sergeant Laurie Naden, has travelled from Gisborne to Ruatoria and uniformed police staff may join them later.

Riria Keelan, the owner of Joe's Bookshop, had carried on the business when her husband died three years ago.

"It's really, really awful," she says, surveying the ruins.

"I haven't quite made up my mind what I should do. I'll try to keep selling papers. I'll have to try to think of some other way until I sort something out. This is the only bookshop in the town. It was on the market. In fact, it was due to change hands at the end of the month. I don't know what the new people want to do. The building is not gutted but it's extensively damaged. It looks as though I have lost all the books. I have to see the insurance assessor."

Perhaps worst hit is Bob Kaa. He was at his mother's tangi when he heard about the fire.

Bob Kaa: I took Kopua in the Air Force with me. We got married in 1961. In the Air Force everyone called her Kaye, cos it was easier for them. But back here she's Kopua because everyone knows Kopua. Before I went to the Air Force, I was living in Rangitukia, just over the river, with my uncle. My father died when I was four-and-a-half years old. He died in an accident. He was milking cows at this farm and he went to take the cream to the road because that's where they picked up the cans. And the horse shied. And he got thrown off the cart and his foot got caught in the spoke. And of course those days, to get to the hospital, you can imagine, there's no roads as they are today. And gangrene set in. He broke his foot and gangrene set in.

It was tough for my mum. I had a younger brother and a younger sister when he died and I was only four and a half.

The arson of the garage blew me away. It blew both my wife and I away. Particularly that they did it at the death of a loved one, when my mother passed away. It was that night when I got word that my garage was on fire. We were in Te Araroa, which is about forty-five kilometres north of here. By the time we got back in the early hours of the morning it was gone. I wasn't even in Ruatoria when the fire happened. I was attending to my mother's funeral. The mourning process takes a couple of days in our tradition. We were only at the first day when it happened. We got a call that the garage was on fire. As we were driving back we could see the glow in the sky. It was too late. Mind you it was a fairly old premises. I understand it was sixty-plus years old.

That sat us back on our butts. We employed five people. I had to satisfy them. There were all those kinds of things. The insurance company accused me of taking advantage of the situation to light it myself so I could claim the insurance. I tell you, it was incredible. It took me eighteen months before they actually paid out. They had their own investigation team. I was screwed by the police. They really gave me the third degree. They thought I took advantage of the situation. And I don't blame them for thinking that way. But fortunately, because I was already involved prior to *my* place getting burnt in terms of trying to *defend* the township, in inverted commas, and its citizens, it helped my case with the insurance company. But it took a long time for them to decide: This guy is up front and we'll pay out. Meantime all my creditors, particularly the IRD and Westpac, were saying, "Hey, when you gonna pay *our* money back."

I kept saying, "Well, hang on, hang on. I gotta get *my* money first."

Did they hit me on that particular date for extra effect?

It's a possibility. Of course, on the Coast when anything happens, whether it's a death or whatever, everyone knows. I heard on the marae this morning for example that someone had died at Waipiro Bay. Whereas, take Gisborne for example: It's much more difficult to know everything that's happening.

So they probably took advantage of the situation, knowing I was away.

But the interesting thing out of all that for us was our children, who were still going to college, and our home were never targeted. We never got any obscene phone calls. A lot of people were getting a whole host of threatening phone calls. That never happened once. I used to get a lot of calls from people who were very scared or who believed they were being intimidated. It was staggering the way the Rastas practically held this community to ransom through fear. It's incredible how their actions actually did that.

Ninety-nine point nine per cent of the people on the Coast are related anyway. Genealogy is part and parcel of our lives, and that's illustrated by funerals and weddings. When we attend these things, in our speeches we always say the reason I'm related to you is because of so and so. We go back maybe three generations. And because of that intimate knowledge of ourselves people were afraid to talk because, "That is my nephew, that is my niece." Or, "That is my aunty, that is my uncle, whether I like it or not." And it was in the back of people's minds. And that's probably why the police had extreme difficulty in getting anyone to talk. They brought all the experts in, so they believe. And they couldn't get anywhere.

Former Ruatoria policeman Steve Tresidder: I first started going down to Ruatoria in mid 1986. I used to live at the Manutahi pub.

I remember the first time I went there. Seven of us graduated from Police College at the same time and we were sent to Gisborne. I'd only been in Gisborne about a month if I was lucky and I got to go up to Ruatoria. And I can still vividly remember driving down the main street of Ruatoria for the first time. One of the shops had been burnt down, and was still half-pie burning. And coming down the road were the Rastas on their horses with the lead guy carrying on a big pole a huge Rastafarian flag. It was like something out of the Wild West. And I thought, "What the hell is this place?" There were heaps of Rastas on horseback behind this lead guy with the flag. And I remember just sitting in the police car, staring in disbelief, and thinking, "What the hell have I walked into here?"

CHAPTER 2

A RADIO STATION IS BORN

Bob Kaa: Such was the hype among the so-called Rastafarians at that time, they believed and in fact they did *say* at three public meetings that, "This township is ours."

After my garage burnt I was rung up in Te Araroa to come back to a public meeting that was held in the St. Johns in the town here. And we had a few Pakeha farmers here then. You had the likes of Colin Williams, John Barton, the Williams family; and they employed a lot of our people, whether they be fencers, shepherds, whatever. Of course, prior to my garage, Colin Williams had already lost two hay barns. John Barton had lost one. Initially they targeted Pakeha. But because our own people, including myself, were standing up against them they thought, "Well stuff it. We're gonna move in and take over."

I arrived back at about half past seven at night. And bugger me days this hall was packed, and I mean packed. And I said, "Well what are we waiting for?"

They said, "Well we want you to chair the meeting."

I knew Colin Williams very well and he said to me, "It's no use me getting up there. It's your people. You go and chair the meeting."

I said, "Okay."

Anyway, I said, "Look, we've got a patrol out there but we're having trouble keeping in touch with each other. We need hand-held VHF radios and we haven't got any money."

Colin Williams never hesitated. He stood up, wrote out a cheque, I think it was for fifteen thousand dollars.

I said to Colin, "You embarrass me, Colin."

He said, "No bloody way." And that started the ball rolling. By the time that meeting finished we had just about thirty thousand dollars on the table. It shows you, such was the feeling of the people in this community, not only the township but I'm talking about the farmers, particularly the Pakeha farmers… and Colin only lived just up the road. And Colin, as I said, used to employ a lot of our people and Colin was a bloody good employer, make no mistake about that. A lot of Maori staff

that stayed with him for twenty-plus years, when they retired, he put'm
in brand new homes. That was their retirement package from his family.
So Colin wasn't a bastard. No way. He just happened to be a Pakeha in
the wrong place at that time.

Anyway, the next day we went and opened a bank account.

Dear Householder,

A meeting of the Ruatoria community was held on Tuesday
26th August to discuss the problems confronting Ruatoria at present…

It is needless to state the problems affecting Ruatoria and its
environs at present. The whole of New Zealand knows.

Indications are that it is going to get worse. It is common
knowledge that the Ruatoria commercial area is under threat. Can you
imagine, what a situation <u>you</u> and your family will be in if our town
closed down, or if it were without power for one week.
These are the realities of what is being proposed. <u>It could be your house
next.</u>

The Neighbourhood Support Group are working in <u>your</u>
interests.

However, their resources are being stretched to the extent that
they may have to withdraw their services. YOUR HELP IS NEEDED, in
whatever shape or form. If you value the work being done by the
Neighbourhood Support Group, consider:

Your children are at risk.

Your homes are at risk.

Your commercial area is at risk.

We appreciate that many people are fearful in coming forward
with information for fear of reprisals. Your information will be treated
with utmost confidence without your name being mentioned or known
by anyone other than the person you confide in.
It is up to you. It is your community…
CONCERNED CITIZENS ASSOCIATION
RUATORIA

Bob Kaa: There were some interesting things came out of the
night patrols; none of the things that we were there to achieve, but
interesting nevertheless. We saw why marriages break up. We would see
people jumping out of windows and over fences. We got the use of those
night vision binoculars. We got them through the police and I think the

police got them through the army. Alex Hope, the local police chief, was a tremendous guy. He said, "Don't tell anyone you've got them, but these might come in handy."

It's amazing what you can see at night.

We were all using these hand-held radios to communicate and we were working out of our homes.

Eventually we talked Alex into letting us use the police station as a base.

There was a building inspector here that year and he had a wooden leg. His wife was a nurse. They stayed in the public nurse's home. I forget his name now. The county council used to have a building inspector domiciled in Ruatoria. The reason I mention him - the poor bugger - he died of a heart attack because two or three of the boys got him on his own so to speak. And they really put the bloody shits up him. Barry…? Barry…? Barry…? His name just eludes me at the moment. His wife was the public health nurse, Thelma Plews.

It was like a home invasion nowadays. They went into his house. He was actually looking after our base radio. We had a guy looking after our base radio every night and we'd change shifts. And we had the patrols going around with radios and they'd be keeping in touch with base.

And this particular night when he was on they went around there like a home invasion and the poor bugger he just bloody… Yeah, that was bloody sad.

They didn't really beat him up like what's happening today. It was similar. But I think it was fear more than anything else. They really put the fear in him and the poor bugger got a heart attack and just bloody… His wife was trying frantically to revive him and not knowing what to do and she was the public health nurse. This all happened during the home invasion.

Former Senior Sergeant John Robinson: That guy in the Neighbourhood Support Group who died of the heart attack, I think he was one of the vigilantes who beat up Paddy Brown, the Rasta Hamana Brown's brother.

These guys saw Paddy and his wife Forli in their car. And the vigilantes all jumped out with their balaclavas on and they beat Paddy up with pick handles and whatnot. But Paddy knew who they were because he could recognise the voices. But once again the police took no action. Paddy made a complaint and the police said they couldn't prove anything. But the police had given the vigilantes these little hand-held radios so they could contact the police quickly if they needed to. It wasn't on the police radio, but they heard these guys talking on their little hand-held radios about how they beat up Paddy Brown. That didn't go down too well when the word got out about what had happened. I don't think the Neighbourhood Support Group lasted too long after that.

Bob Kaa: The other interesting thing that came out of the ashes of this story is the birth of the radio station. We had another public meeting at Hiruharama Marae. And we wanted to gauge the public's feeling as to how things were progressing in the township. And the meeting did say that things weren't as bad as what they'd been but crimes were still being committed.

Anyway, along come two Pakeha guys from Hamilton. One of them used to be a radio announcer with 2ZG (in Gisborne) many years ago. He was working at Radio Waikato. He'd heard about what was happening in Ruatoria. He had affection for this part of the coast and he knew that there was no radio here. So he came in and said, "Can I speak?"

And I said, "Well, who are you?"

He told us who he was and, of course, all of the Maoris looked at this Pakeha and they said, "What!?"

And I said, "No, no. Give him a chance. Let him speak." I didn't know the guy.

It turned out he was the manager of this Radio Waikato in Hamilton. And what he offered the community was thirty days use of their transmission equipment. They brought their radio down here and set it up at no cost to the community and we could talk to one another on the radio.

And, of course, you know what Maori are like. "Aw, you're all shit," and so on and so on.

Anyhow, after a lengthy discussion I put it to a vote. And one lady in front of me was chewing her chewing gum. And she said to me, "Yes, you can never trust these bloody Pakehas."

I said, "Hang on a minute. What's that stuff you've got in your mouth?"

"Chewing gum, of course."

"You know who made that? It wasn't a Maori."

Anyhow, we voted to go along with this guy and have the radio station for thirty days.

They set it up and I tell you what, it really captured the hearts of the people. And I'm talking about here in particular, where the trouble was.

Williams and Kettles had closed down. Wrightsons had closed and they'd moved out and we had two vacant buildings there. As the trouble continued, more and more businesses were moving out of town. So they went to see Williams and Kettles and Williams and Kettles said they could use their building.

Margaret Evans, who went on to become the Mayoress of Hamilton City, came down here and was one of the DJs on the radio station. She's a very, very interesting woman. She was that well liked by this community it was unbelievable. She made a lot of friends here and she's well known here.

Anyway she ran the talkbacks. And I think you could hear it from Tokomaru Bay up to Tikitiki. So it wasn't a big area. They were concentrating on this valley and getting people to talk about the troubles here.

And as the talkback show became popular, in inverted commas, then the Rastas started ringing in. And we'd have some horrendous bloody debates. I mean swearing on the air. And they allowed it. And I said to Margaret, "You've got to stop it."

And she said, "Aw we're supposed to have a delay system on. The law says we've got to have a delay system on it so we can weed out the foul-mouthed callers. Aw, but it's only the coast can hear so it should be all right."

It was a great way for people to clear the air. It certainly was a catalyst in my view, not so much to solving the problems, but to bringing normality back into the community.

Anyhow the talkback became incredibly popular and the radio people were working seven days a week until in the end they pleaded to have a day off. So we gave them Sunday off and when they left we put on a big do for them at the marae by the cross-roads there. And there was a helluva crowd. And I mean that. Even the Rasties were there. And the speeches thanking them for what they'd done were incredible.

And when they left there was a void in the community. And we started saying to each other, "We need a radio station."

So we got back to Margaret and Co. and said, "Hey, can you help us?"

They said, "We knew you'd ask that. But it had to come from you people. Not from us telling you."

And now we've got a radio station that covers the whole coast. It goes right down to Gisborne.

CHAPTER 3

JEREMY WILLIAMS' HOUSE IS BURNED

Satuday, November 8, 1986: *Probably the happiest day of Jeremy Williams' life. It's the day he marries Jane Holden. They hold the reception in a marquee on the tennis court at Jane's parents' home in Whangara, on the coast just north of Gisborne.*

But at midnight, amid the drinking and dancing and celebrations, the happiest day ticks over to be replaced by a day of shock and... well, just shock really.

Jeremy Williams: The first I know that there's been a fire is in the early hours of the morning. The policeman at Whangara rings to say the house has been burnt to the ground. I'm just stunned. I never dreamt that they'd go and do that. We've had a brilliant day. I just can't believe it.

When the police call at about ten to one we're still celebrating. We just tell the immediate family what has happened. And it's quarter past one before we discreetly have a talk about it. We don't tell everybody at the wedding. So a lot of them don't find out until the next day. It's easier to deal with something like that by letting the dust settle. I don't want to deal with lots of people at half past one in the morning. We just stay the night at Jane's parents' place. Our house is all just ashes by that stage. There's nothing I can do.

Only three chimneys are still standing when the Ruatoria Fire Brigade arrives at the two-storey Matahiia homestead, southwest of Ruatoria.

The station's been in the hands of the Williams family since 1883. It was part of the original extensive land purchases by Archdeacon Samuel Williams in the Waiapu district, and Jeremy's the fourth generation of the family to run the property.
The homestead was built in 1939 to replace the one which was destroyed by fire the previous year.

Excerpt from an interview in late 2000 with Ike Campbell, Chris's brother: Chris is not the first one who's done this you know. Two or three of our ancestors before him have protested about the land. This is no new thing that's happened to the Williams. It's not the first time in history their house has been burnt down.

Jeremy Williams: I think they just picked a time when they knew the house was empty. There's an old saying in Gisborne, "If you want to rob a farmer, do it on the day of the Gisborne A and P Show." You just wait until no one's there. It's the same theory. What's the difference?

Lyn Hillock, Gisborne Deputy Fire Chief (now retired and living in Australia): Ian Clark and I go up as soon as the alarm comes in on Jeremy's house. Our biggest concerns are the rifles in the house and the ammunition. I get the bottom of my feet burnt, right through my boots, looking for them. And the same happens to Ian. But we're determined to find these rifles. So we're digging through all these hot embers looking for them. But the rifles are definitely gone. They've been nicked.

There are about twenty-two stolen firearms loose in the community. So people are worried.

Jeremy Williams: I guess I don't have time to feel angry because I actually have no clothes apart from a pair of jeans and a shirt. Other than that all I have is a hired suit, which I'm wearing. We were going to pick up clothes at the house at Matahiia Station on our way to our honeymoon at Lake Rotoiti.

Instead, the first week of married life is spent having to deal with insurance, police, the media. We're lucky that friends of Jane's family have a cottage at Wainui, just north of Gisborne, and we're able to stay there for a week.

See, the house fire doesn't just affect Jane and me. It affects other members of the family. My sister, who's not married, her bedroom had a lot of her personal memorabilia and knick-knacks. That's all been burnt. My aunt, who's married and living in the South Island, her memories of her childhood have gone up in smoke.

THE RASTA CONE OF SILENCE

Rasta Cody Haua reckons he never got into the fires much and he didn't like to know too much about them either. That way, he says, if the cops took him away and beat him up, he still wouldn't be able to tell them anything.

Detective Sergeant Laurie Naden (retired): We had it all wrong. When I say we, I mean the police. We sat down and thought, "They must have these little meetings and then they sit down and decide, 'Right we're going to burn down such and such a house.'" But it wasn't. It was totally cellular. Two guys might be sitting together one night and decide, "Williams, let's go and burn his house." And they would go and do it. *And they wouldn't tell anyone.* In fact, we – the police - would get some of the younger Rastas in and put them through the hoops. And they'd say, "We don't know anything about it, boss." And they bloody *didn't* know.

They used to have these meetings every now and then. I think they called them reasonings. And they'd sit down and they'd smoke dope and they'd say, "Aw, I see the Williams house burnt down." And another one would say, "Yeah." But no one would say, "I did it." They never asked and no one ever said who committed the crime. But collectively they would accept responsibility for it. So it was almost an impossible situation to break into.

Jeremy Williams: We knew the route that the arsonists took because they left a telephone they'd nicked in a ditch. They didn't take much with them when they left, just the rifles and ammo. But they'd been doing that at most arsons. Other times they'd take saddlery.

I was too busy to be angry. And it was summer. We were getting into shearing and having two o'clock breakfasts.

I realised that if I felt angry all the time, it would cripple me. I put it behind me. I'm lucky I was able to do that and get on with my life. Because if you don't you just get bitter and twisted and you can't function. You're stressed out all the time.

We decided we weren't going to build again. We bought a neighbour's property with a house already on it. We bought Stuart Williams' house. He'd already sold the Taitai block. But he had a separate block, which had been part of Matahiia until the end of the First World War. He'd taken that over from an aunt and uncle way back. So that was on the market literally about the time of the house fire. It was an older house and needed some running maintenance but generally it was fine.

After the house fire we got letters from all over the country. Some of them gave us a bit of money, some of them just a note of support. We got $50 from an elderly couple who had shifted from a property in the high country down to a small house in Geraldine. And they just said, "We identify with you and your wife. You are where we were forty years ago. Here's a few bob to get you started again." I can't remember who those people were now but they really gave us strength.

A CLASH OF CULTURES

Hata Thompson, Rastafarian: Guys were always getting bashed by the cops because they wouldn't talk about things. But there were a lot of those fires that to this day I don't know who burnt them. Well, I reckon I know a few, like when old Matahiia Station burnt down. I probably could name a few on that one. But I might be stabbing in the dark because they just rode in in the dark, were there five minutes and rode away. That's no cause to say they did it. But in my mind I'd say it was them. Ha ha ha. You know? And I look at it now and like, that was Ken Williams' place. Jeremy was Ken's son and Jeremy and Chris Campbell had their moments. They used to have their niggles. It was like one education versus another education, a bit of a cat and mouse game. But Chris and him did have their moments. Chris used to say to him, "Fuckin' one day, mate, I'll fuckin' burn your house down, cunt."

And Jeremy would say, "Yeah? Yeah?"

But the bro didn't do it. I can honestly say Chris didn't do it. But it did happen because words were spoken and one of the bros just probably heard Chris talking and thought, "I'll do that."

Chris was disturbed about what happened. I think who did it was frustrated and just went ahead without telling anyone.

Jeremy Williams: Chris Campbell's father Willie was a shearing contractor and Chris used to work for him. Chris and me had a run-in in the woolshed one day. It was after they cut all the fences. It was a fairly minor run-in really. My cousin Stuart was counting the sheep out and I was there because Stuart was using our woolshed. And Chris just made some comment along the lines that when they took over there'd be no more sheep. And he made a veiled threat. But as soon as Stuart asked him if he was threatening us he backed down. That was it.

Versions of the run-in between Chris Campbell, known by some as Kara, and Jeremy Williams are now part of Ruatoria folklore. The bust-up even made its way into the realms of fiction.

Witi Ihimaera, The Dream Swimmer: Among the prime Pakeha targets were members of the Williams dynasty and other members of the Pakeha squatocracy. One day, Jeremy Williams met Kara in the streets of Ruatoria. Kara was reported to have told him that he was going to be living in the Williams' house in six months' time, even if Kara had to put Jeremy in the ground before he moved in...

...One day, Kara saw Jeremy Williams and his men lambing.

"You're wasting your time," Campbell apparently said. "Next year all your stock and your land will be mine, anyway."
The sins of the fathers were visited on Jeremy Williams and his new bride as they suffered a series of lightning attacks, more arson and terrorism.

The opinions expressed in the following excerpt are not presented as statements of fact, but merely as an example of local feeling and how it tied in with the Rasta belief system.

Interview with Rasta John Heeney in early 2000: *When you guys were just coming together - you're talking about early 1980s - you'd just got back from Wellington. Chris, was he coming back from somewhere?*

John: Na, he was still here.

He was still here.

He'd just finished chucking his shearing piece at Jeremy Williams and them, and telling them to shear their own effin' sheep. One day he'll be on that land and they'll have to ask him. He was shearing with the big stereo system on in the shearing shed, playing a bit of Bob Marley. And the farmer got bummed out. But it wasn't affecting their work performances, so in the end he just told the farmer to eff-off and *he'll* be asking *us* from then on. Yeah, he'd had a gutsful because, if you look, a lot of our old people slaved all their lives for those white men. At the end of the day, a lot of those old farmers - they were the old vets from World War Two - they came back, they worked on the Williams' farm all their lives, but when they died their widows and chidren had to *git.*

Out of that land?

Yeah, off that land. And yet those Maoris worked all their lives for them and yet when they died...

Their usefulness had gone.

Yeah. And yet you look at those rehabilitation farms for the World War Two soldiers, when they came back not one soldier got on them. The Williams had already taken them over.

They were supposed to be set up for the men who came back from the Maori Battalion. There were a few of these farms: Matahiia, Pakihirau, some big ones. When all our tipuna went overseas to fight, who was gonna farm the farms?

So the Williams came in did they?

Yeah.

Donna: William Williams, the missionary, brought Christianity to New Zealand. They say the first place Jesus Christ came was here. And he was brought through the missionaries, ay.

That's right.

Donna: They've got a part to play, the Williams, with The Bible. That's why they were picked on so much because they used The Bible and they abused it.

John: Just let Jah judge that. They got burnt out-a here. They got burnt away from here but even though…

Colin did but Jeremy's still here, ay?

Yeah. But, you know, as time comes he soon will be. He's gonna have to forfeit it in the end.

So what's happened to Colin's farm?

He sold that one out to locals. The Americans have got all the pine trees on the land.

So that's back in Maori hands now, Colin Williams's land?

Some of it.

So you'd consider that a victory?

Na. I don't.

You wouldn't even consider that a small victory?

Na.

Na?

Na.

Yeah.

The land was always there. Nothing has improved, ay. If improvements come for us, yeah, but if it doesn't come for us then it's not a victory. Even though people come and go, nothing has changed. In fact, since Colin Williams has gone things might have gone a bit worse because he's withdrawn his money from the community. But aw, you know, I don't worry about that too much because there's higher things that are going on, ay.

Yeah.

Cos the land will always be there. We'll come and go and they'll come and go but that land will still be there.

So did the Williams family come into those rehab farms and push people off?

No. They never pushed anyone off. They went and took them over. They moved on and operated them. And then when the war finished well they were already operating them so you just couldn't pull them out because it was already...

It was already goin' so no one could move in. They couldn't say, "Aw thanks for looking after the farm. You go back to your farm and we'll take over this farm because this is supposed to be for us anyway." You know?

And when you look at it...

Yeah.

…Our ancestors went over there and died there fighting for this country.

The best people too.

Those people that went over, a lot of them died. Those that didn't lost brothers and friends. And yet after all that, they started shitting on them. No wonder we rose up in the way we did because all our people… Hiruharama, Jerusalem, had the highest percentage of injury and death out of all the soldiers in the Maoris that went overseas. We lost the most Maoris, the most that got killed and the most that got wounded.

A bit like Vietnam. These young Americans go over there and they're all told to go over there and then when they come back they're treated like shit.

Yeah, yeah.

And no one understands what they went through.

Donna: When the Maori went over they were put in the front line. The Americans and the English or whatever were in the back line. But they got all the glory.

John: We were just awakening to what was happening around us on our land.

Was there a lot of resentment around Ruatoria ever since that World War Two thing?

Not really.

Cos obviously you guys picked up on it.

Donna: It was a big honour for them to die at war, I reckon. It was the ultimate. I think they were proud.

What about the people who were left? Did they resent that they'd lost such big numbers?

John: Na. We're talking about people we don't even know. We never knew them as human beings. We only know them through a memory and stories. It would affect the older people more because they're the people who suffered the loss. Our mothers, our fathers, their brothers and uncles and friends, they're the ones that lived with them and never got to see them come back home again. And they died for what? You look at the Second World War. You know, going back into Egypt, the Maori people went back into Egypt. That's the same land God led Moses and God's people out of from bondage and slavery. And just not more than fifty years ago our people went back to the same land God chose Moses to lead his people out of. And to have our blood spilt on that land there, not more than fifty years ago. You have a real good look at it, ay.

What does that mean to you?

That means what they said. That's how close the anti-Christ was coming back here. Because they knew if they didn't go, what standing right do we have to claim for this land here? If our blood never got spilled fighting for this land the system could just say, "Ach," you know. "We sent battalions over to fight the Germans and you fullas just stayed at home and…"

"And did nothin'."

"…And did nothin'," yeah, "just like you do on your farms. You fullas can't work your land so we take it off you," sort of thing, ay. They say, "Yeah, that's because you're not giving us any of *that*." Giving it to all their mates and feathering their own nests. And when it comes to the little fish, we're nothing. We don't even exist in their minds unless we're a statistic of crime, ay.

CHAPTER 4

THE MAORI BATTALION

In an article written by Lloyd Ashton and researched by Monty Soutar, published in the April/May 1999 issue of Mana Magazine, then-politician Donna Awatere Huata echoes John Heeney's sentiments about the treatment of Maori soldiers. Awatere Huata's father, Peta, became a legendary commander of the Maori Battalion in World War II. But she recalls that some men had misgivings about going away to fight because many of the old soldiers remembered what had happened to them after World War I.

Donna Awatere Huata: "My own tribes – Ngati Porou and Arawa – formed the backbone of the Pioneer Battalion. They suffered great losses, like the Pakeha.

"But there was a difference when they came home. Maori came back and found they weren't eligible for a war pension. And, even though their tribes had gifted large tracts of land to the government for rehab blocks, none of those blocks went to Maori.

"So our two tribes were mocked for losing so many men for so little reward, and this mockery was a large factor in my father's generation's reluctance to do so again. You may expect to die in battle, but not to be laughed at for so doing."

Many Maori on the East Coast feel their communities have never recovered from the losses of war. And not just from World War II. In World War I, close to five hundred men from the Gisborne-East Coast volunteered for the Native Contingent, later reformed as the Pioneer Battalion. A generation earlier, Tuta Nihoniho, the respected Ngati Porou ancestor of the Rastafarians, offered himself and five hundred Maori troops to fight the Boers in South Africa.

Lloyd Ashton and Monty Soutar, Mana Magazine: Nepia Mahuika grew up in Ruatoria, went to Te Aute College and is a descendent of Porou Rangi. That's one of the reasons why Apirana Ngata went in to bat for him as an officer…

… "I remember in Italy, I was sent over to take a village. It was a daylight attack. No cover, no creeping barrage and the enemy was sitting up there. I saw my men panicking a bit. So I thought, well… 'Ka mate, Ka mate!' I laid down the haka. And the next minute I got the response that sounded all over the battlefield: 'Ka ora, Ka ora!' The men yelled and charged. They got mad. That's the way to get the fear out.

"The Germans had been occupying the houses. We fired at the windows, and any open places. And out came these Italian civilians – hands up, women with babies crying – that knocked the fight right out of my men. Then the Italians told us the Germans had been in the houses with them. But when they heard the haka, they fled."

THE COWBOYS

The 28 Maori Battalion was formed in 1939. It fought in some of the fiercest battles of World War II in Greece, Crete, Egypt, Libya, Tunisia and Italy. Two hundred and fifty of its members are buried in

Italian cemeteries. The unit was made up of 3578 volunteers. Seventy percent of them would become casualties of war. Six hundred and forty nine were killed and many were wounded two or three times. The Maori Battalion had the highest casualty rate of any unit in the New Zealand Division.

The Government had decided that Maori would not be conscripted. But with the great Ngati Porou politician Sir Apirana Ngata leading the cause, Maori up and down the coast joined up in their hundreds. Sir Apirana believed the Battalion would prove that Maori were the equal of Pakeha and deserved to be treated as such, with all the benefits and privileges of New Zealand citizenship. But he was also well aware of the cost to his people. In July, 1941, he said: "We will lose some of the most promising of our young leaders, have lost a few already. But the future of the race as a component and respected part of the New Zealand people will be less precarious."

The Maori Battalion consisted of five companies organised on tribal lines. The C Company was from Gisborne and the East Coast and known as Nga Kaupoi, The Cowboys. Around eighty percent of the Maori men in the C Company district fought in the Battalion. Many of the others also volunteered, but were excluded for health or other reasons. Coastal towns were lonely places for young Maori men left behind by their mates. Nine hundred and fifty five men fought in the C Company. A hundred and seventy two of them were killed. So by the end of the war twenty percent of the men in C Company were dead. And seventy percent of those who came back had been wounded.

Many of the Rastafarians' ancestors fought in C Company's 14 Platoon, which drew its volunteers from Waiapu to Waipiro. In the Maori Battalion, whanau fought side by side. This is thought to be one reason why there were such high casualties: they weren't prepared to let each other down. In the attack on point 209, 14 Platoon, led by John Heeney's uncle Moana Ngarimu, fought to the death. After twelve hours of close-quarter battle only three of the thirty-man platoon were able to walk off the hill.

Sue Nikora (early influence of the Ruatoria Rastafarians):
We had a brother in the Maori Battalion who died in the Second World War. We had cousins that died. At the age of three or four I was able to answer the telephone because my mum lived in constant fear of getting the telephone call that the boys had died.

But it was a great loss. It was a real great loss. We intend to have it addressed in our land claims because we feel it was almost a genocide that occurred to us. The Maori Battalion were sent into the frontline and used as cannon fodder.

It's got to have an impact on the generations that followed. These boys (The Rastas) are the children and grandchildren and nephews and grandnephews of a generation in which most of the males were sent away to be slaughtered. And the feeling of loss is there. Although they may not know it, it's the atmosphere they grew up in. I think we had the heaviest toll throughout the whole of New Zealand. That's the Maori Battalion, C Company. It was made up of guys from Wairoa right around to the Bay of Plenty.

Lloyd Ashton and Monty Soutar, Mana Magazine: Some never got out of war mode. Others found solace in the bottle. For many the RSA's became a form of counseling centre where they relived the trauma and memories of war. There are the women widowed by the war, the parents who lost sons and the children who lost fathers. After the war some of the senior officers of the Battalion found posts in the civil service, particularly within the Maori Affairs Department. And for a while, they were able to work for the good of Maori.

But they were up against a Pakeha bureaucracy – and in 1949 there was a change of Government. That was the cue for the bureaucrats to curb the autonomy and freedom of the welfare officers under Labour.

Government policy compelled people to leave the valley to find work in the towns and cities. The exodus left a few with the responsibility of maintaining the land. In time, the freezing works and the dairy company closed and only a sprinkling of the pre-war population remained. While the drift to the cities may have meant better access to health, housing and schools, it also meant families were cut off from their marae and whanau. The old networks broke down.

VOID IN LEADERSHIP EXPLOITED

Lyn Hillock, former Gisborne Deputy Fire Chief: When you look at the problems we've had on the East Coast you can go back to the Second World War and the Maori Battalion. In my parents' generation we had extremely talented leaders within the community and on the marae. It was all a perfectly functioning social unit. It was like down home for me in the deep south, there was no difference between Maori and Pakeha. I didn't strike that until I came up here from Dunedin. My tribe is Ngai Tahu. When I first came to Gisborne, if you were driving along and knocked over an old white man with dark glasses and a cane sitting in a wheelchair at a pedestrian crossing, that was a hundred points.

When the Maori Battalion went to war, the Poms, being notorious for crap leadership and fighting skills, used the New Zealanders as cannon fodder. And Maoridom lost a whole generation of kaumatua and inspirational leaders. And in Ruatoria and in a lot of communities around the coast, what should have been the natural progression of leadership is broken and there's been a big void and there still is one. So instead of having a leadership with appropriate social behaviour and skills, they've just got this void. If you haven't got strong people remaining then somebody's going to move in and occupy that power gap. And Chris Campbell was one of those guys. He saw a niche in which to develop his thing and he went for it.

I think you can trace a lot of those problems we've encountered on the East Coast back to the loss of those leaders in the Maori Battalion.

Lloyd Ashton and Monty Soutar, Mana Magazine: John Waititi was a commander of C Company… He was born in Opotiki, then they moved to Whakatane, where his father was a slaughterman at a butcher's. His mum Henrietta (a Goldsmith) was Ngati Porou…

… "I was 24 when the war finished. I had a lot of trouble when I came back. This is where I think the Government let the soldiers down.

"They spend months and years training people. You're taught to be a killer. And when they're finished they just turn you loose. And barely say thanks.

"A lot of fellas – even today- still haven't recovered from that. I reckon every man who went through actual combat lost 10 years of his life from the sheer trauma of it all. And the tension that your body has to go through.

"I was like the rest of us, who were finding it very hard to settle down. At that stage public works were calling a lot of men to put roads in. And practically the whole lot of us got on the public works. Just to be with one another.

"That bond was still there – and is still there even today. For two years we were working for the public works. And gradually, gradually we drifted off.

"I was always inclined to the land. I finally got myself into a farm.

"The treatment we received was degrading. You have a farm and you have to borrow money from Maori Affairs and they send a broken-down bloody Pakeha contract painter to administer your finances. You're not even allowed to write your own cheques to pay your bills.

"Every end of the month he'd come around with a cheque book: "Have you got any bills?" Or some of the bills would go directly to him.

"Sometimes I feel very bitter about everything."…

… "When I look at our marae, the fellows that should be kaumatua on our marae, they're not there. They were the young fellows killed over there.

"We've been robbed of a whole generation of our leaders.

"I found out much later what Sir Apirana's theme was, getting Maori to go over in the number they did. I believe he was trying to prove to the Pakeha that we were as good, if not better, than they are.

"Why he had to prove that, I don't know. We are the tangata whenua (the people of the land). Why should we have to prove that?

"The youth were taken away. A whole generation of men. And there was hardship for women and children.

"One of the things I see still happening is the disruption of the whanau. The man's been taken out. The sons and daughters are much older people now and they're still angry about something. There's a lack of parenting. They haven't been taught a few things and they're finding it difficult.

"The mums have been too busy surviving to give the love and comfort children need."

Hughie Hughes, (Pakeha) Ruatoria electrician: During the war there were so many Maori went overseas and got killed. This place was left short of strong Maori leaders. Think of Ngarimu. If he'd made it back he might have had a huge influence on the generations that followed. The young people didn't have many male role models so I don't think they can be totally blamed for what happened in the '80s.

If you go to any of the maraes and churches along the Coast
and look at the honours boards, you'll find in a town of, say, two
hundred that about thirty of them were killed in action.

*According to John Heeney, Chris Campbell had a different way
of looking at all those deaths in the Maori Battalion. Campbell wasn't
concerned that all those leaders might have straightened them out or
given them a clip around the ear or been stronger male role models. He
believed the biggest shame was that they weren't around to have sons.
Campbell believed that if those men had been alive and produced lots of
sons, then Campbell would have had a bigger and stronger army with
which to fight the system and get the land back.*

Nepia Mahuika, quoted in Mana Magazine: What was
gained? For so much loss? I look back on that and really, there was
nothing gained. Nothing.
　　We expected something to come of it – the gains Ngata was
talking about. I haven't seen the benefit.
　　The country was happy to use us. They used to talk about how
great we were, and all that. When we come back home they're going to
do a lot of this, a lot of that to help us. But it never eventuated. I tried to
get a rehab loan to build us a house. I never got it. It was like that before
the war.
　　I was wounded in the war, deafened in one ear and got sand in
my lungs. But it took me 50 years to get a war veteran's disability
pension. I had to go to the Appeal Court in Wellington to get that. The
treatment was insulting.
　　All our sacrifices – these were forgotten.

Hughie Hughes, electrician: The Ngati Porou are a great race.
I don't think they're a violent people. Gangs like the Black Power and
the Mongrel Mob struggle to get a foothold around here because the
Ngati Porou would rather have a couple of beers and a chat than get all
violent.
　　They're a very forgiving race and that might have worked
against them during the troubles. People talk about setting up a Maori
Court, but I don't think it would work here because the older people
aren't hard enough. They look for the easy way out.

The older Maori would say, "Tut, tut, tut, I don't know what these young people are doing. That's naughty." They didn't actually get wild about it or do anything about it.

There was Bob Kaa's group who did the night patrols and they were out to try and stop it. But as far as the grandparents were concerned, "Tut, tut," was about as strong as the language got as far as I know. They didn't realise the implications of what was happening. It was sad.

CHAPTER 5

A SCHOOL BURNS, AN ARREST IS MADE

The Gisborne Herald, Wednesday, November 19, 1986: A Ruatoria couple and their five children were left homeless when a fire damaged their house yesterday afternoon. The Te Weehi family live near a creek. But when the Ruatoria brigade was called just after 3pm it was unable to use it as a source of water because it had run dry. The house was completely burned out. Relatives have taken in the family of two boys, aged six and three, and three girls, aged eight, five and two. Their father is a returned serviceman and the Ruatoria branch of the RSA has made an appeal for relief. Clothing may be left at the RSA room and donations with the secretary.

Saturday, November 29: At 3.15am partygoers in Ruatoria notice a building on fire at the neighbouring Manutahi Primary School. They ring the Ruatoria Fire Service and the school principal, David Goldsmith, who lives on the property and is first on the scene.

"As I walked out the back door I saw the glow in the sky," Goldsmith says a few hours later. "Rather than reaching up, the flames were mushrooming out because of the corrugated iron roof. Perhaps if the flames had been able to get higher it would have been safer. The heat was contained in the building for a long time and endangered other

buildings. People arriving at the fire said they could feel its heat a hundred metres away."

The firemen are on the scene within minutes, with reinforcements from Tikitiki not far behind. But the fire is quicker. It destroys a three-classroom block (the newest part of the school) and scorches the administration offices and the assembly hall. Police are treating the fire as arson and have about fifteen people, including twelve from Gisborne, assigned to the investigation.

Goldsmith, a former pupil and teacher at Manutahi before becoming principal, believes someone tried to set fire to the oldest part of the sixty-six-year-old school, which lies in Tuparoa Road, on the edge of Ruatoria.

"I always thought in Ruatoria the schools and the marae would be safe," he says. "After this morning, nothing is sacred any more, we realise that. There are a lot of angry parents, grandparents, pupils and former pupils who are really uptight. In Ruatoria there is tension, and a lot of stress, which shows itself in all sorts of different ways. Nothing surprises us any more."

Goldsmith's right when he says "nothing is sacred any more", but his final statement is wrong; the people of Ruatoria can still be surprised.

Monday, December 1: *The police are following a number of leads in relation to the Manutahi Primary School arson.*

Deputy Commander of Gisborne police, Chief Inspector Whiro Ratahi, says that within minutes of the flames being noticed, a car in the vicinity was seen "leaving at high speed" by several people. Ratahi's appealing to the public to help find the driver. He says no description of the make or registration of the car is available yet, and police are unsure of the number of occupants.

Dective Senior Sergeant Norm Cook says he's "clearly satisfied" there were at least two efforts to set fire to the school. Police are also sure that entry was gained through a window of a classroom toilet.

That night an unemployed nineteen-year-old Rastafarian is arrested and charged with the arson of Manutahi Primary School. His name is Brent Waihi.

The arrest follows what Senior Sergeant Norm Cook describes as "probably the most intensive police campaign" ever mounted in Ruatoria. Police inquires into the arson are still continuing.

Wednesday, December 3: *Brent Waihi appears in the Gisborne District Court charged with arson. He's remanded without plea in custody until December 10.*

The National Party candidate for the East Cape, Wira Gardiner, challenges the Labour Government to face up to the crime wave on the East Coast. He says that after about thirty suspicious fires in the past year, Ruatoria should be treated as a crisis situation.

"And the government's response is to send their local MP to Ruatoria to talk about GST. The government should address the crime-wave hitting the East Cape community. The people of the East Coast are desperate. They have exhausted every ready means at their disposal. My fear is that they will turn to the ultimate form of retribution – vigilante groups."

Former Sergeant Alex Hope (now a lawyer) interviewed in October 2002: I believe that the whole thing was a classic response to economic and social depression and past injustices mixed up with young people and a Messianic religion. And if you trace the origins of Rastafarianism and then look at what happened in Ruatoria it's not that surprising. You had pre-European autonomy, you had post-European colonialism, but a semblance of autonomy brought about by isolation. That was followed by economic depression. On the Coast, the profitability of all the farms washed out into the sea. People were very wealthy early on while the soil remained on the hills. But when it all disappeared all that wealth disappeared with it.

Then forestry came and although it didn't make the coast wealthy, all the forests they were planting provided jobs and people were spending money.

A guy called Henry Banks is a classic example of what happened to lots of people on the Coast. Henry's wife is a first cousin of Barney Campbell. Anyway, Henry was a good hard-working honest man. He had a good job elsewhere. He was lured back home, you know, "Come back home and build a house. You've got a job for life in the forestry." He came back and bought his house. The forestry wound up and Henry had an investment that he couldn't sell and he could barely pay the mortgage, but he had to stay. I mean that's the classic example. That happened to heaps of people on the Coast, not just to Henry.

And then you have at that time, when those promises were going out the window, you had that New Labour Government, the '84 Labour Government closing down everything, shutting it all down. Regional development was going out the window. And the Coast was in a precarious position. And yes there was a solution to the Rasta situation. But the solutions were economic and social. The solution was not a policing solution. And even those PEP make-work schemes, they might have been a waste of time, but at least they pumped some money into the community and they kept people busy. A lot of marae on the East Coast were fixed up and kohangas were set up. But they even killed off those pathetic work schemes. And people suddenly had lots of time on their hands. The time was ripe for the establishment of a new gang. At the same time it coincided with the renaissance in Maori language. And so instead of having Black Power or Mongrel Mob, you had the same gang framework being filled by people who were also influenced by the renaissance in things Maori.

But I don't think there were policing solutions.

Undoubtedly, poor policing was a problem early on. This might sound arrogant but the policing there was pretty piss poor before I arrived. And I like to think that if I did contribute one thing it was a bit of hard work and honesty to what went on in the place. That's not to say that people were dishonest in the stealing sense. But the management was pathetic. It was tired. I wasn't impressed.

CHAPTER 6

SCHOOL ARSON TRIAL

Monday, August 24, 1987: Twenty-year-old Brent Waihi appears in the High Court in Gisborne charged with burning down Manutahi Primary School last November. He pleads not guilty.

The garbled nature of Waihi's original interviews with police makes it hard for prosecutor Terry Stapleton to nail down a coherent and convincing version of what happened the night of the arson.

But here's Stapleton's version of the next day. The police pick up Waihi at his home near the school in the morning. He's taken to the Ruatoria police station and questioned all that day and into the night, until 4am. At first, Waihi denies all knowledge of the fire and any involvement in it. Later he says he saw four men, two of whom were named Ben and Whetu, setting fire to the school. Then he tells another police officer he started the fire himself, with help from two accomplices, John Boy and Willie from Gisborne. They smashed a window, tipped a can of petrol about the floor and set fire to the classroom. When asked to repeat what he's said for a written statement, Waihi refuses, again denying his involvement and saying he was at home in bed at the time of the arson.

Detective-Sergeant Norm Cook tells Waihi he's interviewed John Boy and Willie and that they've denied involvement in the fire. Again Waihi confesses that no one else was with him, and he describes how he set the classroom on fire with matches and petrol.

"Nobody helped me on Friday night," Waihi tells police. "I did it because I had nothing else to do." The school was close to home so it was easy to get away afterwards, he says. "I was too drunk and stoned. When I was back in bed, I heard the siren go off. I lay listening to everything going on. I was too scared to look out the window."

Stapleton says that all the people Waihi mentioned in connection with the fire have denied having anything to do with it.

Stapleton says that Detective Sergeant Gary Condon examined the scene the day after the arson. Condon believes a pane of glass and a rubbish tin lid found on the floor of the building were placed there before the fire started. Linoleum that was badly burned in the centre but not around the edges indicated the fire was started in the middle of the room.

Damage to Block 4 of the school was severe and little evidence survived the heat and intensity of the blaze. But in Block 1, which was only moderately damaged, clear signs of arson survived. Splashes of accelerant, petrol-soaked materials, matches and charred newspaper were found there. That, says Stapleton, suggests arson was also committed in the more severe fire. (Waihi wasn't charged for the arson of Block 1.)

LENGTH OF INTERVIEW ATTACKED

Tuesday, August 25: *Defence lawyer Russell Fairbrother, of Napier, attacks police over the length of their interviews with Brent Waihi.*

Under cross-examination, Constable John Davies admits that while Waihi was interviewed until 4am, he wasn't warned that he didn't need to answer questions until 1.30am. (A written statement was completed at 3.45am.)

"Had you already been questioning him for four hours?" Fairbrother asks. Constable Davies says this was true, but Waihi was able to leave at any time as he had come to the police station voluntarily.

"Wasn't six hours rather a long time for a nineteen-year-old youth to be questioned? Did you do your best to make him comfortable?" Constable Davies says there were only two officers in the room at one time. Waihi was seated, had cordial to drink and cigarettes. Considering the environment, Waihi was made as comfortable as possible.

"Were you aggressive or non-pressuring when questioning him on points you believed he was being less than frank about?"

"We were matter of fact," says Constable Davies. Waihi had needed prompting on lots of occasions to get his story out.

Another witness, Constable Pani (Barney) Campbell, says he questioned Waihi – nicknamed "Boogie Lights" – on the morning following the fire. Waihi said the first thing he knew about the fire was when someone told him about it at the flea market that morning. He hadn't gone to look at the school because "those old people" would want to blame him because they always said he did these things.

Detective Malcom Thomas says Waihi told him he'd started the fire himself. He said he'd siphoned twenty litres of petrol from his brother's car into a plastic container. He'd walked to the school, smashed a window with a manuka stick, climbed through the window and splashed petrol around the three classrooms of block four, then lit a box of matches, threw them in the window and ran home. Then, on a later occasion, Waihi told Det. Thomas two others, John Boy and Willie, had helped him light the fire.

Wednesday, August 26: *The High Court in Gisborne hears yet another version of what happened the night of the Manutahi Primary School arson.*

Constable Anthony Murrell says he spoke to Waihi after the fire. Waihi told him he'd met a man named Billy Brown on the footpath outside a Ruatoria Hotel on the night of the fire. Brown told him he'd find a plastic container of petrol under pine trees behind an abandoned car yard.

"Burn the building," Brown told Waihi, then mumbled something about a school. "If you don't do it, I'll punch you over." And that, Waihi told Constable Murrell, is why he burned down the school.

During cross-examination, Russell Fairbrother asks Constable Murrell if it was true that Waihi had been questioned by seven different police officers over a period of twenty-four hours.

"No, it was six officers in less than twenty-four hours and Waihi did sleep at times." He'd seemed quite happy during the interviews and wasn't upset.

Fairbrother points out a place in Murrell's notes where it says Waihi was sobbing and seemed to be wandering a bit. "You say he was not upset, yet your notes indicate he was crying for about twenty minutes and you had to call Constable Campbell to reassure him."

"He did burst into tears at one stage of the interview. He said he was upset but scared to tell us what was on his conscience because of the feeling of the town. He wanted to get it off his chest. We gave him some cigarettes."

"Waihi had said he was ready to talk about the fire at 11pm. Why did you keep him talking about his family for another twenty minutes?"

Constable Murrell replies that it wasn't his place to force Waihi to talk about the fire when he wanted to talk about his family first.

Thursday, August 27: *Russell Fairbrother pounces on two niggling aspects of the case and turns them into a solid defence: Waihi's confused state of mind during interviews with police and a lack of evidence from the more severe of the two fires (the one in Block 4, which Waihi is accused of starting).*

In his final address to the jury, Fairbrother describes Brent Waihi as exhausted, bewildered and trying to be co-operative when he tells police how he started the fire, which destroyed part of Manutahi Primary School.

"Bound to a treadmill of confusion and fantasy which he did not know how to stop, the situation got more and more bizarre. Some people need to be protected against themselves – and Waihi is one of them."

Naïve and of limited intelligence, he hadn't known what he had said to the police. He was taken out of a familiar environment and interviewed continuously for nearly twenty-four hours by six different police officers. Things had gotten out of hand, says Fairbrother.

Waihi's brother John and local constable Pani Campbell had tried to stop the developments to no avail. Constable Campbell told Brent Waihi "just to tell the truth" and Waihi said he didn't do it. Detective Malcom Thomas overheard a private interview between Waihi and his brother. John was giving Brent the "third degree" - and still Waihi denied his involvement.

Fairbrother tells the jury it must separate reality from fantasy in Waihi's written statement taken at midnight.

He also brings attention to "an inherent contradiction in the Crown's logic". Prosecutor Terry Stapleton contended that evidence of arson in the less severe fire in Block 1 indicated arson in Block 4 – the block which was destroyed. But fingerprint evidence from the smaller fire indicated Waihi was not responsible for it.

If the prosecution believed Waihi had lit one fire when he hadn't lit the other, that lead to the "ridiculous conclusion" of two arsonists being abroad on the same night at the same time. (The author can't see why this is a "ridiculous conclusion". If what Waihi told police is true - that he did it with the help of two other guys - then it seems quite a logical conclusion.)

Also, Waihi said he had lit the fire with petrol. The windows of Block 4 had fallen inwards, not outwards as one might expect after a petrol fire. There was no sign of the plastic container in which Waihi said he carried petrol. Yet the plastic it was made from would have survived the fire. Waihi's clothes showed no traces of accelerant or glass from the window that he said he broke with his arm.

"And why had Waihi not been charged with the offence until 3.45am – seventeen hours after police started questioning him?"

Following a ninety-minute adjournment, the jury finds Brent Waihi not guilty of arson.

CHAPTER 7

THE FIRE STATION BURNS

Okay, that last trial was in 1987; let's jump back a year now to a few days after the school fire. Waihi's been arrested, but the investigation continues.

The Gisborne Herald, Saturday, December 6, 1986:
Insurance companies do not want to know Ruatoria. The fire-plagued community is getting the industry's cold shoulder and anger is building among those who know about it.

One main street business is uninsured. The owners have been rejected at every turn by companies unwilling to pick up risk in a township where arsons have done hundreds of thousands of dollars worth of damage…

…The community is discovering it has a problem as policies come up for renewal, increased cover or new business is sought…

…Those close to the industry agree that as a public relations exercise, the companies' reluctance to insure is a disaster… …Every major insurance company is unwilling to pick up new risk in the township – in some cases anywhere on the coast.

Friday, December 12: A psychologist warns that Ruatoria could explode like a "powder keg". Dr Ian Miller is the co-ordinator of psychological services for the New Zealand Police. He's been with the police for two years and was with the Justice Department for nine years before that. He's in Gisborne to act as a negotiator in an anti-terrorist exercise at Cook Hospital. Milner says that in such hostage situations, and possibly in Ruatoria, you have to deal with people with two extreme points of view. One group's intent on a "shoot first ask questions later" policy, and the other's on a path of action where too many concessions are made. It's this kind of situation, he says, which provides the ingredients for a violent explosion.

That same Friday, in 1986, at two in the afternoon, a large police party investigating the Manutahi Primary School arson leaves Ruatoria for Gisborne. They should know better than to feel relieved.

One hour and fifteen minutes later the Ruatoria Fire Station burns to the ground. The fire station is in the town's main street, directly opposite the police station. It's destroyed within minutes. Volunteer

*firemen stand by helplessly and watch their equipment burn. Gisborne
police assemble another party to return to Ruatoria.*

*Forest Service workers arrive with their engines within minutes
of the alarm being raised and using water from the police station
quickly extinguish the blaze. But what remains inside the building
reduces bystanders to tears. "Watching the Forest Service pull out the
charred engine really broke us up," says one of the women who raised
the alarm.*

*Two fire engines worth $500,000 and other equipment and a
building worth $100,000 are lost in the fire. A tanker is severely
damaged and is sent to Gisborne for repairs. Gisborne also provides a
relief tanker.*

*By late afternoon police are following strong leads into what
they believe is another arson.*

Ken McKinnon, Ruatoria Fire Chief (retired): The funny
thing was that at about three o'clock I was going to go down and check
what booze we had for the Christmas party that night and order some
more. But a friend of mine came up to my workshop. I said, "We'll
have a cup of tea." So I put the jug on. The next thing the siren went. If
I'd gone straight away as I'd intended to, I'd have caught them.

Tom Heeney, Ruatoria Deputy Fire Chief (retired): When I
get down there I rescue all our old books and records (many of which
have ended up in this book). There's smoke everywhere but I get'm out.
The siren's still going. It's a dismal sound: a siren going while your
station burns down. So I turn that off.

I've been in earlier to set the chiller on to keep the beers cool
for this party we're about to have. I wondered if that might've started
the fire. I think the motor might have jammed or something. But Ian
Clark, the Gisborne fire chief, checks it later. He spins the motor and it
goes round all right. He has a search about the place and finds a brand
new rake. And it's all burnt on top. He assumes the arsonist had a petrol-
soaked rag around the end of the rake. I'd opened a window pretty high
up and they must have put it through there.

We'd sanded all the floors and painted it all up and the station
was looking pretty spot on. I remember Maurice Mataira going to town
on the sander one night about ten o'clock. He said there was nothing the

rest of us could do. We might as well go home and he'd finish the sanding. A couple of weeks later it was flat to the ground.

Lyn Hillock, former Gisborne Deputy Fire Chief: Then they extend themselves and take out the fire station. We've just finished renovating the station. We've done a lot of work up there. It's an old building. Ken McKinnon, Tom Heeney and all the crew up there have done a hell of a good job. They've sanded the floor down to its original timbers, and done a big paint job.

We're answering all 111 calls for the coast in Gisborne. Ian and I are sitting in the office in Gisborne and we hear this call, "The Ruatoria Fire Station's on fire," and we look at each other, thinking, "Aw God. Here we go."

On the way my little Holden's internally hemorrhaging, and not surprisingly. We make Gisborne-Ruatoria, normally a two-hour drive, in fifty-nine minutes. But we're not the only ones hurrying. The officer in charge of Te Puia Station has an old Dodge. And as we drive through Te Puia and all the way to Ruatoria we can see the duel tyre-marks as he's gone around every corner. But we get there and the station's basically destroyed. There are two appliances there that are write-offs. The only thing of use we have left is the communications consul.

*But the people of Ruatoria suspect there is still one more fire to be lit today. It is well known that many of them have happened on the twelfth day of the month. Twelve is a special number in the Ringatu faith. In Maori time, a day lasts from mid-day to mid-day. A Ringatu service runs from midday on the twelfth to midday on the thirteenth. The Rastas incorporate Ringatu into their own beliefs. Part of developing their own unique religion has involved attaching extra significance to the number twelve. For instance, the core Ruatoria Rastafarians refer to themselves as The Twelve. And today is the twelfth day of the twelfth month. So it makes sense to locals: the fire station is just the first of **two** fires.*

*Meanwhile, the men who have to **fight** them are wondering, "What next?" They may not be schooled up on Ringatu. But they come to the same conclusion: another fire is on the way.*

Lyn Hillock: We sit down and have a bit of a think about *why* they've burnt down the fire station. And the general opinion is that they're going to do something else that night. By taking the fire station out they've left the town without protection.

We've got a list of probable targets from the CIB. They include all Government buildings, and any of the Williams' properties.

So we've got about five hours to get something up and running before nightfall. We've salvaged the radio consul and that's crucial. There's a Skyline garage next door that's been used by St. Johns. It's owned by one of the people in town. The owner lets us take it over. We reinstall the communications consul and we've got a workable station up and running by 6.30pm.

So the locals and the firemen have an inkling there'll be another fire. But are they prepared for what happens next? Not at all.

HOLY FIRE

Ken McKinnon, former Ruatoria Fire Chief: So we have our social that night. And it's starting to quieten down about midnight. I get home and about half an hour later off the siren goes again. The church at Mangahanea Marae is on fire.
It's funny. That church is all corrugated iron with a bell tower up fairly high with a wind vein on top. I say to the blokes, "Watch it if you're going under there because there's a bell on top. If the wood catches that bell will drop."

Anyway I look there in the morning and the bell's melted. It's dropped down in a big bronze heap.

Lyn Hillock: Around about 1 o'clock I hear the sirens start up and I look out the window and there's the church down at the marae well ablaze.

We get stuck into that. The local guys like Tom Heeney are just devastated. The kaumatua out there just can't believe that the Rastas have gone this far.

The locals have a hui. But nobody comes forward as to who's done it. It devastates people up there. The fire station is bad enough. The courthouse, well, no one was too bothered about that. But the church really hurts people.

We're tearing our hair out. As far as we can see if it was anywhere else in New Zealand, something would be done about it. There would be that many police and Armed Offenders Squad guys that you couldn't move and they'd clean them out. We're trying to deal with terrorist activity.

One of the most frustrating things for us is that we know *who's* doing it, we know *how* they're doing it but we can't *prosecute* them because we can't *nail* them.

Saturday, December 13, 1986: *Reneti Church is near Mangahanea Marae, about 1.6 kilometres outside Ruatoria. The alarm is raised between 1 and 1.30am. Shortly afterwards, locals are shocked to see a carload of people in the area cheering. In stark contrast, Kawhia Milner is devastated.*

The Mangahanea pakehe lives alone in a house next to the marae. His Maori chanting can be heard above the roar of the flames. Overcome by sadness and anger, he prays for help, for an end to the fires and for justice to be done.

Locals are deeply shocked, even traumatised.

A man who is one of the first on the scene: "We know now that nothing is sacred to these people. After every fire we are asked what we feel – now we have run out of words."

Another eyewitness concurs: "We have no more words; only the one thought: 'Where next?'"

After sifting through the ashes in daylight, police confirm that both fires, the fire station and the church, are being treated as suspicious. Once again, a large police party is carrying out intensive investigations in the area, and reinforcements from other parts of New Zealand are being sent to the Gisborne district.

Mangahanea spokesman Chubby Walker says the people responsible for the fire must be insane.

Reneti Church is eighty-six years old; one of the area's oldest churches. Hundreds of local people have been christened, married and buried there. It was completely restored just four years ago. And now it's completely destroyed. The obvious question is why.

The Governor General, Sir Paul Reeves, is due to visit Mangahanea Marae tomorrow. He's taking part in ceremonies to dedicate the new marae gate carved by Moni Taumaunu. Preparations were well underway when the fire struck. And apart from everything

"HIT LIST" OF TARGETS

Lyn Hillock, former Gisborne Deputy Fire Chief: The whole town, after the first church: the guts just drops out of it. None of the elders will speak; none of the families will speak.

There's real fear in the town. The only ones who will walk right through the middle of them are us and the police. All the other townspeople keep well away.

But the Rastas despise us. We're surplus to requirements. We're interfering with their plan.

The main thing that strikes me is the distress of the kaumatua. The elders come over from the marae. People are in a real state of shock. We sit down and have a debriefing at 11am at the police station. We decide, "Well, this'll be it. This'll be the trigger for somebody coming forward and saying something." But nobody does. It's like the soul has been sapped out of the whole place. It takes a hell of a toll on the families. It affects the kids, the firefighters, their wives. Whai Kaiwai's trying to run a farm and up all night fighting fires. Then they're away from their normal jobs, assisting us for four or five days on the big fires. They're working hard dealing with the arsons, while their own businesses are going downhill. If there's another attack on a Government building or if they try to burn the temporary fire station down again, there'll be quite a few bodybags needed. We've all had as much as we can take.

The reason they're burning everything down is to get rid of the white man from the coast. That's their stated objective and they're well on the way to achieving it. They dropped the price of the land up there. We've estimated that about five million dollars worth of property's been burnt. Anywhere else in the country, the military would have moved in by now. But no one cares because it's the East Coast.

It just keeps going. And it costs us millions of dollars to deal with the situation.

*Another night of heavy eyes and frayed nerves: the
Neighbourhood Support Group is patrolling the streets of Ruatoria. Bob
Kaa, the leader of the group, whose garage burned down four months
ago, is asked if his men are armed.*

*"I am not going to answer that. But you can say we are well
prepared for confrontation."*

*And Kaa has no doubt **whom** they'll be confronting should they
catch the arsonists red handed.*

*"They are anti-social, anti-Crown and anti-authority," he says.
"They are bucking the judicial system, making a mockery of it. The fires
started two years ago. They began with hay barns and woolsheds and
then moved closer to home, to private businesses like mine. They had a
go at the courthouse, then a policeman's house and now they have burnt
down the church, the most sacred thing to Moaris. My personal belief is
that we should bring the Army in under the pretext of an exercise. Now
that ANZUS has gone, soldiers are only sitting around twiddling their
thumbs anyway."*

*Manutahi Hotel manager Dan Harrison says Ruatoria people
are reluctant to talk about the Rastafarians for fear of reprisals. He says
he knows of a "hit list" of town buildings to be burned, but can't see
why people would go to the extreme of burning down a church. "I just
hope the police can sort this out," he says, "so we can enjoy Christmas
like everyone else."*

*Meanwhile, about fifty police from as far afield as Auckland,
Wellington and Palmerston North have been sent to Ruatoria to boost its
usual force of one sergeant and two constables. There are assurances
that security will be tight for the Governor General's visit to
Mangahanea Marae tomorrow.*

Sunday, December 14: *The Governor General Sir Paul
Reeves' visit to Mangahanea Marae goes off without a hitch... and
locals breathe a sigh of relief.*

*"As I go around," Sir Paul says to about two hundred people
at the marae, "I think of all the things that are messing us up. But I also
have confidence in people – that we can sort it out, given time, given
patience and given the support of God.*

*"I am here not to solve problems. I am here to spend the night
in the meeting house, just to do that, and what happens will happen."*

Lyn Hillock, former Gisborne Deputy Fire Chief: Tikitiki people, they do the right thing. It's just after the Rastas burnt down the fire station. And they're heading north towards Tikitiki. So they have a busload of Tikitiki guys come down. "You arseholes step one foot over this mark here you'll disappear." And Tikitiki has no problems with them. "You arseholes stay in Ruatoria. You come up here and look out." So everything stayed within Ruatoria, out to the coast, back into Mount Hikurangi and then down to Te Puia.

CHAPTER 8

PLEAS FOR HELP

Detective Inspector Pat Moore of Wellington arrives in Ruatoria to take over the investigation with Detective Senior Sergeant Rob Marshall of Auckland as his deputy. The Auckland Serious Crime Squad also arrives to join police from a number of other North Island centres.

Pat Moore's first act is to write an open letter. It's put in every letterbox and post office box in Ruatoria and placed in shops and buildings throughout the township. This is what it says.

Residents of Ruatoria,
You do not need me to tell you of the suspicious fires that have occurred in your town over the past two years.
We are anxious to stop any further fires, apprehend the person or persons responsible and return Ruatoria to the peaceful town it used to be. To achieve this end **WE NEED YOUR HELP.** Some of you know the identity of the person or persons responsible for these fires and we want to hear from you… …**HELP US TO HELP YOU.**
P.D MOORE,
Detective Inspector

***Monday, December 15:** The Governor General Sir Paul Reeves slept on Mangahanea Marae last night. He travels to Te Araroa today for the prize-giving at Rerekohu High School.*

Detective Inspector Moore takes over responsibility for the investigation from today. He's split the police into teams, which are spreading out over the township talking to various people. This should take about two days.

Regional Fire Commander Ron Smith of Wellington is also in Ruatoria today, visiting the site of the fire station arson.

Advert in the Gisborne Herald:
<u>REWARD</u>
$5000
We will pay $5000 reward for information leading to the conviction of the person or persons responsible for the burning of the Reneti Church at Mangahanea Marae, Ruatoria.

Any information should be directed to the Gisborne or Ruatoria Police Station and will be treated in the strictest confidence.
ENTERPRISE CARS LTD
Supporting your community

The fires at the church and the fire station take the terror to a new level in Ruatoria. The shadowy threats to burn the town to the ground used to be just that. Now the frightened residents know they're serious. Since the fires, lights are on in almost every house and building late into the night.

*In Ruatoria, speculation is rife about the timing of the fire on the marae. It happened less than forty-eight hours before the Governor-General arrived. When one considers that Bob Kaa's garage was razed while he was attending his mother's tangi and that Jeremy Williams lost his house while he was in Whangara getting married, an element of cruelty appears to be attached to the **timing** of these fires. These arsons aren't just cases of kicking people, but of kicking them when they're down or when they're vulnerable.*

Unfortunately, the timing of the Neighbourhood Watch Group isn't as precise. It's been revealed that one of their patrols stopped briefly on the lonely road by the Mangahanea Marae only minutes before the church went up in flames.

(And doesn't that raise an interesting question for a conspiracy theorist. Is it possible the Rastas didn't light this one? The vigilantes had already been accused of burning down John Heeney's house. Could they have done this, knowing the Rastas would get the blame and the level of outrage that would be directed at them?

I floated the possibility with former detective Hemi Hikawai in February 2009 and he doubted very much that the vigilantes would have been involved because of their connections to the church. I also floated it the next day with a former Rastafarian. He told me three Rastafarians had lit the Reneti Church fire. All three were now dead. Two had died in one freak accident and the third had died in a separate freak accident.

"Why do you think that happened?" I asked.

He replied: "They burnt down a church and they paid the price.")

The church burning is seen as a direct challenge by the Rastas to the authority of the Crown.

Now there are fears for the children, who romanticise about the Rastafarians as horse-riding outlaws.

Tom Heeney, Ruatoria fireman and Rastafarian John Heeney's father: Now they're starting to get all the younger kids joining them. The young kids think these guys are really tough. The kids are even keener to join now that the TV crews have turned up. Every kid wants to be on TV. So they're joining up with this gang and getting into it. The worst thing that happened to us was when the TV crews started turning up.

PROBLEMS FOR TRADESMEN

It's a commonly-held belief in Ruatoria that the spate of fires is a carefully-orchestrated form of revenge for land grievances going back many generations. And the town's self-styled Rastafarians, said to number between a hundred and a hundred and fifty, are the prime suspects.

But still no one comes forward with information. "There are people here who must know something," says Bob Kaa. "They must come forward in the wider interests of the community." He says the

Maori concept of whanau is admirable, but in the situation like that now being faced in Ruatoria, the concept has a major disadvantage: people are closing ranks to protect their own when the protection of the town is more important.

There are now real fears that what doesn't burn down in Ruatoria may end up going anyway. Pakeha farmers are seriously considering the not-too-subtle nudge from Rastas toward greener pastures outside the district. Businesses are struggling. And insurance companies are increasingly uneasy about the town's high-risk properties. And if the town's two stock and station agents close, the effects on Maori farmers could be disastrous.

Hughie Hughes, Pakeha electirician, whose business is on the main street of Ruatoria (interviewed in late 2000): I never seriously thought of leaving Ruatoria. For a start I had nowhere else to go. I also had responsibilities to staff I employed. And anyway this was my town. I went to high school in Gisborne and served an apprenticeship with Ellis and Bull Electrical there. And when the power came up to Ruatoria in 1955, I came up. I've been here ever since. I've been here longer than eighty per cent of the people. It's the same with Ken McKinnon, the former fire chief, and Tom Heeney. Tom's been here longer than I have. Why should we have to move? We provide the services. We do all the work. And of course I was totally involved in the ambulance service in those days.

I remember going around in the ambulance to pick up Dickie Maxwell out the back of the pub here. They'd found him unconscious in the morning. He'd been badly beaten up. This was before the troubles started. But Dickie had already done enough to upset a few people. Dickie had been upsetting people since he was eight. When he was a kid he'd jump school, go round the back and climb into the houses and nick things. This was in the late sixties-early seventies when robbery was rare. And there was almost no unemployment. I remember there were only two unemployed people in town.

The other thing that worries me is that Tom Heeney, Ken McKinnon and myself are more or less the only three tradesmen in town. Tom's a builder, Ken's a plumber and I'm the sparky.

If you go back forty years ago, all my working mates were Maori tradesmen. But these days there are hardly any Maori getting a trade. So they're reliant on just a few of us. I've got three jobs waiting for me today. But I can't get to them. Where are all the young fullas? Every day you see the electricians, the painters, the plumbers, the carpenters all coming through from Gisborne. Why shouldn't it be local?

Having said that, it's very difficult for Maori to be in business up here because the whanau expect you to do it for nothing. And in a lot of cases the ones who have started up have gone broke because of that.

Bob Kaa: The interesting thing about being in business on the coast was my own people were dead against me. Their attitude was: "How come you Maoris can go into business and we can't?" That was at that time.

A couple came in to see us. They said, "Where do you come from?"

I said, "Rangitukia," which is just over the river.

He said, "We'll give you boys six months, then you'll be gone."

And I just couldn't believe the attitude of our own people. I suppose they just thought, "Maoris aren't supposed to go into bloody business." Of course, during those times and before our times all the business people on the Coast were Pakeha. We had no problem from the Pakehas. Once we got to know them we practically had all their business. That's how I met the Colin Williamses, the John Bartons, the Williams and Kettles, the Wrightsons. We had all their business and we got on bloody well. But it was our own people… Maori Affairs was a Crown agency once upon a time. They wouldn't bring any of their work to us. Fuckin' Maori Affairs. Ask yourself. They had a lot of vehicles here then. They'd come with the odd puncture and say, "Bob could you fix this in a hurry." I'd say, "You want your puncture fixed," – and I'd roll the tyre off down the street – "then go chase the bastard."

Hughie Hughes, electrician: Anyway, back to Dickie Maxwell unconscious outside the pub. I took Dickie up to the hospital. And he played dead. He's lying there and the nurse was bending over trying to examine him. And he grabbed her by the bloody hair and pulled her down. He was pulling her hair really hard. And I waited for the cop to hit him over the head with a bloody truncheon or something. But he didn't! And this poor bloody nurse was about to be scalped. And that's the kind of guy Dickie Maxwell was. I don't think he even spoke to the nurse.

Former Ruatoria policeman Steve Tresidder: Dickie Maxwell was a mongrel. Every time you wanted to talk to him, he'd never do anything voluntarily. And I remember one day, there was a warrant out for him. And I didn't want to lock him up. I wanted to tell him that next time he was in Gisborne to sort out the situation, otherwise he was going to get locked up.

And I remember, he was trotting along the road on his horse and I pulled up next to him. And I said, "Hey Dick, you know there's a warrant out for you, ay?"

I'd just got that out of my mouth and the next thing, he just took off on his horse, galloped across the road and leapt the fence and off into the bush on his horse.

I didn't even get the opportunity to explain to him what I wanted to talk to him about. He was just gone. That was the sort of hard case that he was. And I didn't see him for at least three weeks. He just disappeared.

***Tuesday, December 16:** Detective Inspector Pat Moore hits out at the "vigilante" tag given to the Neighbourhood Watch Group by some sectors of the media and some locals. "I have been here for two nights and have not seen anybody that looks like a vigilante," says Moore. The surveillance group and Bob Kaa in particular hate being called vigilantes. Moore has been working closely with them since his arrival and, obviously, wants to keep them on side.*

Police are working in shifts to give the town "24 hour coverage". So far there have been only two phone calls in response to the distribution of more than four hundred leaflets appealing for information. But police are following up on the information they've been given.

Interestingly, while investigating the arsons, police have stumbled across all sorts of other crimes. Since Jeremy Williams' house at Matahiia Station burned down on November 8, they've arrested twenty-two people on a number of charges. That fire was also the catalyst for a change in police procedure. Detective Inspector Barry Hunter in Napier now checks all arson files, and a new investigative pattern has been implemented.

Meanwhile, The Truth newspaper has followed the lead of Enterprise Cars Ltd. It's put up a $5000 reward under its "Secret

Witness Scheme" for information leading to the conviction of Ruatoria's arsonists.

***Tuesday, December 23, 1986:** Detective Inspector Pat Moore of Wellington and other staff from outside the district have now returned home. Moore says he's "saddened" at the lack of response to a police appeal for information.*

Lyn Hillock, Gisborne Deputy Fire Chief (retired): One of the saddest Christmases during this whole saga is the one we spend in the RSA in Ruatoria. That's straight after they've burnt the fire station and everybody's gutted.

It's after midnight and we're all just sitting around with our families. It's not until about two o'clock in the morning, after several cans and bottles, that any of us actually manage to smile. It's just anarchy in the town, like a mini civil war.

The stress on the police and fire fighters is incredible. We're all keeping an eye on each other. If someone's tipping too far, you give him a word in his ear. "Hey mate, you're about to lose it." And hopefully they'll back off for a while.

I know personally there's been one or two times when I've got that frustrated, like when they've threatened our wives, that it's just about been the trigger point for me of going up and cleaning the whole lot out, and to hell with consequences. The consequences don't even enter into the equation when you're that tightly sprung. I've been that close to doing it.

Unfortunately, with the police and ourselves, the first group of people anybody would look at is us.

THE LIST SO FAR

***Saturday, December 27:** Police release a list of twenty-seven suspicious fires in and around Ruatoria since February 15, 1985. Nineteen of them are the subject of active arson inquiries. They are:*

1985
July 1: Stacked hay in paddock, Colin Williams' property, Main Road South.

July 13: Haybarn and contents, same property.
July 27: Haybarn, Horehore Station. Offender was prosecuted successfully.
November 19: Ruatoria Courthouse/Police Station.
December 7: Haybayn, Waiomatatini Station, second in five years.
December 8: Woolshed, Koura Station on Whareponga Road.
December 13: House, Whakapaurangi Road.
December 12: Police house, Mangakino Street, Ruatoria.
December 20: Car burnt out, Waiomatatini Road.
December 26: Small hay fire, Gate Station
1986
February 15: Ruatoria Aero Clubhouse, Pakihiroa Road.
February 22: Forest fires, Whaangiangi Road, Te Araroa.
February 22: Rasta House at the Crossroads. Police prosecuted a suspect, but not convicted.
August 22: Joe's Bookshop, Main Road, Ruatoria.
August 23: Ruatoria Motors, Main Road, Ruatoria.
November 8: Matahiia Station homestead, Makarika.
November 29: Manutahi Primary School classroom block. Suspect arrested, not convicted.
December 12: Ruatoria Fire Station, appliances.
December 13: Reneti Church, Mangahanea.

In relation to those nineteen fires, police have made three arrests, comprising one successful prosecution, one unsuccessful and one pending.
But fire service records show a number of other fires with unknown causes. They are:

1985
February 11: T and S Motors, Ruatoria, rear wall and files.
April 30: Shed, Tuparoa Road.
July 4: House, Tapuaeroa Valley, Maru's property.
November 9: Gilvray House, Te Puia.
November 16: Hedge fire, Whareponga Road.
December 4: Malicious false alarm to Tikitiki House.
1986
January 25: Woolshed, Mangahanea Farms, Tuparoa Road.
April 4: Farm Store Shed, Waiomatatini Road.

NON-RASTA ARSONISTS

Police say they're close to solving a number of the arsons, but haven't enough evidence to go to court. They need to know where certain people were up to an hour before the fires and immediately after the alarms went up. And once again they're appealing to relatives and friends of the offenders for information.

Chief Inspector Whiro Ratahi says public meetings and dialogue with the Ratsas haven't provided answers. "During our investigations we have spoken to nearly every person in Ruatoria, including members of the police, fire service and Neighborhood Support Group. The inquiry does not just stop with the Rastafarian group."

He agrees the group is everyone's favorite suspect because they've talked openly of razing the town and have made similar statements to police. But he says police haven't ruled out the possibility that some of the fires may have nothing to do with the Rastas, that a fire-starter may be hiding behind their bad reputation.

Barney Campbell, former Ruatoria policeman and Chris Campbell's brother: The police did the same thing to the fire department as they did to me over the burning of the police station. They questioned Tom Heeney, the deputy fire chief, extensively over the arson of the fire station.

They got it wrong with Tom and I. But there *were* people other than the Rastas lighting fires up there. There was plenty of *that* going on. Since I left the police force I've been told by people I would-a called good citizens the details of who did what to whom. Some of these people no longer live in Ruatoria and some are still there. It seems there was a bit of people getting their own back. Aw well, fair enough, I suppose. There was a group of locals that everyone called the Vigilantes. And they were supposed to be helping us. But some of them were more trouble than they were worth. There were a couple of incidents where I think we could-a locked a lot more people up. But they were supposed to be on the good side. It didn't help matters. You're trying to sort one lot out and the lot that are supposedly helping you are committing their own little bits of crime. And you're expected to turn a blind eye to what they're doing and come down hard on the Rastas.

Tuesday, December 30: *Gisborne Area Fire Commander Ian McDowall says all sixteen members of the Ruatoria Volunteer Fire Brigade have been talked to by police investigating the arsons. The reason, he says, is to show the community that there's no favouritism in the probe. The volunteers are made up mainly of forestry and rural workers, with a few shopkeepers. McDowall says they've had to fight more fires in the past two years than they would be expected to attend in twenty. He says the brigade keep expecting resignations, but so far there have been none. "They are all good blokes and very loyal."*

Sunday, January 25, 1987: *An arson attempt in the Ruatoria State Forest fails to do much more than scorch the ground. Fires are lit among eight-year-old pines in Whangaangiangi Valley but, thanks to recent rain, can't get a hold. A fire crew spots the blaze and quickly puts it out. The valley, northwest of Ruatoria and just south of Te Araroa, was the scene of a similar incident eleven months ago.*

CHAPTER 9

TWO MORE CHURCHES BURN

Sunday, March 15: *Two more fires are lit just after midnight. Two more historic churches, less than ten kilometres apart, are destroyed. They're both Anglican churches attached to marae. Pioneer family the Williams built Te Aranga Church on Ngati Porou Marae, just south of Ruatoria, around a hundred and thirty years ago. It's still standing after firemen contain the blaze, but is gutted and will have to be demolished. The other fire reduces Mikaere Church on Hiruharama Marae to ashes. The Hiruharama blaze was noticed at 12.15am. On their way there, police and firemen came across the second blaze, at Ngati Porou Marae. About thirty firemen from Ruatoria, Tikitiki and Te Puia Springs, plus forestry fire crew from Ruatoria, fought the fires.*

Tom Heeney: When the church down the road here, Te
Aranga, was set alight, I tore down in my car. The church was burning
so I stopped and ran in and had a look around. Couldn't see anyone. I
called out, "Is anyone in there?" I wasn't sure cos the fire was going
pretty well.

According to Ian Clark, the fire safety officer at the time, he
reckoned they must have been clear of the building by the time I got
there and just sitting there watching me. I came out and I waited. I could
hear the sirens going and I thought, "Aw, the boys'll come along soon."
On our rural watch you always had to go into the station first anyway to
get your gear.

So I opened the gates and waited. No. Still hadn't come. So I
thought, "Maybe the boys are struggling to get a crew. They won't
leave until they get a crew together."

So I tore in to meet the appliance and then we got a call from
Hiruharama that the church there was on fire, too.

Eru Reedy was in the appliance. I said, "You carry on to
Hiruharama and fight that and I'll go into town and get the tanker and
head to the other church. Tikitik are on their way to help me."

We did a pretty good save, but Eru and the boys had a hell of a
battle at Hiruharama. The place was just about burnt out by the time
they got there.

The next day Lyn Hillock and Ian Clark came up. The arch of
the doorway and everything was still standing at Hiruharama. And they
were sifting through the remains. A breeze came along and the whole
arch and everything fell right over the top of them. They were right in
the middle and it missed them. Course we always used to say to Ian,
"Well we always reckoned that if you went to church the building would
come down on you."

Lyn Hillock: The siren goes one night and Tom Heeney stops
at the first church on the intersection. It's fully ablaze. He can't do

anything about it. So he makes his way to the fire station to man the machine back to the fire. And later the police give him a real grilling. Everybody in the brigade gets grilled every time there's a fire. "Where were you? What were you doing?" That puts a lot of pressure on the people up there.

It feels like we're just halfway through this whole episode. But I know personally that the support from Police National Headquarters and the Gisborne Superintendent has just disappeared. They just want it to go away.

Guys like Laurie Naden, Hemi Hikawai, Malcolm Thomas and Lee Pascoe, all the people up there, are just about ready to drop. They're up there all the time, continuously. And the Manutahi pub doesn't have the most comfortable beds in the world.

Tom Heeney: The cops started interrogating me about the fires. They asked all sorts of questions after the fire station and then Hiruharama Church was burned. I always knew I'd have to stick it out. I was ugly enough and big enough to. I could argue with them. I wasn't frightened of them.

Monday, March 16, 1987: Last week Labour's Housing Minister Phil Goff was in Hiruharama launching a new housing project aimed at reviving the village. Obviously, some people had other plans. Today, he's discovering that to get close to events in Ruatoria is to risk getting burned.

"Burning the church is an act of sacrilege," he says, "and an insult to the memory of many young men from the community, including Lieutenant Te Moana Ngarimu, VC, who a generation ago gave their lives for their country." (Lieutenant Ngarimu, John Heeney's uncle, was baptised at the church at Hiruharama.)

AN INSULT TO ELDERS

David Conway, The Gisborne Herald, Monday, March 16: Who could burn a church, desecrate ground so sacred to the Maori people, land containing graves of their families, memories so precious to the elders? Many find it hard to accept another Maori could do this with any degree of sanity, even though the finger points always within their ranks.

They are sad and bewildered at the insanity that continues unchecked. The tears of elderly Ngati Porou, the real victims of the last three fires, say more than the angry words of Ruatoria.

But are those who light the fires there when an old lady clutches a fence post to support her in prayer? Do they see the charred cross of Mikaere lying in the grass overlooking the papakainga that is to be the new Hiruharama? Do they think of Erana Harrison, the church she has lovingly tended on Ngati Porou Marae, the family she has baptised and seen married at Te Aranga?

Married there sixty years ago, Mrs Harrison has maintained Te Aranga since 1927. All those years of work were desecrated along with the church and its history under the cover of darkness. Mrs Harrison could not believe what she was seeing when she rushed from her nearby home at the height of the blaze. Her love for her church extended to cleaning it and putting fresh flowers in it nearly every day. "I can not believe it has gone."

Ngati Porou Marae and its church had been looking a picture since the marae committee, aided by a PEP scheme workforce, had completed a full refurbishing programme. Te Aranga had been reblocked, rotten boards replaced and painted to give it a new lease of life. Now the little church at the Crossroads at the entrance to Ruatoria will have to be demolished.

Excerpt from an interview with Rastafarian John Heeney and his wife Donna at the Crossroads in early 2000: *I was just wondering, was the dope always here or did it come with some sort of stoner sailor, or…?*

Yeah, it's always been here in my life. Well my cousin, he was telling me that twenty-five years ago they were growing dreadlocks and smoking dacc and selling it. But you know they weren't Rastaman then. But they were still the natives, ay. The natives were still there.

Was that round here?

Yeah. Would-a been in the early sixties, late fifties even.

Dreadlocks back then?

Yeah. And my family had them, my first cousins. And I thought, "Gee, no wonder." So when we popped up with dreads and the dacc, the whanau already had seen that but twenty-five years before we'd come in on the scene, ay.

That's right. So it wasn't new.

Yeah. And then they knew straight away how to stomp it: bring the cops in, BANG. Yeah. But it backfired away. As soon as the cops came in well they got a thumping too. They hit us, well, we'll hit them. And it just went back and forward, back and forward. They hit us, we hit them, they hit us, we hit them, they hit us, we hit them.

So there was a lot of standing your ground?

Yeah. You pull out a marijuana crop of ours; we'll go and burn a house down of theirs. And we let it be known that's the price. You play the game; we'll play the game, tit for tat. There's no way we were gonna let them walk on or trample all over us.

What about with the church, when you burnt down the church? Like was that sort of like a real message to the locals?

I reckon that was a real message to everyone, you know, three churches get burnt down by fire.

I was in Gisborne and I was just reading the paper and I thought, "Fuck, the church," you know, "these guys are serious now."

Donna: We didn't do the church fires though ay.

What's that?

We didn't - he didn't do the church fires. You didn't go to jail for the church fires, ay?

John: Na, I only burnt the police houses and the police station, yeah.

(Author's note: Heeney went to trial for the 1986 arson of a police house in Mangakino Street but a jury found him not guilty. The arson of former Sergeant Alex Hope's police house in 1988 has never been solved, although Hope has always believed Heeney was responsible. He explains why later in the book).

John: But there's warriors with two feathers, three feathers and there's warriors with half a feather, ay. There's all different levels, ay. But when the call comes they're all keen. They'll put it into operation but it may not necessarily be where you'd expect them to put it into operation.

Donna: Cos it sort of gave us - you a fright, ay? Ay, us a fright that that church had got burnt, ay?

Aw, not really.

Donna: No, no?

Not really, I was *rapt.*

Donna: Aw yeah, ha ha.

We all laugh. TK, one of two other Rastas sitting with us, has got an awesome low chuckle.

John: I was because, remember, we went to that karakia at Jerusalem (Hiruharama) that night. We went to a prayer. And these old people done it and the last thing this fulla said that night, the last minister, was, "God is a consuming fire." And I told my mate, "Hey, something's going down. I can feel it in my fingers, ay. I feel it in my bones." And so we walked up the hill that night to scout around. I was expecting maybe something fall out from the sky. But then we went back home. Nothing had happened. Fell off to sleep. And then all I remember was seeing the red lights going around the room and the fire engine was outside the old man's place and old lady's place. They were talking to the old man. They asked the old man, which fire should they go and put out. Cos they got called to go and put out the church fire at Hiruharama (Jerusalem) and while they're driving out there the church at Ngati Porou was also on fire.

Everyone laughs.

So they stop half-way between the church fires, at my old man's place and asked him which one. And he reckoned, "Aw which one did you get called to go to?" They reckoned Jeru, so he said, "Go to Jeru then. Go to the one you got called to go to." They both burnt down.

TK: Caught in the middle.

GOD IS NOT IN THE HOUSE

Detective Sergeant Laurie Naden (retired): There are always funny little incidents. There were actually a group of Christians staying in the Hiruharama marae the night the church went up. I remember we were doing inquiries there the day after. And there was one girl and she was a religious bloody zealot… a nice girl. And she said she woke up and she heard the pastor saying, "The church is ablaze, the church is alight." And she's going, "Hallelujah! Hallelujah!" cos she thinks the old flame of God is coming down and they're all being bloody reincarnated. Then she looks up on the hill and goes, "Fuck, it is, too!" And the church is ablaze all right. She's burning down.

Donna Heeney: I think the message at the time was: God is not inside a house. He is inside people.

John: You look at that. He's as big as the whole wide world. And yet he can still live in your heart.

Donna: You can't put God in a house. You go to church every Sunday and you come out and your normal life is ungodly. You go to church and you pray to God and then you come back and you're living ungodly. So I think that was the message of the burning of the churches.

John: Mind you, we were having a bit of a shunting match with the Mihinare church.

Donna: Missionaries.

John: Because we wanted to go back to the old church, the Ringatu church. See at some of these marae around here they're Ringatu churches, ay. What was happening was the big men up in the Mihinare church were coming down and trying to be the big men on the Ringatu church also… (everyone laughs)… because of the carving.

Donna: And they're not Ringatu. They're Anglicans.

John: And that's where a lot of the clashing started: because they left the Ringatu, because before we were all Ringatu people living here, from before the missionaries up to our grandfathers and grandmothers. And then after that when it came to our mothers and fathers, they went to another church. See? They left the church, ay. But those karakia that our grandfathers, our grandmothers, their fathers, their mothers, left , was just too strong, ay. They could walk away from the church but they couldn't walk away from those prayers that got said back by those other generation of old people. And the spirit was left, ay.

And they still recite them?

Yeah. And here's the recitations in young bodies today (John sweeps his arm towards the kids playing in the back of the garage) come alive, ay. See, otherwise you wake up one morning go, "Hey!" Look in the mirror, go, "Phew! That wasn't there yesterday." And it's a whole new world, ay. Because the Lord said if you listen to Him and obey Him he'll give us the land of our ancestors. That's how we gain it.

Lyn Hillock, retired Gisborne Deputy Fire Chief: They take Ian Clark and I off the cases and they send so-called experts up from Wellington. That lasts about five minutes. They don't know what they've let themselves in for and they just hop on the plane and head back to Wellington. They don't have a clue.

In New Zealand, there aren't any more experienced arson investigators than Ian and myself. It's funny as a fit.

Paul Wiseman, the Gisborne police superintendent, hates my guts. I'm the rescue skipper on the rescue boat as well. He used to run it years and years before me. It's his baby and he wants his select people on it. But I'm chairman and I say, "Piss off. You stick to your police stations, mate, and we'll look after the jet rescue stuff." From that day on we don't get on.

After about the 32nd arson he writes a report that we can't find a cause. The fact is we've found a cause for every single fire. But in his opinion he needs more expert investigators. So he takes his CIB team out and brings a new CIB mob in from out of town. And through national headquarters they bring two fire safety investigators up from Wellington. And the whole fuckin' lot last a day and a half. We sit on the fence at the church in Jerusalem (Hiruharama). It's as funny as a fit. We've done most of the investigation and we're right down to the area of origin, which is by the altar. All that's left is this concrete foundation block. We've taken samples of everything. But they've been using meths and it's very, very hard to detect alcohol. All our gas detectors are calibrated for hydro-carbons.

So anyway the mob arrives from Wellington. The big boys arrive in. So Thommo, Laurie, Brett Kane, myself, Ian Clark, Tom Heeney and Ken McKinnon, we all take all our tools outside and put them down. And we just sit on the fence and watch these guys.

They're saying, "Aw, where'd ya start?"

"Sorry, you're the experts. All yours. Your scene. We can't come in. Bye."

So we fuck off to the pub. And the shit hits the fan. They're ringing national headquarters. We've got the national commander ringing up. "You get back!"

"Sorry, the experts, you sent 'em."

Tuesday, March 17, 1987: *The police make more desperate pleas for information.*

Chief Inspector Whiro Ratahi: "A young child or an old person who cannot move quickly could be in one of these buildings when a fire starts. Even a fit adult can be overcome by smoke and flames."

Sergeant Alan Dawes, police media liaison officer: "People must know who lit these fires. The people have not been helpful at all. It is a close-knit community where everyone knows each other and that has to be the reason they are unwilling to come forward. Someone is going to die either in one of these fires or at the hands of a community vigilante group. The people who light these fires cannot be sure that no one will be hurt; it could be one of the firemen sent to fight the fires."

Wednesday, March 18: *It's four days after the burning down of the two churches and not one call to police from anyone with information. Police install a confidential hotline direct to the man in charge of the inquiry, Detective Inspector Barry Hunter.*

Hunter says an accelerant of some sort was used at the Hiruharama church and samples will be sent to the DSIR for testing.

Thursday, March 19: *Ruatoria people are getting over the initial shock of the two latest church fires. Now they're starting to respond to police requests for information.*

Detective Inspector Barry Hunter: "Perhaps they have had time to think about it and reconsider. There is a much better response from the local community. I am happy with what we are starting to receive. But obviously we want more."

Police and firemen have now completed their scene investigations of the two churches. It's been established that accelerants were used in both cases.

CHAPTER 10

THE REAL PRIME MINISTER

*Sue Nikora made the national news in 2005 when she ended up in court after declaring herself the **real** Prime Minister of New Zealand (thanks to her bloodline). She had sent a burly relative around some motels in Gisborne to collect rent she believed was rightfully hers (even though she didn't legally own the motels).*

In 2008 Sue and her husband Noel were living in Haig Street, just around the corner from my parents. But when I made my second trip home to collect interviews for this book, probably in 2001, they lived in Gladstone Road, Gisborne's main street, in the suburb of Te Hapara. They had a tidy white weatherboard bungalow with a corrugated iron roof and a white picket fence out the front. There were a couple of cars in the concrete driveway so I parked my black Honda City on the road.

Two women were also there: Bob Kaa's sister and Sue's niece, one of the Browns. I can't remember their names. They were all mature women. And once they found out my intentions, they were keen to weigh up the young Pakeha who wanted to write about Ruatoria. And that was fair enough.

We sat in the living room, spread out on the brown velvet lounge suite with white lace antimacassars on the arms. The walls were covered with framed pictures of various family members, some in traditional Maori dress. That was common in most if not all Maori homes I'd visited. My parents' was the only Pakeha home in which I'd seen the same practice. Dad had turned our living room walls into a crushing victory of family pride over interior decorating. But Sue's arrangement of photographs was tastefully done. She served me tea in a cup and saucer and emptied a packet of Chocomints onto a plate for me. Somehow she reminded me of visiting my big Scottish grandma when I was a kid.

The way the Rastas' opponents talked about Sue and how she'd fired up the youngsters in the early days, I'd expected to meet an ogress with one baleful eye in the middle of her forehead. But she struck me immediately as a person with a very warm smile and a ready laugh. She was quite big, with a happy round face and white hair, a real cuddly teddy bear. But I could see she was also a strong character.

Her niece looked like an old friend and Gisborne Herald workmate, Kathy Akuhata-Brown. It turned out Kathy, the daughter of Sonny Brown, was in fact closely related to her and Sue. The niece was a real joker, the epitome of the laidback East Coast Maori, easy to get along with and a real good sort. She was quite big, too, with wavy black hair and a very expressive face.

Bob's sister, like Bob, was a lighter skinned Maori with blue eyes. There was something severe about her. I always felt like she was weighing me up. When I talked to Sue and her niece, I made jokes. But when I talked to Bob's sister I gave well thought-out, serious answers in

*an effort to convince her I could be trusted. She struck me as a bit of an
intellectual who had in-built x-ray goggles when it came to bullshit.*

*Noel, Sue's husband, was a quiet, affable character. He had
coke bottle glasses, prominent front teeth and a Norman Gunston
hairstyle. He stayed in the kitchen most of the time.*

Bob's sister asked me why I wanted to write the book.

*I told them I'd been a reporter at the Gisborne Herald when
the troubles in Ruatoria were at their peak. And though I'd never
worked on the story because I was just starting out in journalism, I
followed developments closely. I said I was overwhelmed by the sheer
volume of incidents and court cases and curious as to what made the
Rastafarians tick. I'd always believed there was a book in the
Rastafarians because their rise had turned that part of the Coast into
something like the Wild West for a time.*

*I'd always intended to interview Chris Campbell when he was
in prison. While I was living in Wellington and working at The
Dominion, I toyed with the idea of a book on people who lived on the
fringes of society. I figured I could include Chris in that book. I even did
a few interviews for different profiles I was going to write. But I lost
momentum. The project was never completed and I didn't interview
Chris. But the idea of a book on the Rastas and Ruatoria was still
percolating away in my head. The next thing I knew Chris was dead and
Luke Donnelly had got off for shooting him.*

*Then early in 1999, when I was working for TV3 in Auckland, I
read a short two paragraph story in the New Zealand Herald. The man
who had killed Rastafarian Dickie Maxwell in a knife fight had been
found not guilty on grounds of self defence and the crowd in the
Gisborne court had cheered when the verdict was read out. I didn't even
know Maxwell had been killed.*

"This whole thing's still going on," I thought.
*It renewed my interest. I talked to my father about how keen I was to
write a book on Ruatoria and the Rastas. He talked me out of it. The
wounds were too fresh, he said. Better to let sleeping dogs lie. It's too
dangerous. The Rastas are too unpredictable. There'd be a limited
market. Who would buy such a book?*

"He's probably right," I thought. I tried to forget the idea.

*About six months later I was back in Gisborne and saw a one-
page article about the Ruatoria troubles in a Gisborne Herald
supplement on the 1980s. The newspaper had published a supplement on*

every decade of the century as part of their build-up to the new millennium. Reading Marianne Gillingham's article about arson, homicide and religion, I became excited again. A publisher had recently asked me to write a book about a prominent New Zealand sportsman because I'd already written a biography on league player Matthew Ridge. I sent Gillingham's article to the publisher with a note saying, the sportsman doesn't interest me, but this does.

He said, "Okay, give it a go." (As it turns out, I've had to finance and publish the Ngati Dread series myself because mainstream and even Maori publishers weren't interested).

I told the women that I wasn't out to hang the Rastas, and I wasn't out to apologise for them or to promote them either. My only loyalty was to the story. It had become an obsession to me. It was a fantastic story and I couldn't believe I was the only person pushing really hard to want to write it. I felt as if I'd been picked to tell this story. And the more I got into it, the more I realised that there were all sorts of different layers to it. It worked on all sorts of levels, some of which I was just discovering, others I probably still hadn't discovered.

Anyway, I convinced Sue to agree to an interview and we set a date when I should go round to see her. Noel sat in the living room with us this time. I still found Sue great company. I really enjoyed the cups of tea and the biscuits. And while, apart from a short denial, she didn't really bite when I repeated claims I kept hearing wherever I went that she was the real mastermind behind the Rastas, all her stories were strange and fascinating.

SUE'S STRANGE LETTER

Sue Nikora: Burning? I don't believe they burnt anything. I have evidence here.

Our Anglican church at Hiruharama burnt and I happened to be in Ruatoria at the time. I'm the chairperson of the papakainga. That's where all those houses were built just inside there. Ten houses were being built and I was the organiser for that and given a million dollars to build them. And I happened to be there. I had a home in Ruatoria given to me by the Maori Affairs Department. And I happened to be there when our church was burnt.

At the same time our church was burnt, another church was burnt on the other side of town.

The church was still burning when I got there in the morning. Well, I was met at the gate. There were cops everywhere, about a hundred cops. And the first thing they said: "The Rastas have burnt the church down."

I was devastated. I went in there and gosh I couldn't believe it.

So we all went into the marae and we had a karakia and we had a hui. And then they said the newspaper and the television are coming. And so the people decided that my cousin and myself would be the spokespeople to front up to the media.

So anyhow when it came to my turn I spoke. They asked questions and I said, "I don't know who would have done this."

And they said, "Do you think it was the Rastafarian people?"

I said, "You know, I don't want to say who did it. But from my knowledge of those children, they hold the church in awe. They would be too scared because it was told to them and they've always known how sacred it's been to us. But we'll soon find out if they did. And somebody will go mad if they really did that. I can't believe who would have done it. I'm not committing myself to who's done this. But whoever it is must pay in the end."

Anyhow about three weeks later I got this letter.

Selwyn Parata came and brought it to me. It was addressed to Sue, Maori Affairs Department, Ruatoria. I had a look and opened it. It was from this lady called Fran Yule. I didn't know her from a bar of soap. She said to me, As soon as the TV came on and I saw you on there I felt pity, not just for you but for all you people for the loss of your church. I was happy with what you said because I do believe it wasn't the Rastafarian people who did it.

Then she continued to say, But the person who did it, and described this guy to a T. She's never been to Ruatoria. She didn't know us from a bar of soap. But she was psychic. I was a bit sceptical. I looked at this letter. I thought, "What the hell would she be writing to me for?" She was a Pakeha person from Australia living in Auckland. I eventually went to Auckland and made it my duty to meet her.

You know this letter was so weird and uncanny. She drew a map. She described the road from Te Puia Springs and it would have gone straight through over the blue bridge at Hiruharama. And there's Whareponga Road coming over here. But when she got to Hiruharama, she came along the flat and the road turned right. There's no road there any more. And there was this old bridge that's been taken down years ago. Anyway, on her map she went across the old bridge straight into Whareponga Road. For someone who's never been there to draw that is incredible. Then she described the house where the person she believed lit the fires lived on the right hand side of Whareponga Road. She described it to a T. She said, There's a line across the front part of the house. And there's this white car without wheels. And there's this blue line around the car, and this red line around the car. And on the mantel piece in the house is a fireman's helmet with a fireman's badge on the helmet. Then she drew this road going into Ruatoria to the petrol bowsers where Bob Kaa's garage used to be on the left-hand side. The line on the map Fran had drawn went along from Whareponga Road to Ruatoria and it pinpointed the other church as well. It was the same person who lit both fires. She was saying it was a fireman who was an expert in explosions. He had a bulbous nose and all that and that he had had an appendix operation.

So we had a hui on the Sunday. I had needed to come back to Gisborne because our boy was going to school and we had to fix up all the things for him here and then we went back on the Sunday to have a meeting with the people.

I presented it to them. The letter went around and my secretary got it. A long time she studied it. And I said, "So what are we going to do?"

All our old people said, "Right we'll have to ring the police. Get the sergeant to come and give a photocopy to the sergeant. His name was John Robinson."

Anyway, he came and looked at it and said, "Okay, I'll take it away."

I had no inkling who the person described in the letter was. I didn't want to think it was anyone in the community. So later that day I drove my secretary home, to her house on the right hand side of Whareponga Road. I parked the car and went into the yard. The line in front of the house, mentioned in the letter, was there: a line full of clothes. But I wasn't even thinking of the letter at this stage. So I went inside and she said, "I'll go and get us a cup of tea, Aunty."

I sat down and right in front of me on the mantel piece there was this photo. It had a policeman's helmet and the badge on the helmet. It had the bulbous nose and everything.

So anyhow we came out and there's this white car in the yard.
It had blocks underneath it and blue and red lines on the ground around
it, and that was mentioned in the letter, too.

But I didn't have the person on. You see, diplomacy is the best
way. Nobody at the hui except me figured out who it was. And I tell you
the Rastafarians took that flak for those fires. They weren't perfect but I
don't think they should have taken that flak.

Then I waited for John Robinson, the sergeant, to do something
but he never did.

Just the other day I saw John and I was having a talk with him
and Lois, and I said, "Do you remember, John, that letter I gave you."

Oh yes he remembered all right. And he said, "Yes, I gave it to
my superior and nothing was done."

I said, "Oh, that's all right."

But in my mind at the time, the guy was married to my niece.
They had two children. He was an ex-policeman. And he happened to be
an explosives expert whereby he can set an explosion here and it will go
off over there. That is why there was a few seconds between the two
fires. The Rastafarians had been blamed. They were thick and hard
enough to take the flak. Why stir up the hornets' nest?

That's as far as I'd like to go with this story because he is the
father of my two mokopuna. I did confront him with it once, in anger,
which is the worst thing that could ever happen. He took off. He took off
from the onslaught.

I'm not saying he was responsible for other fires. All I'm
saying is these two fires were quite explicit and they happened almost at
the same time.

Cody Haua, former Rastafarian: That's not right. I wouldn't
believe that. That sounds like a load of rubbish to me.

Sergeant John Robinson (retired): Yes, I remember that.
They called me down to Hiruharama Marae one Sunday morning. She'd
received a letter from a woman who was psychic. She described the
person who lit the fire at the church at Hiruharama and she described the
house he lived in. And it was Sergeant Hope who was the person they
were talking about.

Sue said, "We drove around Ruatoria and we actually saw the
house this psychic woman described."

I just passed it on. If I'd done nothing and something was in it, they would have crucified me. So I just wrote down on a job sheet what they said and sent it in and I never heard any more about it.

They were saying that Sergeant Hope was the person who'd burnt the churches.

Alex Hope: Sue's talking about the guy being married to her niece. Well, my ex-wife's not her niece. I didn't have two children; I had four. And I'm not an explosives expert. I wouldn't know anything about them. And I've never been in the Fire Brigade and I've never owned a fireman's helmet.

John Heeney, Rastafarian: I don't know. If someone told you that the Rastas didn't burn down those two churches, you write that because that makes us look more innocent. And that's good. We want to look more innocent. We want people to know that we're the good guys in all this, and that the people in the system are the bad guys.

Friday, March 20, 1987: Nineteen-year-old Rastafarian Lee Wayne Kirikino is sentenced to a year in jail for five charges of wilful damage arising from a December fence-cutting spree.

CHAPTER 11

ARSON ARRESTS

Former Detective Sergeant Hemi Hikawai: David Mataira, the son of Maurice Mataira, who was a volunteer fireman, did the police station. Catching him was the breakthrough that the police had waited years and years for.

It was a Sunday and we'd been given the day off and I had some paperwork that I had to tidy up. And his name had been mentioned as a possibility as a suspect or someone worth talking to as far as the police station was concerned. I believe he'd already been spoken to previously because of his association with the Rastafarians. So it was really just a shot in the dark.

I went there first thing on a Sunday morning and brought him in. And most of the boys were either still at the hotel having a sleep-in or some guys were finishing off a bit of paperwork. And I was interviewing David at a house a couple of doors along from the police station. So I put a series of questions to him and during the questioning he broke down and confessed to burning not only the police station, but also the courthouse and also another building belonging to the Williams family, from memory a hay-barn, Colin Williams's hay-barn that he burnt down as well.

And during that interview he admitted to me that John Heeney had been the person who had assisted him. So you had a situation in a small town where the sons of two volunteer firemen were working as a team to commit arsons. David was charged with the arsons. He dropped Heeney in it. A couple of people were sent to grab Heeney, who I think was living in Kawerau at that time. And Heeney coughed. Yeah, he admitted it. And he also admitted, I think, another six fires that he had been involved in. And so you had all these fires that had been stacking up for years that were unsolved. The only other person who had been convicted of arson was a guy Tuck Morice, Eruera Ranfurly Morice, and I'd locked him up as well for the Horehore hay-barn, which he burnt down early on. And he was the only one that had been convicted of any of those arsons.

Now Mataira coughed, Heeney coughed, we're on a roll and Heeney was prepared to name more. At that stage Chris Campbell was in jail. But they wanted to get together and they were prepared to come clean and own up to everything. It was the breakthrough we'd been waiting fuckin' years for, mate. The unfortunate thing that occurred and what stopped all that was that a couple of days after we had moved on Heeney and them we had police being flown up there from Wellington to investigate us because Dickie Maxwell had gone in there the following day and alleged that he'd been kidnapped.

And so we were stopped right in our tracks. The department thought it was more appropriate that they pursue these wild allegations made by this madman called Maxwell rather than we do what we were there for and that was investigate arsons.

Monday, March 23, 1987: John Heeney and David Mataira are arrested for the arson of the Ruatoria courthouse-police station on November 19, 1985. Detective Inspector Barry Hunter says police work since the fire plus information gleaned during the inquiry into the two latest church arsons led to the arrests.

Ken McKinnon, Ruatoria Voluntary Fire Brigade Chief: Tom Heeney and Maurice Mataira, their two boys burnt down the courthouse. When they found out who it was they came straight in and gave me their resignations.

I said, "I'm not accepting them."

They said they were going to write to Gisborne.

I said, "You didn't do it. Your kids did it."

So the fire chief from Gisborne, Ian McDowall, rung up and he said, "Have you accepted it?"

I said, "No."

"Well neither will I. I'll tear mine up."

I knew the pressure and stress were building up for Tom and Maurice. They were both very upset about what had happened. So I told them, "I'm not going to take your resignations. But if the next fire comes along and you don't want to go to it, have a spell. There are plenty of other fires you can help me with, not only arsons."

Tuesday, March 24, 1987: David Mataira appears in the Gisborne District Court.

Duty solicitor Neil Mackie appeals for bail, saying his client has a delicate family situation at present.

Sergeant Chester Haar of Gisborne opposes the bail application. He says it's against the public interest. "The local community is at breaking point." He concedes that Mataira made a frank acknowledgement of his involvement in the courthouse-police station arson. But he adds that Mataira also implicated Rastafarian John Heeney and that some in Ruatoria fear there might be retaliation.

Justice of the Peace Harry Johansen decides not to grant bail. Mataira's remanded without plea in custody.

Meanwhile, John Heeney appears in Whakatane District Court and is also remanded without plea.

HOLLOW RING TO LANGE'S COMMENTS

The troubles in Ruatoria are once again national news. Even Prime Minister David Lange talks about them at his post-Cabinet press conference.

He says Ruatoria is already a community under stress. "You have a series of underlying tensions. You have all of those which are associated with the rural economy, with the resettlement of people from the cities, with the question of the Rastafarian cult. You have the land issues. You have a whole variety of issues which are stress enough in themselves. These are already overtaxing the traditional people.

"And then you have this guerilla campaign which actually strikes at the heart of the traditions of the people, which must be awfully provocative to the people who have set their hearts to achieving some sort of reconciliation – and then they go and torch a church."

Lange says all available police resources are being deployed in the "further sad saga".

The Prime Minister's comments are well intentioned. But they have a hollow ring for the likes of Neighbourhood Support Group chairman Bob Kaa.

He knows the group's patrols can't go on indefinitely without support. He also knows Ruatoria will soon be full of able but redundant forestry workers who could tackle security as a fulltime paid job. With that in mind he's applied to the Community Organisations Grants Scheme to fund security jobs in the town. But his application has just been turned down. This probably has something to do with the strong-arm tactics employed by some of the group. Nevertheless Kaa's angry and disillusioned. "It was one of the saddest things for me when this was turned down," he says. And some would argue that Ruatoria's been incredibly restrained in its response to the destruction.

The proposal was to employ two men, with a vehicle and support services, for night patrol work on a six-month basis. That would save Kaa's group having to do everything voluntarily.

Kaa says his proposal meets the desired criteria for the grants in all respects. And, more importantly, Ruatoria is a town with a crisis.

Ironically, the group will have to keep relying on funds from sources such as demolition tenders on arson-hit buildings. (In the past *fifteen months, the group's spent over $10,000, mainly on its radio system.)*

Wednesday, April 1: *Police arrest Cyrus Kennedy: a nineteen-year-old farmhand and a fringe member of the Rastas. They charge him with the arson of Joe's Bookshop, the arson of Ruatoria Motors and the attempted arson of Carlyle's Drapery on August 22 last year. The businesses were all located in the Main Road of Ruatoria.*

Chris Bunyan, a thirty-year-old Gisborne man, who bears a striking resemblance to the American actor William H. Macey (but with fiery red hair), graduates from Police College in Porirua to take up a posting in Ruatoria. Bunyan's family have lived and worked in the saddlery business in Gisborne for thirty-five years. District Commander Superintendent Paul Wiseman recruited him with Ruatoria in mind.

When his posting's read out at the graduation ceremony, an audible murmur of surprise rises from the crowd. Bunyan isn't worried though. "It's in the news and it's a topical hot potato, but to me it's just part of the job." He stopped reading newspapers and listening to the news about Ruatoria when he began training in October. He says he's looking forward to fishing, gardening, rearing "a few chooks", and perhaps adding to his family. He starts work in Ruatoria next Wednesday.

Thursday, April 2: *John Heeney's charged with three more Ruatoria arsons. As well as burning down the Ruatoria courthouse-police station on November 19, 1985, he's now accused of wilfully setting fire to:*
The police house on Mangakino Street on December 12, 1985.
A haybarn on Colin Williams' Kaharau Stud Farm on July 1, 1985.
A hay barn on the same property on July 13, 1985.

*Heeney's been living in Kawerau, in the Bay of Plenty. He's described in court as a **former** Ruatoria Rastafarian.*
Police no longer oppose bail for him and he's remanded on all four charges. After hearing the application in chambers, Judge J. D. Hole announces his reasons for granting bail in open court. They are:
All the fires happened over a year ago.

He's been living in a stable relationship and has the support of a church, the Salvation Army, which also supports him in his work situation.

There has been no indication from police of a likelihood of reoffending.

Heeney's lawyer Doug Rishworth picks up on the word "reoffending". He points out that Heeney has entered no pleas and that the defence has made no indication of accepting guilt. Judge Hole notes that Rishworth is quite right.

ANOTHER ARSON INVESTIGATION

Friday, April 4: *Police launch another arson investigation. It follows the discovery of a gutted house in Whareponga Road, outside Ruatoria. Police believe the unoccupied Kawhia Homestead was burnt down last Friday, March 27. But a photo of the remains in a Ruatoria Fire Service scrapbook has the caption: "The brigade was not notified of fire until three days later. The Kawhia homestead was burnt down on either the 23rd or 24th of March, 1987."*

The homestead belongs to Eddie and Sue Harrison, the publicans of the Manutahi Hotel on the main road in Ruatoria. Their son is Rex Harrison, a Gisborne detective already investigating other suspicious fires in the area. The Harrisons are deeply involved in the Ngati Porou Marae and the church there, Te Aranga, which was burnt down on March 15.

So why would someone want to hurt a respected Maori family like the Harrisons? There are a few theories.

The Harrisons have a line of Anglican ministers in the family. The Rastas rail against symbols of colonialism.

Some say the Rastas believe the Ngati Porou Marae was supposed to face Mt Hikurangi, but didn't. And the Rastas were upset about that.

The Rastas also didn't like the Harrisons putting up the police in the Manutahi Pub. (On the other hand, some police didn't like the Harrisons making money off the town's troubles. Members of the Gisborne CIB staff even went so far as to start rumours that the Harrisons were burning down some of the buildings themselves! This is generally considered petty spitefulness with no foundation.)

*And of course Rex's involvement in the arson inquiries
probably didn't go down too well with the Rastas either.*

*There was one other thing about Ngati Porou Marae that
particularly upset Chris Campbell. He believed that while he, Cody
Haua and Hata Thompson were being "hunted in the bush like
animals" following the kidnapping of Detective Sergeant Laurie Naden,
their hunters – the police – were being put up at Ngati Porou. And what
really infuriated Campbell was talk that members of the police force had
taken women there and had sex with them in the marae.*

Retired Senior Sergeant Alan Davidson: I remember helping
out the internal inquiry team looking into Dick Maxwell's allegations of
assault by police officers. I went down to the scene and came across
another house that had burnt down. Nobody even knew about it. I was
driving along and there were some sheep on the road. And I stopped to
talk to some cockies. And they said, "Aw there was smoke coming up
from behind there yesterday."

I said, "What's happened?"

"The old Harrison homestead was up there. It's empty. But I
think someone might have burnt it down."

"Really?" So I got up there and I got out of the car and walked
up. Sure enough, the house had been burnt to the bloody ground. It was
the house that Rex Harrison the cop's mother or father had been brought
up in.

Saturday, April 4: *Gisborne police arrest two more men in
connection with the Ruatoria arsons: unemployed teenagers and fringe
Rasta members Tony Tuhou and Jonathan McClutchie. Along with
Cyrus Kennedy, they're jointly charged with the arson of Joe's
Bookshop and Ruatoria Motors and the attempted arson of Carlyle's
Drapery.*

WELCOME TO RUATORIA

**Constable Chris Bunyan, interviewed at the community
police station where he worked in Kaiti Mall, Gisborne, in late 2001:**
I guess it was in the early '80s when things started to happen in
Ruatoria. You'd see the name Chris Campbell attached to it and a few of

us who used to go to school with him would go, "Hell, what happened to Chris?" He disappeared and then started calling himself a Rastafarian and getting involved in incidents like the dragging of the horse. And that was before I joined the police.

And when I joined the police in 1986 I was recruited to go to Ruatoria directly from the Police College.

And the night of my graduation, I'll always recall, the patron of our wing was Judge Gillies, and he said, "I want to watch this TV programme." He was a little grey-headed fulla with glasses, a really nice old guy. So we watched that and I think Mike Valintine did the report. Dickie Maxwell had had his hair cut and he was riding along in the sunset and that sort of thing.

***Wednesday, April 8:** Constable Chris Bunyan begins his posting in Ruatoria.*

Constable Chris Bunyan: During that week, being my first week, the sergeant came out with me on the Friday night and we went through the hotels. And I always recall going into the Manutahi Hotel and there would-a been sixty guys out in the car park, cos that was the big thing, some of them sitting on their horses and sitting in cars with stereos going. These are all the young guys, the riff-raff they called them. There was the odd Rasta around. But generally the Rastas in those days weren't into drinking alcohol. They were tucked up in the hill country smoking dope or out at Makarika there or up at Whakaahu.

We went through the hotel and there were, like, the rugby boys and the older people from the community were in having a beer and I was introduced to a few and we came outside and we were leaving to walk across the road to where the kai cart was. The vehicle was parked there. And basically I guess I'd been set up. And there was a young fulla who'd been waiting in the car park to have a crack at me. And he came running flat out at me from behind. And just before he got to us, we realised what was happening. He was coming right into my back with his arms extended. And I managed to move slightly and he glanced off me, came back and went for my throat. Well, I was three weeks out of Police College, so I'd just finished all this wonderful hand-to-hand combat training. I just somehow or another twisted him, put him in a choker hold and he went limp in my arms. I escorted him across the road and into the vehicle.

From that day on I think I gained a certain amount of respect. I was just so bloody lucky that that had happened. I didn't have anyone else, apart from the odd verbal (and Dickie Maxwell with an axe) have a crack at me the whole time I was in Ruatoria. I think they thought I was some sort of martial arts expert.

And realistically they're not fighters, those boys up there. They might have the odd fight among themselves. But that's about it.

I remember other occasions with the Rastas when I was first up there. They had this vehicle that was a chassis with four wheels, an engine and a couple of seats with a manuka pole and a flag sticking up. That was it. And they used to drive through Ruatoria at fifty-sixty miles per hour with balaclavas on, so you wouldn't recognise them. But you'd hear this thing coming. You'd get out, get the Nissan Patrol started. But by the time you'd got out of the driveway of the police station, they'd gone. And they'd just do it every now and then, no rhyme or reason or timing. This thing would just come tearing past. It really was as funny as a fart, ay. But it was just intimidation. It was just to say, "Fuck you guys. We can do this."

And there'd be occasions when half a dozen or more of them would be on horseback. One of them would be leading. Or they might have their balaclavas on. And they'd have their big flag and they'd clip clop through town and stop outside the police station and make sure you knew they were there and then off they'd go again…

…There was a lot of fence-cutting going on. It was just prolific. It was partly, "This is our land, we'll do what we want." You'd be a metre from a gate and they'd cut a piece of fence out. It was totally frustrating for the farmers because the stock starts wandering.

We went out on horseback. But what you've got to remember is that these guys were expert horsemen… expert. They didn't need saddles. They liked to have them but they didn't need them. And we'd never catch them. It was a joke. It was like putting an eighty-year old on a skateboard trying to catch a ten-year-old kid. It just doesn't happen.

You'd only see them once every three weeks, when they'd come down to get supplies. They were quite happy living up in the bush. They lived very primitively. That's probably the easiest way to describe it.

Wednesday, September 9: Cyrus Kennedy is committed for trial in the High Court on charges of burning down Joe's Bookshop and

*trying to burn down Carlyle's Drapery. After a depositions hearing,
Kennedy pleads not guilty and is remanded on bail until October 19.*

***Thursday, September 24:** John Heeney and David Mataira are
committed for trial in the High Court on charges of wilfully setting fire
to Ruatoria's courthouse and police station. After the depositions
hearing, they plead not guilty to the joint charge. Heeney also pleads
not guilty to further charges of setting fire to an unoccupied police
house and to two hay barns on Colin Williams' farm.*

*So, in quick succession, two big arson trials involving the
Ruatoria Rastafarians have been scheduled. It would be ideal for our
story to just jump forward in time, and to write up both trials now, one
after the other, while the details are still reasonably fresh in our minds.
But the only one I'll deal with now is Cyrus Kennedy and the arson of
Bob Kaa's garage, Joe's Bookshop and Carlyle's Drapery. I'll leave the
trial of Heeney and Mataira until later. There are things that happened
in the lead-up to that trial (Heeney and Dick Maxwell escaped from
police custody and went on the run) that make more sense if left in the
right chronological order.*

CRAZY BALDHEADS

"We're gonna chase them crazy baldheads out of my town." –
Bob Marley, Crazy Baldheads

Detective Rex Harrison, Gisborne CIB (retired): Having
come from that area I was fortunate that I received some information
and Laurie Naden and I went to Tolaga Bay and there we spoke to a
person – I just can't remember his name – who admitted lighting the
arsons at Joe's Book Shop, Ruatoria Motors and Carlyle's. He said
basically they used either a can or a cup with diesel and fuel in it. After
they tried to light the third fire the cup was thrown over the bank. And
we went back and found the cup. That was actually a breakthrough. I
arrested this guy and charged him.

Tuesday, February 16, 1988: *Rasta Cyrus Kennedy pleads not guilty to the arson, on the night of August 22, 1986, of Joe's Bookshop and Ruatoria Motors and the attempted arson of Carlyle's Drapery.*

The Crown prosecutor tells the court the Tokomaru Bay man and two associates, Tony Tuhou and Jonathan McClutchie, planned to burn the three premises, using an arson kit of diesel, tins and rags.

While it was Tuhou and McClutchie who lit the fires under the garage and bookshop, Kennedy was present and encouraged them, thereby assisting; that's why he was later charged as a party to the arsons.

Wednesday, February 17: *Detective Rex Harrison tells the court he interviewed Kennedy on April 1, 1987.*

Kennedy told him how he, Tuhou and McClutchie lit the fire because they wanted to close down the town. Their aim was to make the "baldheads" - Pakehas and all people who supported the system – move away. They wanted the baldheads out to make it more comfortable for the Rastafarians to live.

Kennedy has classed himself as a Rastafarian since joining the sect two years ago, but says he doesn't think like the others, whose main thoughts are of burning, fighting and stealing.

He tells Harrison they decided to burn the three shops so they would go up at the same time. Tuhou and McClutchie put tins of diesel under the garage and bookshop and lit them in that order, using rags for wicks.

Then Kennedy took an enamel mug of diesel around the side of the drapery and lit the wick. Just then he looked across the road to the bakery restaurant and saw people having a meal there. Startled, he quickly put out the flames, threw the mug over the bank and ran off to meet McClutchie and Tuhou under a bridge.

They went to a friend's place and drank some beer until they heard a siren about an hour later. Smirking to themselves, they walked back into town to have a look. The bookshop was on fire and they felt excited.

Eventually, they went back to their friend's place, watched television and went to sleep.

At breakfast the next morning, the friend asked if they'd heard a second siren and told them the garage had burned down, too.

Thursday, February 18: *Cyrus Kennedy takes the witness stand in his own defence.*

This is his version of events, starting on the afternoon of August 22, 1986.

He's hanging out with Jonathan McClutchie and Tony Tuhou. McClutchie suggests burning Ngata College, but Kennedy disagrees. He says they should not burn a school.

McClutchie's next idea is to burn down Joe's Bookshop, Ruatoria Motors and Carlyle's Drapery.

McClutchie goes away for about half an hour and returns with a flagon of diesel.

They wait until dark and then head down to the area behind the garage and bookshop.

Kennedy moves away from Tuhou and McClutchie, who fill the cans with diesel.

Tuhou places one under a water tank. The pair then move out of sight for about thirty seconds.

Kennedy doesn't run off because he's frightened of Rastafarian retribution. He's heard of people being tied up and beaten with plastic hoses when they don't do what they're told. He's heard talk of informants having their tongues cut out.

Tuhou and McClutchie move along the bank to the back of the garage while he walks along the front of the shops. He walks down the side of the garage and meets the other two after about two minutes.

McClutchie gives Tuhou two tins and gives Kennedy an enamel mug. McClutchie fills the tins and the mug with diesel and then tells him to go across to the drapery.

Kennedy doesn't see anything lit, either behind the bookshop or the garage.

He heads across to the drapery, places the mug underneath, lights it and, after about five seconds, puts it out again.

"I put it out because I couldn't bring myself to burn it (the drapery) down."

During cross-examination, the Crown prosecutor asks Kennedy why there was a difference between his answers to Detective Harrison during his interview and his evidence to court.

Kennedy replies he was "muddled up" when he was interviewed and made his written statement to police.

To a question from defence counsel Phil Cooper, Kennedy concedes he took all the blame on himself during his first interview with police and says he did it so the other Rastafarians would not get in trouble because he was scared of them.

"I was protecting myself from other Rastafarians, not the police."

Kennedy is found guilty for the arson of Joe's Bookshop and the attempted arson of Carlyle's Drapery. He's found not guilty of the arson of Ruatoria Motors, which went up in flames later in the night.

March 24, 1988: *In the High Court in Auckland, Cyrus Kennedy is sentenced to do flood relief work for arson and attempted arson.*

May 26, 1988: *During a depositions hearing, Gisborne police withdraw charges of arson against Tony Tuhou, twenty, and Jonathan McClutchie, nineteen, after a key prosecution witness (Cyrus Kennedy) fails to show up.*

It's the second time the police have withdrawn the same charges without prejudice.

Like Cyrus Kennedy, Tuhou and McClutchie were charged with the arson of Joe's Bookshop and Ruatoria Motors and the attempted arson of Carlyle's Drapery.

Why didn't Kennedy, the young man who during his own trial spoke about his fear of reprisals from the Rastafarians, show up in court? Maybe he feared reprisals from the Rastafarians. The police must have been highly frustrated. All those man hours investigating the three fires resulted in Cyrus Kennedy doing a bit of flood relief work. McClutchie and Tuhou got nothing. The owners of Joe's Bookshop, Ruatoria Motors and Carlyle's Drapery must have been frustrated, too.

PART 5
COPS ON TRIAL

CHAPTER 1

CLOSE UP WITH DICKIE MAXWELL

Sergeant Alex Hope, former head of Ruatoria police: I was at a meeting in the meal room at the Ruatoria police station. Stuart McEwen was there. He was Assistant Commissioner Crime, so he was the most senior detective in the country. I was there. Barry Hunter was there. He was the Detective Inspector in Napier and he was very well regarded. His first involvement in Ruatoria was Lance Kupenga's murder. He did that one. Then he came up and did some of the arsons.

Anyway, I remember McEwen coming up and getting a briefing from everybody, me included. It was a selective group at this meeting. Norm Cook was there. Laurie Naden was there. And Paul Wiseman was there.

McEwen said, and I paraphrase here – I can't remember the exact words – but he did say, "This needs old fashioned policing." And he used those words "old-fashioned policing". "You need to target the offenders. You need to take them away to a place out of their safety zones. You need to target these people and you need to get them to dob their mates in." And the "old-fashioned policing" was like saying, Get admissions the hard way, whack it out of them, do whatever, isolate them, one at a time, not in the police station where their mates can hear them yelling and screaming and that sort of thing. That was the implication and it was a *clear* implication. It was *clear*. We all knew that Stu McEwen was saying take them out of town and beat it out of them. That's what Stu McEwen was saying to us. I interpreted it that way and I know that Laurie Naden interpreted it that way, I know that Barry Hunter interpreted it that way and I know that Norm Cook did because incidentally we've all discussed it. When I say we've all discussed it, we didn't discuss it together. Over the years I have discussed that meeting with those guys. I haven't discussed it with Paul Wiseman and I haven't discussed it with McEwen.

And this was just before the whole Dickie Maxwell thing went down and the heat was coming on.

Monday, March 30, 1987: An internal investigation is launched into the actions of some police officers investigating the Ruatoria arsons.

Police Association president Keith Morrow and the association's industrial advocate Graham Harding meet with Gisborne staff. Afterwards, Morrow requests a copy of the complaint under the Official Information Act, but is declined on the grounds its release might prejudice the inquiry.

Tuesday, March 31: Keith Morrow says details of the allegations still haven't been made known. Gisborne police don't know how many officers are involved, who's being investigated or how many people will have to be interviewed. Morrow is adamant the internal inquiry won't impede police work in Ruatoria. "In no way are we going to be distracted by the presence of an internal investigation," he says. "If anybody thinks they've put us into a tailspin they can start thinking again."

The Gisborne Herald - LATE NEWS - *TV Special*: "Close Up" special on Ruatoria, featuring interviews with local Rastafarian leader Dickie Maxwell, to screen Thursday night. Accusations by Maxwell led to investigations of police conduct during arson inquiries.

Wednesday, April 1: It's revealed that Maxwell has told a Close Up television crew that he was abducted, bound and gagged, beaten and had his dreadlocks cut off by police.

Close Up producer Michael Valintine says locals took he and reporter Amanda Millar to a house to meet Dickie Maxwell. He told them he'd tried to shoot his abductors, who included some policemen. After recording the interview Valintine and Millar approached the police with the allegations.

Detective Superintendent Brian Hartley heads a four-member police team, which will investigate the police conduct and report directly to Minister of Police Ann Hercus.

"POSSIBILITY OF CIVIL WAR"

Thursday, April 2: *At the High Court in Wellington, Dr Don Mathieson QC's talking about the possibility of civil war in Ruatoria. He's trying to convince Mr Justice McGechan to put an interim injunction on Close Up's Dickie Maxwell interview, scheduled to go to air tonight.*

"This is a matter where there is in Ruatoria – and I speak moderately – feeling running high, where there is some danger of local civil war breaking out. There is a danger of vigilante groups exceeding their role in a Neighborhood Support Group and a danger of people who align themselves - Rastafarians like Maxwell - aligning themselves behind him and using violence against their perceived enemies."

A constable has applied for the interim injunction based on defamation. He believes he's accused in the interview of misconduct towards Maxwell and of seriously insulting him in the course of an investigation.

The court is shown a copy of the programme without the voice-over. Once it's established that the constable is not identified in the pictures or mentioned in the commentary, Mr Justice McGechan refuses the application for an interim injunction.

Close Up goes to air with the Dickie Maxwell interview. He alleges he was abducted, beaten and had his dreadlocks cut by two men who questioned him about fires in Ruatoria. He says two policemen arrested him and drove him to a derelict area, and then left him. According to Maxwell, two masked and armed men then held him at gunpoint and in a struggle, he snatched a .308 calibre gun and pulled the trigger, but there were no bullets in it. He was then bound and blindfolded, bundled into a blue Commodore stationwagon and taken to a house about twenty minutes away.

"They took me and questioned me, kicked me in the shoulders, stood on my head and asked me about these fires. I told them all I knew, which was nothing." He also alleges the men threatened to kill him.

The programme shows cuts and bruises on Maxwell's body, and his cut hair.

Friday, April 3: Police Association president Keith Morrow says last night's television interview with Dick Maxwell poses no threats to police staff. "As a policeman myself and having some knowledge of the matter I was able to detect a couple of technical flaws in the version of events by Mr Maxwell. No doubt the inquiry team who are far closer than I am will have spotted those two or more."

Morrow has a meeting with Gisborne police staff today to review the week's activities. "I doubt whether they will have seen any threat arising from the programme. They will be quite relaxed about that."

Letter to the Editor, The Gisborne Herald, Thursday, April 9, 1987: Sir. – The "Close Up" television programme on East Coast problems made the comment that it was obvious a struggle had taken place. It looked more like a cow had slept there.

It said Maxwell showed signs of a beating. I would have preferred the words "alleged beating".

It made no comment about how in one week there were 33 out on bail in Ruatoria, and how the police have tried to do their job but the system has often let them down. It says they preach peace on horseback, yet my heart went out to the horses more than the riders.

To me the programme came across as a bad attempt to give substance to the "Rastas'" claims and did not counter them with the rights of those ordinary people to live, worship, raise families and earn a living as most New Zealanders expect to.

I feel it did no credit to those who made it, but made them look like cheap headline grabbers.
MOURNER
P.S. - I have always signed my name to any letter I have written, but for the sake of my family on the Coast I have restrained myself with regret.

NICE ONE, STU

Sergeant Alex Hope, former head of Ruatoria police: Later, when everyone realised that there was a big investigation and that cops were in trouble, Laurie Naden and them were looking towards Stu McEwen (the head of the New Zealand CIB) and they were wanting help. And McEwen went to Australia. When the shit hit the fan,

McEwen went. I can't remember the exact details of the timing. But at the time when people wanted McEwen's support, he'd gone to Oz. Stu McEwen was conspicuous by his absence and his silence when these guys got in trouble for following what he'd virtually instructed them to do. He was talking to the people who were trying to sort out the Ruatoria situation: the CIB, the Gisborne police and the Ruatoria police.

There were other court cases in which cops were accused of beating up Rastas. But they all arose out of the same instruction: Basically, get hard. The frustrating thing was that we didn't ever have a suspect. We had interviewed everyone and we were stuck. No one, apart from Dickie, would dob anyone in. Dickie Maxwell didn't ever admit that he had dobbed in Mataira and Heeney. And Whiro Ratahi told me that they knew Dickie had dobbed Mataira and Heeney in but he would not admit it to them. Whiro was frustrated by that and told me that they would have succeeded in their trials against the cops if they'd got that evidence showing the connection between Dickie and those guys (Mataira and Heeney) and the violence Dickie suffered. But Dick was too staunch to ever admit he'd dobbed his mates in even though it would have helped his case.

Tuesday, April 14: Gisborne District Commander Superintendent Paul Wiseman says the team investigating alleged misconduct by police during the Ruatoria arson inquiry won't be finished for at least two weeks. When it's finished, the four-member CIB team from Wellington, led by Detective Superintendent Brian Hartley, will make its report to Deputy Police Commissioner John Jamieson.

Friday, May 22: Dick Maxwell appeals, in the High Court in Gisborne, against a sentence of two months in jail for burgling the Te Puia fire station. Justice Thorpe rejects the appeal.

EDITORIAL ANGERS POLICE

This editorial in The Gisborne Herald on May 23, 1987, written by Iain Gillies (author's father) angered police because it suggested there were grounds for an internal inquiry: Our sympathies are with the police who have had so many thankless months working on the Ruatoria arson inquiries.

Not only has their work been long, involved and carried out in adverse circumstances, but it has been subjected to these long drawn-out investigations into the way in which they have acted during their quest for solutions.

Police Association industrial advocate Graham Harding has already voiced his concern at the length of the investigations. Police and their families in Gisborne have carried the burden of the investigations and the men have had to continue their normal police duties. We agree with Mr Harding that the whole investigation has taken far too long.

It was all sparked by allegations made by Ruatoria Rastafarian Dick Maxwell during an interview by Television New Zealand.

We accept that in a democracy the police can only operate effectively with the consent and trust of the people they serve. Any reduction in public confidence in the police reduces the effectiveness of the service they provide and lowers the level of public cooperation.

So any investigations into allegations against the police must not just be thorough, they must be seen to be thorough.

But this investigation is beginning to resemble an inquisition.

We don't suggest for a moment that Mr Maxwell has no rights because associated with a group of people who have not exactly endeared themselves to the East Coast populace. We don't know, for instance, that this group of people is linked to all the arson that has taken place in and around the area. But there is no doubt that Mr Maxwell and his associates have contributed considerably to the transformation of a comparatively happy, easy-going East Coast community to a district being strangled by frustration, anger and suspicion. It does not seem so far-fetched that someone could have dealt out some rough justice. We are sure, for instance, that a few decades ago, the Ruatoria sergeant or constable would have given a few people a good kick in the pants and told them to get on their way. The next day it would have been a laughing matter and something to joke about over a few beers. But that way of life is gone forever because a policeman must mind his manners even when the bottles and bricks are flying in his direction.

We don't dispute for a moment that Mr Maxwell has a right to lodge his complaints. Nor do we blame Television New Zealand for passing on these complaints for investigation.

But rights and freedoms carry a measure of responsibility. And when people abuse the human rights of their neighbors, and refuse to accept the responsibility which goes hand in hand with the freedom bestowed upon us in a democratic society, then there is little sympathy for them when they start to squeal.

We are sure that law-abiding citizens around New Zealand are angered by the length of time this investigation is taking.

***Monday, July 13, 1987:** Deputy Police Commissioner John Jamieson announces seven officers from Gisborne and one from Hastings will appear in the Gisborne District Court to face a variety of serious charges on July 22. He says they've all been suspended from duty as it was inappropriate they should continue to work with the charges hanging over them.*

***Wednesday, July 15:** Lawyer Tony Adeane releases the names of seven of the eight detectives and the charges they face.*
"A man who calls himself 'Diesel' Dick Maxwell had made a television complaint against the police as a result of which Detective Sergeant Laurie Naden and detectives Malcolm Thomas, Dave Neilson, Hemi Hikawai and Mike Wilkinson (Hastings) have now been charged with kidnapping and assaulting Maxwell," says Adeane.
"In the wake of that complaint, further allegations have been made by three associates of Maxwell. Detective Sergeant Eric Newman and Detective-Constable Neilson have been charged with assaulting a youth called Jonathan McClutchie. Detectives Thomas and Brett Kane have been charged with assaulting a youth called Michael Paiti. Detective Constable Wilkinson has been charged with assaulting a man called (Tony) Tuhou."

CHAPTER 2

THE STORY OF DICKIE V THE COPS

I'm about to start writing up the trial of the five CIB detectives accused of the kidnap and assault of "Diesel" Dick Maxwell. It's a long and involved case full of outrageous claims and counter-claims. I'll write it up in the present tense, as I've written up most of this book. But the date today is February 9, 2009, in other words, twenty-two years after the fact. I know how it all ended up. And anyone who remembers the case will also know. The police officers were found not guilty.

Personally, I believe the jury got it wrong. I believe the detectives were guilty and many other people do, too. I've heard second hand that even some of the jury members have said they were convinced that Maxwell had been kidnapped and assaulted and that the police were involved but that, for whatever personal reasons, they couldn't find the accused guilty. The readers can make up their own minds.

Just remember while you're reading this: much of what is used to discredit Maxwell amounts to small differences in detail as he tells and retells his version of events to TV crews, to the police involved in the internal inquiry and before the court. This is Dick Maxwell. I never met him. But I feel I know enough about him now to say he had a hazy memory and was almost certainly a bullshit artist of the first order. I'm confident most readers will feel the same way. Of course Maxwell's going to embellish such a great yarn every time he tells it, just as he'd embellish a great yarn about a fight at the pub, a sexual conquest or a lucrative dope deal.

So it comes down to details. And if we entertain the possibility that Maxwell **was** *assaulted, we must remember that he was expected to have committed these details to memory while having the crap beaten out of him. Now I work in TV news. And I often can't remember what we've put to air from one week to the next. If someone asked me to stand in court and recite the stories we put to air in a certain week at different times months apart, I'd stuff it up completely. Who wouldn't? Lawyers know that. The police know that. We all know that.*

The other thing to remember is this: Dick Maxwell was a crafty little bugger. But was he really as crafty as we're expected to believe?

One last selfish little thing I'd like the reader to remember: I'm not out to right past wrongs or rewrite history. I don't have a vendetta against the police officers. Hemi Hikawai, Laurie Naden and the other cops I talked to are great guys. I like them. I'd feel terrible if anything I wrote got them into trouble again. I haven't set out to do anything special in this account of the Ruatoria troubles other than tell a version as close to the truth as I can. And that's all I'm trying to do with this. Under the circumstances in which they worked, I don't blame the police officers for what I believe they did (and, of course, I could be wrong). One old guy on the coast told me what Dick Maxwell did to his daughter. Other people told me how he left his brother with serious head injuries in a fight. Another old guy was terrorised with a gun in a home invasion. And if I stay subjective for a moment, I think Dick Maxwell probably deserved a good hiding. If, as the old saying suggests, we reap what we sow, then Dick Maxwell had it coming to him... God rest his soul.

Wednesday, July 22, 1987: *It's obvious who the sentimental favourites are in this case... and Dick Maxwell isn't one of them. There's standing room only in court two when the detectives make a brief appearance. Supporters of the policemen pack the small chamber and spill out across the public foyer. It's considered the largest expression of support ever seen at the Gisborne Courthouse. A small group is picketing the entrance to the courthouse with placards supporting the police.*

When the detectives appear together before the court, the people standing outside in the foyer open the courtroom doors. But the short preliminaries can't be heard. It's all over in minutes.

Thursday, September 15: *Seven policemen appear in a packed Gisborne courtroom. Here's the list of charges.*

Malcolm Thomas, Dave Neilson, Hemi Hikawai and Mike Wilkinson: *Kidnapping Rasta Dick Maxwell.*

Thomas, Laurie Naden, Neilson, Hikawai and Wilkinson: *Assaulting Maxwell with intent to facilitate the crime of wilfully attempting to pervert the course of justice.*

Naden, Neilson, Hikawai and Wilkinson: *Assaulting Maxwell to facilitate the crime of kidnapping.*

Thomas and Brett Kane: *Assaulting Rasta Mike Paiti with intent to facilitate the crime of attempting to pervert the course of justice.*

Neilson and Eric Newman: *Assaulting Jonathan McClutchie with intent to facilitate the crime of attempting to pervert the course of justice.*

Naden: *Knowing Thomas, Neilson, Hikawai and Wilkinson to have been parties to the charge of kidnapping Maxwell, and assisting them in order to enable them to avoid arrest or conviction.*

Wilkinson: *Two charges of assaulting Rasta Tony Tuhou.*

Chief Inspector Whiro Ratahi (retired) interviewed on Thursday, December 11, 2008 (Ratahi now lives in Upper Hutt): I heard about the Dickie Maxwell incident from Paul Wiseman, the superintendent up there at the time. I'm not sure of the sequence of events, which led to Paul hearing about it, but Paul told me he wanted the Dickie Maxwell allegations investigated, which I did. But it took me a long time. Dealing with the Rastas, they're never available when you want them. The neat thing is trying to tail them down. They're readily available once you turn up. But it's getting there at the right time that's hard.

With Dickie, I had to get through the confidence things because he knew I was a cop and he'd already been worked over by police. And an interesting thing is, Angus, he told me, "Oh, I don't mind the bash," because he had the bash from police before and he had the bash from other gang members before. But he said the thing that hurt him most was his dreads. They cut the dreads. If they'd just given him the bash, that was okay. He had no problem with that. There would have been no complaint from Dickie Maxwell and no trial if they'd just given him the bash. He told me that. But, once they cut the dreads, that was a crime in his book.

When I first went around to Dickie's place to talk to him it was a bit of a shock really. He smelt like he hadn't washed for a while. He had that smell of stale cannabis smoke on his breath and on his clothes. There were a lot of dishes on the sink. It looked like the kitchen of a bachelor. There was food up on the bench, some food on the kitchen table. And the dishes had been there for several days if not maybe weeks.

And, that typical Maori on Maori, he said, "Hey, you want a hot drink? I'll make you a Milo." That's typical of Maori wherever you go. There's always an offer of food.

And I said, "Yep, I'll have one with you," because from my perspective it would have been hugely impolite if I'd declined and I didn't want to do that. If I come to your home and you invite me to have coffee, it's impolite not to have some. And it's the same if there's a feed. So that's what I did with Dickie.

And then we just slowly worked our way through what it was all about. And very early in that piece I realised he was telling the truth because you could see the hair where it's been gouged out. Even if he'd cut it himself he could have done a better job. Certain sides of the head there was obviously a big gouge out where it wasn't clean, it wasn't a clean cut, like it was in a hurry. Even a shearer would have done the job better because there's a way of doing that.

Plus the other thing that very clearly he told me, he said, "Listen, if it's not done properly, someone will be shot." So we had to take it seriously because he said, "Hey, you won't see the bullet coming." He wasn't threatening me. He was threatening the individuals who he believed to have been involved. And he named them. They were the main guys who were arrested.

He could tell who they were because he could hear them talking and by height because he wasn't a little guy. He was lean but quite strong, wiry. He didn't have much guts on him. He was quite a strong individual but he was also quite tall. He was inclined to lean forward a little bit. But when you see him standing up he was about three or four inches taller than me.

PROSECUTION OUTLINES CASE AGAINST COPS

Monday, September 28: The depositions hearing into Dick Maxwell's allegations against police gets underway in the Gisborne District Court.

This, says New Plymouth Crown Prosecutor John Laurenson, is how events transpired leading up to and during the alleged kidnapping of Diesel Dick Maxwell.

On March 17 the investigating team held a special briefing session, where the seeds were sown for the kidnapping plan.

"The prosecution alleges that the accused decided to deliberately isolate and terrorise certain members of the Rastafarian group who, they thought, would be able to give them information regarding the fires."

An elaborate plan was devised to kidnap Maxwell. First he'd be isolated from Ruatoria in circumstances which would make it appear later that the police weren't involved. After that, he'd be carried off to an even more isolated location where he'd have information beaten or terrorised out of him.

On March 21, Thomas and Wilkinson called at a property Maxwell was visiting and told him to accompany them to the police station. There was no reason for Maxwell to do that because he'd already been questioned by another officer that afternoon and evidence available suggested he hadn't been involved in the church fires.

But it had been pre-arranged that while they were in the police vehicle the officers would receive a call requesting them to detour to the old Reedy homestead five kilometres out of town.

A call was received and they drove to the old house. Wilkinson and Thomas left the car to see if anybody was about. Both then ran off out of sight, apparently chasing someone, leaving Maxwell alone in the car.

Minutes later four men appeared disguised in overalls with pillow slips over their heads. Two were armed. They tied up Maxwell and put a pillow slip and a sugar bag over his head. During the struggle Maxwell bit one of them on the finger.

Later Thomas and Wilkinson radioed back to the station saying they'd returned to the car only to find Maxwell had escaped.

*They later went to the house from where they'd collected Maxwell and asked the occupier if she knew where he was. The officers knew she wouldn't know. This visit was just to make it appear **they** didn't know.*

Laurenson says the four men in overalls drove Maxwell to a disused house on Whareponga Road. There he was assaulted and interrogated by them. Some of his hair was cut off and most of his clothing was removed.

He was then taken back to Hiruharama Marae, ten kilometres out of town, from where he made his way back into Ruatoria. He later confronted some police officers at the hotel. But no effort was made to detain him.

The following day he met the television crew and some of the events of the previous day were recorded. As a result, the police investigated Maxwell's complaints.

Maxwell was so familiar with Whareponga Road he was able to take members of the investigating team there. DSIR scientists found evidence of people having been there recently. This included small portions of hair consistent with having come from Maxwell and pieces of jute, which could have come from a sugar bag.

The investigating team were told a call directing the two men to the old Reedy homestead was made from the base by Naden, following an anonymous phone call. But this made no sense because Naden had already left the base before the call was made. And another constable,

Steve Tresidder, told investigators he'd heard Hikawai making the call from a police car. It's also alleged that, later, Hikawai admitted making the call. (Hikawai, to this day, denies making this admission).

With the help of the DSIR, the police investigating team found a fibre, consistent with having come from the police car, on Maxwell's clothing. This was seen as supporting evidence that, after the kidnapping and assault, the car being driven by Hikawai had brought Maxwell back from Whareponga to Ruatoria.

The following day Neilson went to Gisborne Hospital and received treatment for a bitten finger. While there, he told hospital staff he'd received the bite from a human. The bite wound was consistent with having occurred about twenty-four hours previously.

The prosecution explains why each of the defendants is implicated in the crime:

Thomas and Wilkinson collected Maxwell, setting the scene for his alleged disappearance. Then they drove him to the disused house in Whareponga, later calling at the house from which they uplifted him to add force to the subterfuge. As such they were parties to the two assaults and the kidnapping.

Hikawai allegedly made the call from the police car to Thomas and Wilkinson. This provided the pretext for taking Maxwell to the Reedy homestead.

Neilson was implicated because of his bitten finger. There was also evidence of alterations to times entered in his workbook. And the same applied to other records of their hours worked.

Naden's job was to provide a reason for the apparently chance redirection of the police car; that reason was the "anonymous" phone call. He was either involved in the plan originally or became involved as an accessory after the fact, when it was realised an explanation for the "redirection" was necessary.

Whiro Ratahi, December 11, 2008: *Was there any evidence that sealed it for you that this did happen?*

Right from the very beginning when I took the first complaint from Dickie Maxwell. His demeanour. His body language and the cuts to his hair. On his hand there were grazes. And Dickie Maxwell wouldn't want to talk to a cop at the best of times. He wouldn't want me in his house otherwise. When you stack all those up it helps towards his credibility. Then that guided me on, "Well, what am I gonna do next?"

Then I just said to Dickie, "Let's go into Ruatoria now and move on to the next step, take it a step further."

During the ten years spent researching Ngati Dread, I literally inched my way toward my version of what happened on March 21, 1987. I started by reading the newspaper clippings. I got a bit closer by reading the trial notes. The internal inquiry team had done remarkably well to get so close to the truth. But they hadn't made a few crucial connections. Even Dickie Maxwell's version of what happened had holes, because he had no idea of what had been planned for him. It wasn't until I started talking to the people involved in the case and their acquaintances that previously-hidden pieces of the jigsaw puzzle began to reveal themselves and slip into place. As the years had passed following the court case, more and more snippets of what really occurred had leaked out from under the cone of silence. And these made their way, often through a few degrees of separation, to me, where they were reassembled.

I won't recount my version. But I'll point out where it differs from those offered by the Crown and by Dickie Maxwell.

For example, I've heard that there weren't four assailants in hoods. There were only three, including one who escaped being charged in this case. According to my version, Thomas and Wilkinson did not drive Maxwell from the Reedy homestead to the disused house in Whareponga. They had already left the scene. And it wasn't Hikawai who made the original call to which Thomas and Wilkinson responded. It was Naden.

I suppose the next obvious question is: Who was the police officer who wasn't charged?

The answer: Detective Sergeant Eric Newman.

This wasn't made public but was common knowledge among those investigating and accused of being involved.

My first inkling was when I noticed that two comments about Eric Newman, gleaned from my interviews, didn't seem to fit where I thought they should. They were made by former police officers when the conversation was about the Maxwell case but, because I didn't connect Newman with Maxwell, I originally added them into this book during the coverage of Newman and Neilson's trial for the alleged assault of Rasta Jonathan McClutchie. But they seemed out of place. Here they are.

__Angus:__ Your daughter sent an email to me that she saw the jury nudging and winking and all the rest of it with the accused. Did you see anything like that?

Whiro Ratahi (December 11, 2008): No, but I soon realised that when I walked in the room there was real hostility. I would give my evidence as I'm professionally required to do and walk out because there's no point in me hanging around there just to antagonise those in the courtroom. There were a lot of police officers and obviously their friends and families. The sad thing is that I babysat some of their children and I looked after their house when they were on holiday. One of the detective sergeants, Eric Newman, I looked after his children and his house when they were away.

Sergeant Alex Hope (retired, now a lawyer): Eric Newman was the weak link. And I know that he was panicking when all the others were battening down, staying tight-lipped. And I know through a former cop who was close to those guys that Eric Newman was the weak link. They were scared that Newman would blow it because he was terrified.

I should add that neither Hope nor Ratahi were trying to drop Newman in it or reveal anything they thought I didn't know. The comments were delivered so matter-of-factly that I didn't read anything into them at first. Hope's comment sat on its own in my computer, making no sense, for six years before I interviewed Ratahi. Then Ratahi's comment got me wondering. Either comment, on its own, wouldn't have been enough. But, eventually, together, they hit me. Newman was involved in the alleged assault on Maxwell. I made some more calls and was assured that, yes, Newman was originally in line to be charged along with the other detectives. There wasn't enough evidence to link him to the chain of events, so he escaped charges. Of course, that's just my theory.

Oh, and there was that awkward moment in court during the trial of the five detectives. One of the female witnesses, a kitchen-worker at the Manutahi Hotel, was asked to identify the police officers who were late back for a meal on the night of the alleged kidnapping. She identified Hikawai and Neilson and then pointed at Eric Newman, who was sitting behind them in the public gallery. Everyone involved in the case was stunned: The prosecution, the defence and some people in the public gallery, who giggled because she had identified someone who was sitting on the other side of the bench separating the accused from the public.

Newman wasn't seen around the courthouse much for the rest of the trial.

MAXWELL GIVES HIS VERSION OF EVENTS

Tuesday, September 29, 1987: *Dickie Maxwell gives the court his version of what happened on March 21. This is how he describes it.*

He's at his sister-in-law's home. As he gets out of his car he feels Malcolm Thomas put a hand on his shoulder. Thomas says he wants to talk to him about the fires.

Maxwell thinks, "I'll play their stinking little game," and agrees to go with Thomas and Wilkinson. He takes with him a Bible, cigarettes and a yellow plastic lighter.

Mike Wilkinson's driving. As they drive through Ruatoria a radio message mentions the Reedy house. Maxwell's asked if he wants to go to the police station or go with them while they attend to that inquiry.

"I knew it was a little game," he tells the court, " and I was willing to play."

Thomas asks Maxwell where the Reedy homestead is. He directs them but Wilkinson goes up the wrong drive. At the house, Wilkinson disappears, then comes hurrying back.

Thomas jumps out of the car. They call out "halt police", and both go over a fence and down a bank.

Maxwell's alone in the car for about ten minutes. Suddenly a back door opens and "some clown's there in green overalls".

He has a light green pillowslip over his head with a couple of eye-holes in it. He tells Maxwell to get out of the car. There are three others outside dressed the same. One has a .30 handgun, another a .303 rifle. The pillowslips look new and he sees a light blue dress shirt.

Maxwell's pulled out of the car in a struggle. The man pulling him out speaks in syllables − "You... get... out... car... lie... down... on... ground."

He tells Maxwell to put his hands behind his back. Maxwell is face down in the grass. One of the men is sitting on his back.

"You... no... struggle," he is repeatedly told.

The man with the rifle puts it down a short distance away. Maxwell grabs at it, with the intention of shooting. He gets his right hand to the barrel and his left thumb in the trigger guard. But nothing happens when he pulls the trigger. The gun's empty. The man who put it down, wrests it back off him.

Maxwell's wrists are tied up his back with what feels like electric fencing wire. While all this is happening, he notices that one of his captors is a Pakeha with light green-blue eyes.

A wet pillowslip is put over Maxwell's head and an attempt is made to stuff something into his mouth. He manages to bite a finger – a forefinger, he thinks - hard enough to make the person say ouch.

A wet sugar bag is put over the top of the pillowslip and some sort of binding is put around his throat, tight enough to restrict his breathing when he turns his head.

The men stand him up and put him back in the car. They drive around the old house and back up the driveway. The men take him for a drive around Ruatoria's roads. But, even with his eyes covered, Maxwell knows everywhere they go because of his knowledge of the roads and the turnoffs and the sound of the tyres on the shingle, tarseal, bridges and cattle stops. He realises they're taking him along Whareponga Road and senses them pull up at a building near Koura Station.

He's ordered out and walks up some steps into a building. "Lie down on the floor," he's told. The floor has bare boards and smells old and dusty.

Someone stamps around his head and he hears the bolt of the .303 rifle being worked.

In the same jerky syllables as before, he's asked who burned down the churches, the police station and the fire station.

"I don't know," he says. A boot is squashed into the back of his head and insults fly about Maxwell's fellow Rastas. Another voice in the room says to him several times: "We will kill you." Someone pulls off Maxwell's gumboots and the soles of his feet are kicked. Maxwell recites The Lord's Prayer. His captors remove Maxwell's jeans and sweatshirt, leaving him lying in his underpants.

"You don't go to police," he's told. "We will kill you. If we don't get you we'll get your family. Go to Te Araroa, grow your herb and don't come back."

His hands are untied and someone helps to work the circulation back into his fingers. He's feeling "bloody sore".

His hands are tied again, this time in front of him, and the hoods are removed but replaced with a blindfold. Someone says, "We cut dreadlocks now." Maxwell tells them to do it.

After his hair is cut, Maxwell's reminded not to go to the police. He's put in a different car, a Falcon he's seen driven around by detectives, dropped off at Hiruharama by two of the men, told to count to fifty and given his clothes.

He showers at the marae to warm up, then makes his way to his father-in-law's home, where he changes into dry clothes and recounts what has happened.

He then goes to another house and gets a lift into Ruatoria to retrieve his car. The keys are gone but he notices someone has put his Bible and cigarettes back on the seat. The lighter though is still missing. Maxwell last saw the items at the Reedy homestead.

He goes looking for his brother and then for detectives in the house bar of the local pub. The main person he's looking for is Malcolm Thomas. But he's not there.

Maxwell tells the police officers in the bar that their worst mistake was letting him go. They should have cut his throat instead of cutting his hair.

During the kidnapping, he's suffered a nylon burn to one wrist, a cut to the other, scratches to a shoulder, a leg and his forehead, bruising to the back of the neck and the upper arm, and the soles of his feet are sore.

There is also evidence today from other witnesses. One of them seems to back up Maxwell's assertion that he managed to bite the finger of one of his alleged assailants.

Nurse Raewyn Rickard (former Rasta Beau Tuhura's sister, who will later marry Ruatoria Rasta Tony Tuhou) says she treated a bite injury on the little finger of Constable David Neilson.

Nurse Rickard says there were puncture marks at the base of the nail and that Neilson told her it was a human bite. They discussed briefly the fact he had been working at Ruatoria and he told her "a dog's mouth would be cleaner than this guy's mouth".

The Gisborne Hospital receptionist produces a written record of his arrival at the accident and emergency department for a tetanus injection.

ENTER CONSTABLE TRESIDDER

One of the crucial witnesses is Constable Steve Tresidder, who will always be (at least) disliked by the accused officers for the evidence he gives today. He tells the court how he overheard an exchange on the police radio while on patrol in Ruatoria between 5.30 and 6pm on March 21. The Crown contends this conversation was staged to cover up the real reason why Maxwell was taken to the Reedy house (to be assaulted). Tresidder says he heard Detective Hikawai call someone and say: "Something is going on there. As we drove past someone ducked down and hid. Could you have a look?"

He didn't hear a reply. But fifteen minutes later he heard Thomas say, "You're right, there was something going on here. We chased them but we lost them. We had Dickie Maxwell in the car but he's gone." He then heard Hikawai reply that it didn't matter; they could pick up Maxwell another time.

Constable Tresidder comes under intense cross-examination on the exact timing and wording of the messages he heard.

Nigel Hampton, for Hikawai and Thomas, has him go over his recollection of the messages several times, and he trips up over the exact wording. He says he didn't hear Thomas ask for assistance to find Maxwell, nor did he himself go on air to offer help, even though his initial reaction was that Maxwell was an escaped suspect. He agrees that when Hikawai gave his message he had no idea who it was directed at or that it involved the Reedy homestead. But by the time he discussed the radio conversation with Hikawai, he knew more about the incident from general discussion and from seeing the Close Up television programme. When he told Hikawai what he'd heard on the radio, the detective said, "That's okay." (It should be noted that Hikawai still vehemently denies that this conversation ever took place).

There are questions over what time Tresidder saw Laurie Naden entering the Ruatoria Police Station. Tresidder believes he was at the station until 5.30pm, so Naden must have entered the station before that.

Representing Naden and Neilson, Tony Adeane asks: "If two witnesses later say Naden was drinking coffee in the police house at that time, would they be incorrect?"
Tresidder replies: "Possibly, yes."

Twenty-one year old Te Aroha Daniels tells of a detective who came to her home on the evening of March 21. The detective told her to tell Maxwell they were looking for him. Later Maxwell came in and she glanced at him to give him the message. The next day Maxwell was working outside on his car when two men came to the gate. Maxwell became angry and upset. Daniels saw him crying and hitting her shed. "You did this," he cried and pulled a towel from his head. Daniels saw that his face was grazed and his hair had been cut. "He was angry," she tells the court, "really angry." She's asked if she knew at the time who the two men were. She recognised one, she says. She thought they were "clothed" policemen.

Wednesday, September 30, 1987: *The main witness on the third day of depositions is Close Up TV producer Mike Valintine. This is how Valintine remembers March 22, 1987.*

He's in Ruatoria with a film crew, working on a follow-up story on the troubles there. He's approached in the main street and as a result of that conversation, he says he'd like to speak with Maxwell, who he meets later that day at a house. Maxwell winces as Valintine shakes his hand. Valintine notices Maxwell's hands are bruised, bleeding and swollen (but he concedes Maxwell also told him he'd punched a tin shed earlier, when the cops came to see him). Maxwell also has bruising to his forehead and upper arm. There are marks on his wrists and most of his dreadlocks have been cut off. He interviews Maxwell and finds him upset, frightened and angry.

Maxwell takes Valintine and the film crew to the Reedy house and shows them an area of flattened grass. Lying on the ground is a yellow cigarette lighter with green writing on it. Valintine tells Maxwell to leave it there until they've filmed it. (In court, Valintine is shown an exhibit lighter, but says it isn't the same one. The one he saw had something like Tolaga Bay Garage written on it.) Then they go to the Rastafarian headquarters in Makarika, where another interview is shot.

CHAPTER 3

BAD DAY FOR MAXWELL

Thursday, October 8, 1987: This is not a good day for Dickie Maxwell for three reasons.

1: Te Aroha Daniels says she didn't see anything wrong with his dreadlocks the same night police are alleged to have cut them off.

2: Detective Senior Sergeant Norm Cook tells the court that Maxwell was a main suspect in the church arsons, and that the investigations into them dried up within days of the Rastafarian's allegations against police. That raises the possibility once again that Maxwell made up the story to sabotage the investigations.

3: It's revealed that Chief Inspector Whiro Ratahi rendered most of the exhibits taken from the scene useless. He didn't put his exhibits in plastic bags, allowing them to become contaminated.

Te Aroha Daniels made her statements in two interviews conducted by Senior Sergeant Alan Davidson of Gisborne – as part of the internal police investigation - eight days after the alleged assault of Maxwell. Daniels told Davidson about a visit by Maxwell on the night of the alleged kidnapping.

Asked if Daniels told him Maxwell was wearing nothing on his head, Davidson says the wording was: "I can't remember what he was wearing. Nothing on his head, I would have noticed." Daniels said his dreadlocks were a foot long and hung down his back.

Les Atkins (for the accused Mike Wilkinson): Did she tell you that if anything was wrong with Maxwell's hair, she would have noticed? - Yes.

Did she tell you there was nothing wrong with his hair that night, that she would have seen it? - Yes, there was nothing unusual.

Did she also tell you she first saw the cut dreadlocks the next morning when Maxwell asked her to take a photograph of them? - Correct.

Davidson tells counsel he took two statements from Daniels on March 29. The notes were read back to her and she signed them as a true record. Davidson also made up job sheets from the interviews,

**Retired Senior Sergeant Alan Davidson, interviewed at his
home in Gisborne in the early 2000s (he belongs to my father's
Catholic men's group, so later I see him occasionally on Saturday
mornings when I'm in Gisborne staying at my parents' place and
Dad's hosting the group):** After the depositions hearings, I was grilled
by Chief Inspector Bruce Scott at the DB hotel. He accused me of
passing information on to the defence.

There was that piece in my notebook where the woman said
that Diesel still had the hair on his head after the alleged incident with
the police. Well the prosecution claimed that I'd passed that information
on. And I said, "No I did not."

And it was only by a fluke really that the defence *found* it.
What had happened was Tony Adeane, the lawyer, had asked to look at
my notebook and was reading through my notebook although I had
indicated to Malcolm Thomas or somebody that there was stuff in my
notebook that was *more* than interesting. And they knew they had to get
access. So they asked for my notebook. They checked through. They
checked the information I'd written down about firearms. They checked
the numbers. And that's when Adeane spotted my notes about this
woman.

Often Chris's brother Barney (Campbell) and I would go for
drives and we were very much aware of the equipment that the police
had for bugging people. And I didn't know whether the people which I
physically saw from Wellington, namely Hartley, Scott and Marsden,
were the only ones there working on the case.

The police brought in covert gear and planted it around to try
and pick up evidence against the cops on trial.

I remember Barn and I were working together one day and we
were thinking, "The offenders had green overalls. So where would they
get green overalls from?"

And remember it was raining that night when the alleged
incident involving Dickie Maxwell took place. Well, bugger me days, I
recall vividly going down to the fire station and there were these fuckin'
green overalls. And they were wet.

And of course we can't talk because we don't know whether
people are listening to us somehow or not. And we're thinking,

"They're not that fuckin' foolish. They're *not* that foolish. Surely, they wouldn't put them back wet. You wouldn't do it." That is, assuming the incident had happened.

So I remember Barney and I walked out without saying anything to each other. We drove away, saying nothing, stopped and walked into the middle of a paddock so we could sort out, "What do we do about these overalls?"

In the end I said to Barney, "I've got enough faith in these guys that if this thing *did* happen then *these* green overalls *can't* be the same ones."

MAXWELL CLAIMS STALL INVESTIGATIONS

Detective Senior Sergeant Norm Cook tells the court the inquiry into the Ruatoria arsons had been moving forward well, but lost impetus after the alleged kidnapping and assault of Maxwell on March 21. He says it's still his view the Rastafarians lit the fires but the "heat" swung away from them and on to the police. He's cross-examined by Les Atkins.

What happened to the church arsons once Maxwell's allegations had been made? – They went on a day or two but certainly lost a lot of impetus.

After the inquiry, who was the heat on? – The police... very much so.

Had the fire inquiry files moved forward since the allegations were made? – No, not at all.

Open but dormant? – They would remain open while unsolved.

Had the Rastafarians been cleared of suspicion? – No, they had not.

Where in the hierarchy did he place Maxwell? – Of those left in the community, at the top.

Cook agrees with defence counsel Tony Adeane that Maxwell still hasn't been excluded from the church arson suspect list.

Asked if he's aware how many criminal convictions Maxwell has, Cook agrees that sixty-three sounds a correct figure.

Cook's also asked if an injury report was filed by Neilson in respect of his finger bite. There was none and he agrees the accused had a duty to report it.

Gisborne's Deputy District Commander, Chief Inspector Whiro Ratahi, carried out the initial investigation before the internal inquiry team arrived. Today he comes under intense cross-examination from defence counsel.

Les Atkins asks why he accepted exhibits from Maxwell yet, knowing they would undergo forensic testing, did nothing to protect them from contamination.

Ratahi admits he put them in the boot of a police vehicle and took no steps to obtain plastic bags. He agrees it's fundamental practice to protect exhibits as soon as possible.

Atkins: Did it not occur that any persons charged might deserve proper handling of exhibits?

Ratahi: It was not until later that I realised the significance of the items.

Did he take steps to put the items into bags on his return to Ruatoria? – No, not until he passed them on to another officer the next day.

Did he consider that they were so hopelessly contaminated that they were no good at all? – No.

Chief Inspector Ratahi also admits he didn't discover Maxwell had handed him the wrong cigarette lighter as an exhibit until it was revealed much later, on August 29.

Ratahi says he didn't post a scene guard. His role was fact finding and at that stage he was still assessing the allegation.

Ratahi tells lawyer Nigel Hampton that he stored the exhibits overnight in his hotel room wardrobe, where he also had one police shirt. He doesn't recall whether he put the exhibits on the floor or the shelf and can't recall if there was carpet on the floor. The next day they were put into a box obtained from the hotel. He believes he handed the box over in his room at around 9.30 that morning.

Hampton says it might surprise him that Davidson says the hand-over of the exhibits actually happened at 9am at the car.

Senior Sergeant Alan Davidson tells the court he took possession of exhibits, including three police vehicles. He says Ratahi gave him socks, jeans, a T-shirt, gumboots, a cigarette lighter, newspaper and human hair, which he kept in his possession until handing them on to the investigating officers.

Whiro Ratahi, interviewed on Thursday, December 11, 2008: We were up in the middle of Ruatoria and we had to try and secure any information we were able to pick up. We didn't have an investigation at that time. We were really a fact-finding mission. And in retrospect I should have called the CIB's Detective Senior Sergeant in, Norm Cook. I don't think Norm was involved in any shape or form with what happened to Dickie. I think it was the next tier down who was involved. Norm wouldn't have sanctioned any of this. I could be wrong but I don't think so.

If I'd got Norm in as an officer in charge of the scene, he would have closed down the scene and bagged all the exhibits. We were really just listening to the claims and as we looked at it a bit closer we were starting to realise, "Shit, this is more serious than we thought."

We were still trying to work out whether there was a case to answer. And we stored the exhibits at the hotel overnight. Then there were the claims of contamination and all that.

What did you think of that? Was that a fair thing or were they just leaping on something to try and take the focus away from the accused?

That's just sheer defence. Defence's role is to weaken any case regardless of what the case is. That's their game. And taking me personally, I was fair game because as Chief Inspector you're meant to be above all that.

Were you kicking yourself?

Not really, because I was still on a fact-finding mission. I said to Mr Wiseman, "Listen, there's substance in this complaint." The next day I was going to Wellington. Wiseman phoned me and said I'd better get back. Then when I got back to Gisborne, the investigation was growing.

"IF YOU KNEW WHAT I KNEW"

Alan Davidson: You've got to remember that nobody was getting caught for nothing in Ruatoria. And I recall Stu McEwen, the Assistant Commissioner, coming up from Wellington and talking to Paul Wiseman, who was the District Commander here, and Whiro Ratahi must have been in the office. Norm Cook, who was in charge of the CIB, must have been in that office, too.

And I recall vividly McEwen telling us that we had to start thinking outside the square when it came to dealing with the Rastafarians. The traditional proven methods of investigation were obviously not working. There was a massive hint there that we had to do whatever it took to get convictions against the Rastas...

... The next thing I've heard a rumour that something's happened up there to Dickie Maxwell. And I've heard the names of those who are allegedly involved.

Now I remember talking to Paul Wiseman, our District Commander, over the bar at the police canteen. And I said, "You look worried, Paul. What's your problem?"

He said, "If you knew what I knew."

And I thought, 'Yeah, I fuckin' does.' Only, I thought, 'I fuckin' does more.'

And that gave me a real shock when he said that. I thought, "Ooh fuck."

Then Wiseman submitted a report to Whiro Ratahi. Whiro came and told me there was a report on his desk that I shouldn't be reading but that if I went into his office in the next fifteen minutes he wouldn't be there. So I went in and it was Wiseman's report to Whiro telling him to get up and investigate an allegation that Diesel had been kidnapped by these policemen and had his hair cut and all that sort of stuff.

Then about ten o'clock that night I got a phone call at home. And it was from Ratahi. He'd gone up that afternoon and taken a lengthy statement off Dickie Maxwell.

And he said, "You've got to come up."

So I went up the next day with the police typist Kaye Andrew. She was going steady at the time with a cop called Steve Tresidder who was involved in the Gisborne team working in Ruatoria.

Now when I arrived there Whiro went off and picked Dickie Maxwell up and they went and had a look at the scene where the incident allegedly took place...

... When Whiro Ratahi arrived back from being with Dickie, he was about to leave Ruatoria so he had to show me a few things. He had all the exhibits in a cardboard box. And I remember telling him, "They're fucked. You've contaminated the exhibits."

This box had some long dreadlocks in it. I said, "Where did you get this hair from? From the scene?"

The answer was, "No." Diesel had cut the rest of his hair off and given it to Whiro.

They were alleged to have cut off Diesel's hair and he'd apparently gone into the pub where the police drank, screaming, "Look what you've done!"

Then he'd gone to an address in College Street after it had happened. And there was a woman there who said that Dickie had had his hair *on* his head at that stage. I recall taking a statement from the woman about that. And that came out in the trial.

Anyway, Whiro Ratahi then went and showed me the scene and where he'd been. I thought, "He's been *all over* the scene… *with* Diesel Dick. He's driven onto the scene over any possible tyre tracks. Aw well, the scene's fucked, too."

So Whiro had to go to Wellington. And he took Kaye back with him. So they left me alone overnight in the Manutahi pub with this box of evidence. And I was certain that Hemi, Mal Thomas, David Neilson and Laurie Naden and these guys would be very keen to get their hands on it. Mate, I had no fear of the Rastafarians at that stage. And, oh yes, I was pretty shit scared. Because of what I'd heard on the rumour machine prior to me even hearing about it from Whiro, I was pretty sure that something had possibly happened. And I knew the names.

And I thought, "If they find out that I'm up here and I've got that stuff here…" And I thought that stuff in that box was pretty damning sort of stuff. As it turned out it wasn't because it was so contaminated… but Hemi and the guys didn't know that.

So I took over Whiro's room. And I put the box of evidence into a wardrobe. Then I shifted the dresser over to block the door off. I shut the window. I took the mattress off the bed and lay down directly below the window. See, the Manutahi Pub's a u-shape. And I know you could look across from one window to another. And I think there was a fire escape nearby, too. I was totally concerned that anything could get in, coming through the windows or coming through the door. So I had a police issue 38 there with me and it was loaded and I slept with it that night.

I didn't sleep that well. And bugger me days about two or three in the morning there's this BANG, BANG, BANG. It turned out to be Peter Clark, who's now currently a sergeant here in Gisborne. But I didn't know this Peter Clark back then. I'd had no dealings with him. I knew *of* him. But I didn't know him.

He says, "It's Peter Clark."

"Who?"

"Peter Clark. I'm the constable at Ruatoria."

"Whadya want?"

"Whiro wants me to pick up something from this room?"

"What?" I thought this might be a ploy to get hold of the evidence.

"He says he's left his shaving gear behind."

"Do you know where it is?"

"Yes. It's in the wardrobe."

Well, that's where I had all the exhibits. I had a quick check. Yes, there was shaving gear there. "Okay." I shifted the dresser and let him in.

As he came in I said, "I've got the light off. And I want the light to stay off."

It was the old typical thing, standing in the corner with a loaded 38 on him. And I don't think to this day he'd know that I had a loaded gun pointed at him the whole time he was in the room.

The following day three fellas I'd never met before came to town: Detective Superintendent Brian Hartley, Chief Inspector Bruce Scott (not to be confused with another Bruce Scott who was Chief Superintendent), and John Marsden, who was a detective senior sergeant from Lower Hutt. The other two guys would have called the shots but Marsden was the guy who had the best feel for what was happening. They were the team who investigated whether Hemi and the other guys should face any charges. They never stayed in Ruatoria. They stayed in Hicks Bay, to get a bit of distance from the rest of the action.

Now I was the same rank as Marsden, but I was shunted to one side because I was a Gisborne bloke and I'm sure they would have been worried that I might pass on stuff to the guys being investigated. They tasked me. I was tasked to look after Diesel Maxwell on a couple of occasions. But I didn't take part in their conferences. And I probably brought a lot of that on myself.

We were having dinner at the pub one night about two or three days into the investigation. And I made it very clear to these fellas, "I will not be locking up my mates from Gisborne."

And I remember Hartley telling me, even though we were on a first name basis, "Senior Sergeant," - and I thought, 'Here's a lecture,' - "if we had senior sergeants who make those statements about criminal activities and criminals throughout New Zealand then I'm afraid we'd have no police force. You will do what you're directed to do."

"Well I'm telling you clearly now what my thoughts are on this. And I want to make it patently clear that I won't be going out of *my* way to ensure that my fellow officers are locked up because I've been in Gisborne longer than you guys have." How much clearer could I make that message?

I was quite surprised how close they got to what really happened. That was one of the big surprises to me: When policemen got arrested, just *who* got arrested. The arrests seemed to correlate quite accurately with the rumours I'd heard. Then again, the jury said they got it wrong.

Retired Senior Sergeant John Robinson, interviewed at his home in Tokomaru Bay in the early 2000s (his son Anthony was one of my best mates at school and I remember staying at their house when I was a kid): After the police station got burnt down they had a high-level conference. Thompson, the Assistant Commissioner, came up. So did Stuart McEwen, the leader of the CIB. And they were asking us why weren't we getting any results. And we said, because they're attacking at night and getting away on horses, cutting fences as they go. And they won't talk to us.

So the word went out from this conference that they were to be picked up and interviewed away from their mates. And they were. There were picked up, and they were threatened. There were a lot of incidents before the Dickie Maxwell one. Michael Paiti was held over a cliff, I heard, and threatened he'd be dropped over if he didn't cooperate.

This is how stupid the Police Department was. When the Dickie Maxwell thing broke they sent up Brian Hartley, Bruce Scott and John Marsden. And we got a call from Ruatoria that there was a big inquiry and certain police cars were to be seized and locked up. And the guys who had to seize them were the guys who were the suspects.

I mean, we were all suspects for the Dickie Maxwell incident, all the police who were in Ruatoria. And they're ringing us up and getting us to do stuff for them.

But these three guys get up there and the more they delve into it, the more they realise, "There's something in this. This is not just some Rasta ranting away."

They asked for more staff so they wouldn't have to use suspects to investigate themselves. But headquarters apparently said no. So they had to use us to get evidence against our own mates, the CIB.

I know one local sergeant who went to go into one of the cars. And he was stopped. The policeman looking after the cars said, "Aw sorry, it's all under quarantine."

And this sergeant said, "There's nothing in it anyway."

"Then what do you want to go in it for?"

"I just want to see if I've got anything there."

"Sorry."

And the sergeant said, "Aw well, you won't find nothing anyway. We hoovered it out before you got here." Comments like that didn't help, ay.

I don't know if that stuff came up in the trial or not. I didn't bother to read any of the evidence at the trial because most of it was lies.

Senior Sergeant Alan Davidson was a uniform cop in charge of all these exhibits. And he goes out one day and he calls up on the radio, "Aw look, I left some exhibits out on the porch of the police station. Can you put them in the room." And it was a pair of gumboots that belonged to someone. So we put them in the exhibit room. And when he gave evidence he inferred that he'd left all the exhibits out, everything, unattended. He was suggesting all the evidence could have been tampered with or contaminated. But all it was was just one pair of bloody gumboots. I know because I picked them up and put them in the exhibit room.

Whiro Ratahi, interviewed on Thursday, December 11, 2008: *How hard was your life made during the investigation?...*

...There were those who were in that tight group who made it awkward for the genuine police officers because some of those genuines were being pulled in for interview and they were ostracised. The photographer was ostracised, Danny Batchelor. He was given a hell of a time by the detectives because they all worked together. He had to take photographs of the hut and the car and in the end DSIR had to come out because they still found hair in the hut and in the motor vehicles. So they didn't clean them up very good.

Was this after they'd tried to get rid of evidence?

Yeah. It had obviously been swept out. After I took the initial interview, Dickie and I, we went up to Ruatoria. We were up there for about three hours. He took me to the hut where it happened...

... The cops involved in the assault swept up the shack but the experts found stuff that was still there. It was an old shack and there were some traces of human hair in the corners and some down in the cracks and quite clearly it was traced to Dickie. And they even found some in the car.

COMMITTED FOR TRIAL

Saturday, October 10, 1987: The five detectives charged with kidnapping and assaulting Dick Maxwell are committed for trial in the High Court in Gisborne. Judge Peter Trapski takes only a few minutes to deliver his decision, which he says is based on the need to put so much conflicting evidence before a jury. But some of the people who pack the public gallery are obviously stunned.

Neilson, Thomas and Wilkinson are also remanded for the hearing of depositions on three separate matters involving alleged assault. Three other detectives are also involved in these hearings.

Email received by the author from David Neilson on November 29, 2008 (Neilson had been working in Iraq for four years as a training coordinator for TMG Threat Management Group): Well mate I don't know what people have told you about the Dick Maxwell trial but I'll tell you the guy was a terrorist, an arsonist and a perjurer and I will not be inferring in any commentary that anyone in the police assaulted him other than in the lawful execution of their duty.

Re the kidnapping trial, as you know we didn't have to get up and give evidence as the prosecution witness's testimony had been totally discredited along with any evidence that was presented by the prosecution.

I don't know if you have been told but this whole matter was going to be thrown out of court at depositions by Judge Peter Trapski. We know this as our lawyers were told this by Trapski himself at the end of the defence submissions at depositions. However, overnight due to interference by the solicitor general, the five of us were remanded for trial.

ALEX HOPE: The former Ruatoria police boss is now a lawyer. He was a straight and hard-working police officer with empathy for Maori grievances.

RELIEF: Constable Dave Neilson (with the moustache and suit) celebrates the not guilty verdict in the Dick Maxwell case. With him from left to right are Dave's dad, Geoff Dods and Detective Sergeant Eric Newman.

CELEBRATION: Hemi Hikawai, Laurie Naden and Mal Thomas break open the champers after being cleared of kidnapping and assaulting Dick Maxwell.

SHEPHERD SYKE MANUEL: Disbelief and sadness at the destruction on Matahiia Station where he worked for thirty years. Behind him the remains of what used to be home.

CHARRED RUINS: All that's left of Matahiia farmer Jeremy Williams' woolshed, tractor and fuel drums.

THE pad in Makarika where "Secret Service types", who'd bugged it, were caught by the Rastafarians.

TOUGH CALL: Assistant Commissioner at the time Stuart McEwen (right) told Gisborne and East Coast officers to use "old-fashioned policing" to get information that would lead to arrests. They did as instructed and, as a result, were charged with kidnapping and assault. Whiro Ratahi's on the left.

UP IN FLAMES: The Ruatoria Courthouse/Police Station at the height of the fire. John Heeney and David Mataira were later convicted of its arson.

A BUSINESS IN ASHES: Bob Kaa in the remains of his garage on Ruatoria's main street. A shed on the site was later lent to the community for Radio Ruatoria, the forerunner of Radio Ngati Porou.

The day after Joe's Bookshop is burned down, it's business as usual.

The scene at the Reneti Church site on Mangahanea Marae after forestry labour and heavy machinery cleaned up the remains of the arson.

The Governor General Sir Paul Reeves (white hair) visits Mangahanea Marae, as planned, straight after the arson of Reneti Church.

Sir Paul Reeves surveys the devastation left by the arson of Reneti Church.

Welcome to Ruatoria…

Volunteer fire fighters douse down Reneti Church.

BURNING DOWN THE HOUSE OF GOD: what was left of Te Aranga Church after the fire at Ngati Porou Marae.

STILL STANDING… JUST: The ruins of Te Aranga Church.

Radio Ruatoria… born out of the troubles in the East Coast town.

WELCOME TO THE AIRWAVES: The team who introduced Ruatoria locals to the experience of having their own radio station.

Support outside the Gisborne court for the five officers on trial for the kidnap and assault of Rasta Dick Maxwell.

CHIEF INSPECTOR WHIRO RATAHI: Did the initial police interview with Dick Maxwell that led to the internal investigation and the trial of five CIB detectives.

NOTHING IS SACRED: the scorched frame of the Ngati Porou Marae burned down by Dion Hutana and Hurae Wairau, Hawke's Bay disciples of Chris Campbell.

CLEANING UP: Volunteer fireman Tom Heeney shovels some of the mess left by the Ngati Porou Marae arson into a wheelbarrow.

DICK MAXWELL: The Rastafarian who accused
police of kidnapping him and cutting off his
dreadlocks.

DION HUTANA: Was convicted of burning down
the Ngati Porou meeting house and of attempted
arson of the Manutahi Hotel.

Due to the huge interest in the prosecution I guess the Justice Department wanted to be seen to be totally impartial and not be seen to be acquitting cops but would rather leave that role up to the community.

Email from the author to David Neilson on November 30, 2008: I agree that Dick Maxwell was a terrorist, an arsonist and a perjurer. They all probably were. But put aside the prosecution's case and the trial altogether for a sec. All I'm wondering is what happened that night. Did nothing happen that night? Or did something happen that night?

Email from David Neilson on December 2, 2008: Well mate I guess something happened that night from Dick's perspective, if you can believe Dick. I remember having a beer one night, can't remember the date, with the rest of the enquiry team in the house bar at the Manutahi Hotel and at one stage in the evening Dick came in ranting and raving and pointing at his head. He was clearly aggressive and abusive but this was normal behaviour for that idiot.

He had obviously taken off his dreadlocks.

I didn't take too much notice of him; I think Rex Harrison told him to leave.

Saturday, October 17, 1987: The Crown seeks to move the High Court trial of the five policemen from Gisborne to another location. Its lawyers have argued in an application to the High Court in Auckland for a transfer on the grounds that the trial needs to be fair and impartial. They say there's evidence of strong public prejudice in favour of police in Gisborne.

Crown counsel John Laurenson produces twelve affadavits from prominent citizens, expressing reaction ranging from disbelief and utter dismay to anger, sadness and shock over the decision to charge the police. Several residents say if the trial was held in Gisborne, there would be bias in favour of the police.

Defence lawyer Tony Adeane refers to affidavits filed by the defence from people who'd served on such juries. They were unanimous in saying they could confront the issues involved in such cases and deal with them properly. Mr Justice Tompkins decides the High Court trial will go ahead in Gisborne as planned.

CHAPTER 4

FIVE COPS ON TRIAL IN THE HIGH COURT

Tuesday, November 24, 1987: The Crown's opening address in the case against the five CIB detectives covers the same ground as its opening address in the depositions hearing.

Then, once again, Dick Maxwell is called to the witness stand to give his version of events on March 21, 1987. That's the same story he's told before, too, although he does manage to add some new and interesting details that help to paint a better picture of what might have happened.

Maxwell says he waited alone in the car at the Reedy homestead with the windows and doors closed for ten to fifteen minutes. He was about to have a cigarette when a back door was opened. He looked up to see a man in green overalls with a light green pillowslip over his head. The man told him: "Get out of the car you shit-head."

To which Maxwell replied: "Get fucked."

Maxwell also describes the men's footwear. This time he says three of them wore Army-issue black lace-up boots, whereas at the depositions hearing he talked about only two of them wearing black boots and a third wearing brown riding-style boots. The defence lawyers will pounce on such discrepancies.

He goes on to tell the prosecutor that he thinks the finger he bit was one of the outside fingers. In depositions, it was revealed that the first time Maxwell mentioned biting a finger was in response to a police interview question and the answer was: "I felt that it was either the index or middle finger of his right hand." Since then of course Raewyn Rickard has said in court that she treated Dave Neilson's little finger.

Maybe what Raewyn said jogged Maxwell's memory. Maybe he was just being opportunistic, changing his story to match Raewyn's. Anyway, small as it is, the choice of fingers is another discrepancy between one version and another.

Thursday, November 26: Sure enough, lawyer Nigel Hampton absolutely grills Maxwell over the discrepancies in his story.

*The Gisborne Herald's report on the trial is headlined:
Difference in "minor details" examined.*

*Hampton starts by telling Maxwell that his allegations depend
to a great extent on the evidence that after he was hooded he was put
back in the same police car that picked him up. He then reads Maxwell a
transcript of part of his interview for Close Up. He's quoted as saying:
"There was one vehicle there, the one driven by a demon (detective)
with a demon passenger." He says he heard it drive away while he lay
on the ground with a .308 to his head. "If those demons had nothing to
do with it, they would not have just driven off." Then Maxwell is quoted
as correcting himself and saying they did not drive off but dumped him
in the back of the vehicle and took him with them.*

Hampton: Do you remember saying those words?

*Maxwell: No. (The author believes Maxwell's first statement
was correct: Thomas and Wilkinson drove off and, therefore, he was
taken to the second house in another car. It's also possible that Maxwell
received such a beating at the Reedy homestead that he lost
consciousness and his memory of those moments was a bit unreliable).*

*Anyway, for the next two and a half hours, Hampton takes
Maxwell through his testimony, his depositions evidence, statements to
police and interviews with Close Up. All the while, he's highlighting
differences in Maxwell's accounts of what happened.*

*The Gisborne Herald reporter who covered the trial, Dave
Conway, captured the quick-fire cross-examination brilliantly.*

Dave Conway, The Gisborne Herald: When it was put to him
that the light green pillowslips were described by him to both television
and Chief Inspector Whiro Ratahi as being white in colour, KKK style,
Maxwell said it might have been a slip of the tongue. He could not
remember the colour of the slip put over his head. He took no notice.

Did he say two hooded men kidnapped him when describing
the incident to Close Up?

He did not recall.

Did he say at depositions that he held his lighter in his left
hand?

He might have.

Did he say to the TV interviewer that he had a Bible in his hand
and a lighter in his pocket?

He could not recall.

Was the lighter in his pocket?

No, in his hand.

Did he say, "That's my lighter there, I haven't planted it, I haven't been out here"?

He might have.

Why say he had not planted it?

He couldn't recall.

Hampton asked him about comments he might have made about the fires being the work of the hand of God. Was it his belief that they were, rather than the hand of man?

It could've been the hand of man that held the match.

Was he aware the fires were started with a mix of methylated spirits and diesel?

He had not taken any notice.

Was his nickname Diesel, connected with fires?

He hoped not.

Had he ever suggested the police may have lit the fires themselves?

He might have.

Was that what he believed?

No.

Had he suggested to the TV interviewer he would not have put it past those who came into the town under the guise of law enforcement to light them?

He could not recall.

Hampton took him over his descriptions of a "dark" police car, variously described in his statements as black, dark, green or dark blue.

The witness said his interpretation was that black was dark. He meant the same thing.

Asked why he knew Ruatoria's Manutahi Hotel as "Jericho" the witness told the jury it was a place of deceit, a gathering place of heathens, a synagogue of Satan.

Did he drink alcohol?

No.

Did he smoke the herb?

Yes.

Asked about differences in his descriptions of times the officers were away from the car at the Reedy house, Maxwell said he was not good on times.

Why had he described the rifle first as a .308 then later as a .303?

It was a .303 but he was confused by his desire for revenge and the fact a .308 was within his reach. He had thought of getting it and "shooting them".

Asked about the difference of handguns, pistols and revolvers, the witness said there was no difference to him.

He had described grabbing the rifle and pulling the trigger with his left thumb. Then, in a statement to Ratahi, he said the right hand.

At that time he was still "aggro".

Hampton referred him to a difference in deposition and trial evidence on the number of pairs of black boots he saw.

Maxwell told him he did not know whether he saw one pair of combat boots three times or three pairs once. Maxwell said he just saw black boots three times…

…Hampton turned his attention to the hair-cutting incident and the fact the witness had described himself as having his hands bound behind him, and in front.

Maxwell said it was correct that they were in front.

Why had he said to Chief Inspector Ratahi on April 6 that they were behind his back?

An error.

In the end another lawyer, Tony Adeane, puts it to Maxwell that his accusations against the detectives are a clever, devious plan to take the heat off the Rastas over the Ruatoria church fires. The arson investigations have gone nowhere, Adeane points out, since Maxwell made his allegations against police.

Friday, November 27: *As she did at the depositions hearing, Te Aroha Daniels testifies that she saw Maxwell later that night, after he was allegedly abducted, and that his dreadlocks, at that time, had not been cut. She says she was watching TV and looked over her shoulder at him for about eight seconds.*

On the other hand, Barney Rangi Wharepapa, one of the Rastas, says Maxwell visited his house that night to change his wet clothing in the bathroom. Wharepapa says Maxwell's hair had been cut, leaving only about three dreadlocks.

Of the alleged cutting itself, Maxwell says pretty sharp scissors were used. He was able to tell they were scissors because there "wasn't much pulling". The only pieces that weren't removed were those under the blindfold.

Sixteen-year-old Fredrick William Meyrick says he also saw Maxwell with his dreadlocks cut that night. Maxwell had woken him at about 9pm and had wanted to be taken home. He was wearing a Swann Dri with a hood on his head. Maxwell took off the hood to show how his hair had been cut. Earlier in the morning he had seen him with long dreadlocks below the neck. When he saw him that night he saw a couple of short lengths of dreadlock sticking out.

Lawyer Nigel Hampton says there's evidence that when Maxwell went into the house at College Street there was nothing untoward about his hair.

But the witness maintains that when Maxwell showed him his hair, it was cut.

Monday, November 30: *Senior Sergeant Alan Davidson's in the witness box today. He's one of the officers that this case has put in a very awkward position. He's good mates with Hemi Hikawai and the other CIB detectives on trial but he's also been forced to work on the internal inquiry.*

There are two main subjects about which Davidson is cross-examined. One is the way he handled exhibits; the other is the accuracy of Constable Steve Tresidder, a witness for the prosecution.

Davidson says he took possession of two police cars and a number of exhibits: The personal belongings of Dick Maxwell, including a cigarette lighter and a quantity of head hair. He placed the exhibits in a carton and kept them with him in a vehicle, a hotel room and at the police station.

He concedes that he left them unguarded for about forty-five minutes at the Ruatoria Police Station and didn't realise it until he was driving to Whareponga. He radioed back and had the exhibits locked away.

Davidson tells the court the exhibits were loose in the boot of a police car when he took possession of them. So he grabbed a cardboard box from the hotel and put them in that. He placed the carton and its contents in his hotel wardrobe.

He did not label or mark each item, make a note of them, or place them in plastic bags. The next day he put them in the boot of a police car and took them to Ruatoria Police Station.

Laurie Naden's lawyer, Tony Adeane, takes Davidson on a different tack. Had he ever taken Tresidder to task over accuracy? (Tresidder will give evidence over a police radio message he heard.)

Davidson tells of an incident during the inquiry. The constable claimed a drunken Dick Maxwell had abused him at the hotel. Davidson put it to Tresidder that he was mistaken. He had himself just left Maxwell ten minutes earlier at his brother's house. Maxwell did not drink and he was sober.

Another time Tresidder made a mistake in regard to identification of a disqualified driver.

"EVERY METHOD" ORDER REVEALED

Wednesday, December 2, 1987: *CIB Detective Barry Hunter reveals an "every method" order from police.*

Hunter was in charge of the inquiry into the church fires and attended a special meeting of NCOs in Ruatoria on March 17. He told the meeting that while there wasn't enough evidence to point at the Rastafarians he considered them the main suspects.

It was decided to target the younger Rastafarians in an effort to obtain information. If someone had to be picked up at midnight that was the detective's decision.

"Use every method you can to get information out of them," the meeting was told.

These strategies were passed on to the suspect squad, which was increased from four to ten.

Detective Senior Sergeant Norman Cook, who until recently was in charge of Gisborne CIB, says after March 15 there had been thirty-two suspicious fires in Ruatoria, most occurring between early November 1986 and late March 1987. As the fires stacked up, so did the pressure on police from top to bottom. "There was considerable pressure on me from my superiors and through myself to my staff," says Cook.

Cook says he heard Naden's voice on the radio in the police station watch-house the night of the alleged assault. "He was speaking to Mal or Malcolm and was telling him to go somewhere in response to some information which had been received and because of its suspicious nature he wanted it checked out."

A couple of strange entries in the staff time sheets are also revealed. Cook describes altering Naden's finishing time on the personnel deployment sheet because he saw him arrive at the hotel. The other entry involves Hikawai. He was scheduled to see an informant that night and had ordered backup. Yet the time sheet for Hikawai showed him finishing at 1800 hours.

Thursday, December 3: *Nothing much new today. Just a bit more about the time sheets. As second in charge of the operation, Cook says that where figures were altered, they were the ones to be relied upon.*

He concedes it was his duty to be a watchdog, to check operations and time sheets and agrees that twelve amendments to officers' starting times appeared to be in his writing.

Friday, December 4: *The defence lawyers decided long ago that the best tactic in this case was attack. The weed-befuddled Rastas are unreliable witnesses at the best of times and Whiro Ratahi has also proved to be an unexpected bonus. So, just as they pointed out every minor inconsistency in Maxwell's various testimonies, the defence lawyers now set out, once again, to discredit the uncertain chief inspector. The second week of the trial ends with Ratahi in the witness stand taking a verbal hammering from a tag team of lawyers.*

Les Atkins gets stuck into him about the contamination of exhibits such as Maxwell's clothing, his lighter and hair cuttings. Ratahi should have protetected them by placing them in plastic bags. But he just left them in the boot of his car.
And his memory is poor.

At one time he described taking the exhibits to his hotel room on March 25 and handing them over on the morning of March 26. Now he's certain he left them in his car on the 25th and handed them over on the evening of the 26th.

Also, at the depositions he said Maxwell brought him the exhibits in three lots, but now he accepts it was two.

Robert Wolff pulls him up on two lights he reckons he saw outside Hiruharama Marae in March. They weren't actually installed until September.

Peter Kaye pings him because he thought Dave Neilson was still a member of the Armed Offenders Squad but he hadn't been since April 1986.

He also notes that Ratahi said somewhere that he started taking Maxwell's original statement in a derelict shelter on Whareponga Beach at noon but it had actually been 4pm.

The lawyers sell these minor discrepancies to the jury as full-blown calamities. Stumbling on a real prize such as the contamination of exhibits they seek to maximise its value by searching out other mistakes, any mistakes, no matter how tiny, as long as they help paint a picture of all-round incompetence. And by such means, right or wrong, truth or falsehood, guilt or innocence, is decided.

Ratahi describes picking up Maxwell on March 25, four days after the alleged kidnap and assault. He says Maxwell pulled up his trousers and showed him cuts to his leg. Maxwell had cuts on his right hand and cuts, scratches and bruises on his forehead. Also, the area above his left eye was slightly swollen and his hair was cut jagged.

Monday, December 7: *Ratahi's accused of coaching Maxwell for the trial. He denies it.*

"Did you give him, Mr Maxwell, a statement of evidence before the trial?" counsel Peter Kaye asks him.

Ratahi says he went to Ruatoria on November 22 with a two to three page document to invite Maxwell to refresh his memory on the complexities and inconsistencies of his evidence, which appeared at the depositions hearing. He says he went because he was directed to do so.

Nigel Hampton asks if they had discussed the use of the term 'as far as I can recall'. Maxwell had used the expression several times and Ratahi also used it several times last Friday.

Ratahi says it wasn't discussed.

Ratahi's also asked why he drove Maxwell to court twice during this trial. He says it's because he's been appointed the police liaison for the complainant.

A DSIR forensic scientist, Dr Harry John van Enckevort, also gives evidence today.

He talks about finding two-centimetre long cylindrical clumps of hair in the house where Maxwell was allegedly assaulted.

At first they looked like animal droppings. Only by getting down close was he able to see that the clumps on the floor of the bedroom were hair.

A number of partial footprints and a gumboot print were found on the porch. Two tyre tracks were found at the rear of the house and lighter tracks appeared to have been made by a wheel that was spinning.

Pieces of string found in the bedroom had some jute fibre similar to that in scrim, hessian, the backing of carpet, rope, twine or sugar sacks.

"Did you think it could have been put there as a construction?" asks prosecutor Philip Smith.

"It was my opinion that only a person with extensive knowledge of forensic science could have constructed the scene," says Dr van Enckevort. He says there's nothing to lead him to believe it was constructed. The scene in the bedroom was subtle: pieces of hair, relatively small and only a small amount of fibre attached to it all.

HIDDEN TOLL OF TRIAL

Excerpt from an email received by the author on December 4, 2008: My name is Christine Webster (nee Ratahi) and I am the daughter of Chief Inspector Whiro Ratahi. Our family moved to Gisborne in 1985 and as a family we had many great experiences living amongst the Ngati Porou iwi. I was at Ilminster (Intermediate) School in 1986 and Gisborne Girls High in 1987. As the daughter of one of the top cops in Gisborne I saw and heard a lot of things that have significantly impacted my life.

It was good to read your book and hear what was going on for people at the time we lived up there as I often heard conversations, phone calls and stories about what was happening and as time has passed the connections and related memories were lost until I read your book. It was interesting that you said that this was a dark story as when we left Gisborne I carried a lot of anger with me. I went back to Gisborne when I turned 30 to make peace with the place and to find some release. This anger I had was mainly directed at the police and authority and was a result of the incident when Dickie Maxwell was kidnapped and the investigation that followed (and the impact this had on our family).

I am really interested in the next volume of your story and I hope that the truth is told. Our family suffered from abusive phone calls, threats and verbal abuse on the street and sadly this was often from police family and friends. I was only young at the time and I also attended court when my Dad gave evidence against the policemen charged with kidnapping Dickie Maxwell. I saw the defendants winking and smiling at the jurors and also felt the tension in the air as my Dad walked out of the court after giving evidence. I was really angry with the way my father was treated and how our family was treated.

My Dad is a humble man and as a Maori policeman he was often put in a position where he had to make a choice that others would not like and he would not be popular. Dad has always been pushed to the front of incidents where race has been a factor (such as the 1981 Springbok tour, Bastion Point, Queen Street riots, Moutua Gardens and the Ruatoria incidents). I am proud that my Dad chose to make a stand for truth and justice.

I learnt during this time that police could not be trusted and that police could be corrupt. The police culture meant that they closed ranks and did what they liked and nothing happened to them. Looking back, I wasn't old enough or strong enough at the time to have more of a voice and I did what I could to support my Dad.

Anyway, all I ask is that the truth is told and nothing is left out. Is anyone ready to hear and speak the truth though? Kia kaha.

Whiro Ratahi, interviewed on Thursday, December 11, 2008: *What sort of personal toll did it take?*

There were a lot of sad aspects to it actually. There were a lot of threatening phone calls to our home. So whoever picked up the phone got the message. So instead of shooting me they were shooting my children or my wife. And interestingly we tried to trace those and we went to the P&T but we couldn't trace those calls.

So what does that suggest, do you think?

Well, the technicians didn't want to find it. We know the calls were made…

… What sort of things were they saying? Were they threats?

Yeah they were actually. And they were abusive and hoping that I'd die of cancer and all my children the same. So those were the sad things because it was a beautiful place. Normally they were really neat people. It was not only adults saying these things. I think it was teenagers rather than young, young kids... ...And I felt really sorry for these kids because what was coming out of their mouths, I'd think, "Gees... goodness me."

From what they were saying it was obviously someone who knew we were involved in the investigation.

__Tuesday, December 8, 1987:__ A nineteen-year-old Rastafarian, Jonathan McClutchie, is in the witness box.

He says that two days after the church fires, Neilson and Detective Sergeant Eric Newman took him to Horehore, near Ruatoria, to question him.

They covered his head and handcuffed him and one of them kicked and punched him. They stopped and the three of them had lunch. Then they beat him again.

Defence Counsel Peter Kaye: That is nothing but a blatant pack of lies isn't it.

McClutchie: No.

This is Kaye's version of events. McClutchie attacked Newman while Neilson was out of the room. When he returned, Neilson joined in the fight to get McClutchie off. It was during this struggle that Neilson was bitten on the finger (this is a ploy by the defence to explain away the only evidence that links Neilson to Maxwell: The bitten finger). Threatened with being charged with assaulting the two police officers, McClutchie informed on two of his brethren. He told the police officers that Joe Campbell, Chris's brother, had cannabis and that Dick Maxwell had lit some of the fires.

McClutchie admits he informed on Campbell, who has since been arrested and dealt with. But he denies informing on him to avoid being charged with assault. He also denies informing on Maxwell. And he denies biting Neilson on the finger.

The court also hears evidence from a handwriting expert, Alfred Denys Crawford, the retired chief document examiner for the police, who describes changes made to workbooks belonging to Neilson and Malcolm Thomas.

He says thirty-five of the ninety-six leaves in Neilson's workbook were missing.

An electronic static document analyser was used to produce an image from indentations on one leaf. Those indentations had come from another leaf, which had later been removed. This showed a timetable for a period finishing on March 26, 1987.

Another timetable, further in the book, was for a fortnight ending on March 27. The only difference between the two timetables was that the finishing time for March 21 (the day of the alleged kidnapping) had been changed from 2100 hours to 1930.

Crawford says he found it strange that two timetables were completed for the same period within a couple of pages of each other.

Thomas's workbook showed that a number of finishing times had been altered and on March 21 the finishing time had been altered from 1700 to 1900.

Wednesday, December 9, 1987: *Constable Stephen Tresidder is in the witness box today, giving evidence about the two conversations he says he heard on the police radio the day of the alleged assault.*

Nigel Hampton questions him at length as to how he knew Mal Thomas was involved in the first conversation. Tresidder says it's because he heard Hemi Hikawai say, "Thanks Mal."

Hampton: "You're making this up as you go along."

Constable Tresidder: "No. I don't need to do that Mr Hampton."

Hampton asks if he remembers Hikawai saying at the police station that a lot of people would be interviewed and that he hoped they would tell the truth and not go assuming things. Tresidder says he doesn't remember that.

Friday, December 11, 1987: *Gisborne Crown Solicitor Terry Stapleton tells the High Court he's resigned so that he can give evidence of character for the policemen facing trial.*

Stapleton's been crown solicitor from July 1979 until yesterday. Asked to give evidence, he realised there would be a conflict of interest and he didn't want to compromise the office of Crown Solicitor in Gisborne.

There's no need to repeat what he said about each officer. He reckoned they were all good guys who were respected in the community.

Stapleton's the last witness in the trial of the five policemen.

CHAPTER 5

AND THE VERDICT IS...

Monday, December 14, 1987: The fourth week of the trial kicks off with the final addresses. The defence says that Maxwell's a liar and the police have been set up. The Crown says that Maxwell was kidnapped and assaulted in a premeditated attack and reminds the jury to put away their preconceived ideas: Maxwell (the Rastafarian with the long list of convictions) has the same rights as anyone else.

Laurie Naden: We weren't in custody, except, once the jury retired we were technically in custody. We went back to the police station and we were in the mess room. And the meals were coming over from the DB. And it was like the Last Supper. They sent over these beautiful steaks and it was a superb meal. None of us ate it.

Back at the court, we weren't in the cells but we were kept in a secure room. The jury room was above us and they had windows open. You couldn't hear what they were saying. But you could hear them mumbling away. Every so often you'd hear a laugh and you'd think, "Aw shit, that sounds all right."

Then you'd hear, "No, no, no, no." And you'd think, "Aw shit, that doesn't sound too good."

They'd gone out and then they'd gone for a meal. Then they came back. It probably took them about four hours to deliver.

And of course as a policeman you're always sussing out the jury. The first look you get is when the foreman or foreperson walks in. You'd always look and see if they looked at the defendant. If they did you could almost say they've found him guilty. Well shit, old Mike Brittenden - he was the foreman – he walked in and didn't look at us. And of course everyone was acquitted and that was it.

The whoops and hollers begin as the jury foreman reads the not guilty verdicts on the crucial charge of kidnap. It's clear by now that the aggravated assault and accessory charges will go the same way. And applause breaks out as the final verdict is entered.

Friends and fellow officers descend on the five acquitted detectives. They are whisked away down the back stairs to the corridor

Laurie Naden: We were pretty bloody happy, of course. We went down the back stairs of the court, down into the jail area where most of our wives were waiting. Peter Bush, the newspaperman, was there going mad with a camera. We had a little bit of a celebration. Then we adjourned to the fire station because we were still suspended and couldn't drink at the police station. And we had a fair session down there. Of course the phones started going silly and we started getting phone calls from cops and ex-cops all round the country.

And I sort of woke up the next morning and of course Hikawai and I - the others still had charges to face – had to go back into work for the first time in about seven months. The suspension notice had banned us from the station until we were otherwise dealt with. So Tony Adeane, the lawyer, came with us. He came because he didn't know how we were going to react when we saw Ratahi. We walked in and Wiseman had run away, as he had during almost the entire inquiry. He'd just shot through.

So we arrived there and Ratahi was rather sheepish. But Hemi and I had decided, "Right, we're not putting any shit in. It's finished."

He said, "Welcome back."

"Aw, thanks very much."

"Now whaddya wanna do?"

"We'll go on leave." We'd built up a huge amount of leave.

He said, "Yeah, yeah." And he opened this bloody leave book he had. And he's got six names all underlined. And he had something at the end of it, the words "pay out" or something, which would have happened if we'd gone to jail. They would have then paid our spouses the equivalent amount of leave.

I said, "You're a bit quick putting that down weren't you?"

"No, no, it doesn't mean that, it doesn't mean that."

"Look, we're not gonna bullshit you. We're just going on holiday for six weeks."

"Aw, go."

Hemi and I just walked out and we went on leave.

So that's how convinced Ratahi had been we'd all go to jail. He'd worked out to the last cent how much our spouses were going to get. It was a little bit presumptuous.

The trial and the controversy didn't have a great adverse effect on anyone's career path. It did take a toll on lives though.

I remember my girls. Caroline would've been about twelve. And although we tried to keep her away from it, because it was such a topic of conversation, on the odd occasion my wife would have to bring the girls in for half an hour after school. For a long period of time there was a lot of tension in the house, probably because we knew what was happening, it was easier for us than our wives. It was harder for them.

I remember going to a bloody school dress-making thing one night and I walked in and I would say ninety percent of the heads turned round. I just thought, "Who gives a shit." It didn't worry me. But my youngest daughter come up and she said, "Why's everyone looking at you, Dad?"

And I said, "Aw, because of what's happening down the courthouse."

So there was a bit of a drama there for *them*, not so much for me.

And of course there were seven of us charged and five of us were in the main trial. And we were close. We kept close. We talked to each other all the time. We had lawyers to discuss things with. We knew where we were, the women didn't. And that was bloody difficult.

I remember the day that we got suspended. I got called down. I think I was the last. And they handed me these papers and I shook their hands. I said, "Thanks very much. I'll see you in court."

And the District Commander at the time, Paul Wiseman, he was shocked that I actually shook their hands. And I said, "Well they're only doing their job. They're not going to convict us."

He couldn't believe it.

I said, "Well you started it. You could've gone up there and sorted it out. But no you sent your 2IC Whiro Ratahi up there."

They lived in the realms of fairyland, some of these cops in the internal inquiry team. They kept shifting motels because they believed we had the ability to bug their motels. Well, who gives a shit about bugging their motels. But I'm bloody sure there were things happened to some of our houses which were totally illegal, too. One night I attended a Police Association meeting, which was held in the house of a fellow suspended member. And the following day one of the persons who was not suspended but had attended the meeting was fronted by the District Commander and all sorts of things were put to her which could only have come from the meeting. And I think they certainly over-stepped their mark. They had surveillance squads following us around. That didn't worry us. I know staff were sent from Christchurch, monitoring staff. They denied that any electronic surveillance had been done because they didn't have any warrants.

The Police Complaints Authority was just starting to come into play at that time. They overview all police inquiries. And policemen right through the ranks didn't want the Police Complaints Authority. So it was probably an opportune time for them to show the public, "We'll go out and do a competent and full inquiry." We had no problem with that as long as they played by the same rules as everyone else. But I believe that they used illegal tactics.

Lyn Hillock, former Gisborne Deputy Fire Chief: That team up there was the best team of police I've ever worked with. But they were just down-graded, derided by Paul Wiseman and their other commanding officers.

When Diesel Dick made his accusations that they shaved his head, all that team were banned from the police canteen. They weren't allowed anywhere near it. This was while they were suspended from the police.

I said to Ian McDowall, my chief, "This has gone too far. These guys are coming down to our canteen here at the fire station."

Paul Wiseman came down about five days later, marched into the office and said, "You realise you've got criminals drinking in your bar?"

I said, "Woo-woo, arsehole. Excuse me?"

"You've got criminals drinking in your bar."

"Would you mind taking your person off the fire station premises. Thanks very much, you're no longer welcome here."

He came back when Ian McDowall arrived back in. Ian called me into the office and old Wiseman ranted on that we were hiding criminals and they shouldn't be drinking on our premises, etc, etc, etc. And we told him to *fuck off*.

Everyone assembled for the verdict in the fire station canteen. Shit, there were heaps and heaps of us. The verdict came through and up went the town siren. "Yahoo!"

Wiseman, of course, was totally slutted. They'd treated their staff like shit during this whole thing. They treated criminals better than they treated their own staff. It was bad enough being up there in Ruatoria, let alone having that sort of pressure coming down on you from within your own organisation.

Peter Brown from the CIB came up with the best song to ever come out of that area. It was "No Dreadlocks No Cry" sung to the tune of Bob Marley's "No Woman No Cry". It was all about Dickie Maxwell claiming he'd had his head shaved by the cops. We were sitting on the staircase inside at the Ruatoria pub. There was Hemi, Laurie, Thommo, Brownie. And they come out with a guitar and away she went. Christ, it was about the only time in two weeks we'd cracked up laughing, and we were just rolling around on the floor.

My feeling on the whole Dickie Maxwell thing? Couldn't happen to a nicer guy.

You look at normal society; they ram you in prison or put you in the Army or whatever and the first thing they do is cut your hair. That's the area where you lose some of your mana. It's one way of saying, "Listen, arsehole. You're not twenty foot tall and bullet-proof, Jocko. We'll just give you a little reminder." A lot better could've been done to him. He's just lucky we never caught him with an emasculator because we would've ringed him with it.

BUT WAS IT THE RIGHT VERDICT?

As I said when I started writing up the trial of the detectives, I believe the jury got it wrong. Now I'm not saying that the prosecution got it right on every point (that would be a near-impossible feat without a confession). But I do believe that Dick Maxwell was kidnapped and assaulted by police. Alex Hope is now retired from the police force. At the time of the Maxwell case, he was in charge of the Ruatoria police. These days he lives in Hamilton and is a partner in a law firm, Waihere Hope. I interviewed him on October 5, 2002.

Alex: I reckon I must've been the only cop who wasn't interviewed about the Dickie Maxwell kidnapping. I guess I was just over-looked.

Q: Do you think they did it?

... I was talking to Hemi after Mataira and Heeney had been arrested for the arson on the police station. They were arrested about eighteen months after it, out of the blue. And Hemi was involved in the arrest. I think he locked them up. And I said to Hemi, "How did you get on to those two? It's been well over a year since that fire."

And he said, "When does Dickie Maxwell reckon he got his haircut?" It was a Friday or a Saturday. At that stage I don't think a complaint had been made but the rumour was going round that Dickie had had a haircut and that the cops had given him it. And then he said to me, "And what day did I arrest Mataira?" which was, I think, a day or two later. And he said, "Well, where do *you* think I got the information."

It went basically like that. And then he just laughed and that was the end of the conversation. I didn't want to know any more. That was it.

That was Hemi's way of telling me, I believe, somebody had bashed out of Maxwell the answer. He'd dobbed those two in and on that basis they'd been interviewed and they'd admitted it.

Napier lawyer and long-time Labour MP Russell Fairbrother is another who's convinced the detectives were involved in the kidnapping and assault of Dickie Maxwell.

Russell Fairbrother: I acted for Dickie Maxwell for a number of years. The police knew this and Whiro Ratahi contacted me. He was in charge of the Gisborne station and of investigating the allegations against police. He wanted me to be a coordinator between them and Dick Maxwell because Dick wanted me to be involved.

The night before the trial I drove through to Ruatoria with Whiro and met up with Dickie Maxwell and he'd had a chart prepared of inconsistencies in what the policemen had said, which was being used for the crown prosecutor. And we virtually went through what Dickie had to say and confirmed that the inconsistencies existed. It was quite a detailed meeting and Dick was very nervous. He wasn't used to being on the same side as the police.

And as I recall it we brought him back and provided him with somewhere to stay in Gisborne that night before he gave evidence at the trial.

I didn't go to the trial. I stayed in Gisborne. I was asked to stay in Gisborne. But I stayed away from the trial so that it wouldn't become obvious that Dick was getting other advice as well. But he had such a history he was always going to be an easy target for good lawyers.

But I've heard things since from some of the officers involved - things said both directly and indirectly – that have confirmed that what Dickie Maxwell was saying was right. And we tried to bring a civil action against the Crown. The trouble with Dick though, he was a heavy dope smoker. And he'd go walkabout. Then he'd suddenly re-emerge, and usually when he was put in prison. And he'd ring up and he'd say, "Well, how's the claim going?" And we'd get on to it. Then he'd disappear. I thought at one stage we were close to a settlement. But I couldn't get any instructions. Then I heard from him ten years after the event, and, of course, the time limit's six years. He wanted to settle it there and then. But we'd run out of time by that stage.

I think we were on good ground for settlement. The Internal Affairs department of the police had investigated and believed he'd been kidnapped and assaulted. And that's why they prosecuted. I spoke to two detectives involved and they seemed pretty clear-headed and convinced that they were right. And I can't see that the Police Department would have ever said, no, we won't settle. I think it was more a question of how much more than anything else. And if I'd received some instructions from Dickie, both he and I might have been very rich.

But Dick was just a wanderer. When he went back to Ruatoria he would beg and smoke dope. I think people saw him as a bit of a pest. I think he had a higher opinion of himself than most other people had.

Soon after Volume One of this series came out I got a call from one of my best friends from Gisborne, John Taituha. A former Poverty Bay rugby league rep and an old school-and-band-mate of mine, John was in Auckland to watch the Warriors in the 2008 playoffs and he wanted me to drop off a copy of the book to him at a house in Papatoetoe where he was staying.

I took him the book and, while we were having a chat out by my car, he flicked through it. "Hemi Hikawai," he said, noticing the former detective's name on one of the pages. "He gave me a hiding down at the Gisborne Police Station when I was just a young little Catholic kid straight out of school."

"That's right," I said. "I remember you got beaten up by the cops when we were teenagers. Was that Hemi?"

"Yeah. He reckoned I stole some band gear. I didn't know anything about it. But he beat me up. Then he took me upstairs where one of the other CIB guys was and I had to hold my arms up while I was punched some more. I was there for hours and in the end I was so upset I signed a confession."

"Even though you didn't steal anything?"

"I just wanted it to stop."

"Did it ever go to court?"

"Na. My old man got on to Peter Bradley (a policeman back then and also the father of a couple of our schoolmates) and Mister Bradley sorted it out with Hemi. It never went anywhere after that."

I put this story to Hikawai in February 2009 and he didn't deny it but said he honestly couldn't remember it. I believed him. And, of course, I believed my mate Taituha as well.

Whiro Ratahi: I remember Hemi coming around to my place in Gisborne one night. He was a detective at this stage. And he said, "Aw, I just smashed someone. And I don't think there's going to be any complaint."

I don't think there's going to be a complaint?

Yeah.

Heh heh heh.

Hemi was having a drink at a bar, one of those out of town bars, and this guy started putting the jugs up one on top of the other, you know how people do when they've had a few jugs, one on top, then another on top. And he had it about eight high.

And the barman said, "Sir, can you stop doing that. I'm frightened that it will fall over."

And this guy carried on. So Hemi came over, pulled him aside, whacked him and said, "The barman said stop." He smashed him. And then he came and told me.

He said, "Look, I thought I'd better give you a heads-up in case a complaint's made."

Luckily, there was no complaint.

I remember him telling me when I interviewed him that he'd put away more murderers than anyone in New Zealand, but probably had more complaints against him, too. I'd say that was part of his...

That's his psyche, I think. He'd been on undercover for a long time and he was always on edge.

That story you just told me, do you mind if I use it?

No, no. It happened. What people don't realise is that he had an open door to my private home. He just knocked on my door and said, "Hey, boss, I need to talk to you a minute." When you've got Maori on Maori it's okay to do that. The only difference was that I was Chief Inspector and he was Detective. And he'd bring over paua, a sheep, stuff like that. He wouldn't be wanting a favour for it, none of that. It was just aroha, or koha, from him. Farmers would give him stuff and he couldn't eat it all.

I ran this story past Hikawai and he said, "That's not true?"
"What do you mean?" I asked.
"There were five guys stacking the jugs, not one."

CHAPTER 6

HIKAWAI VERSUS TRESIDDER

Before moving on from this case, there's one other perplexing aspect to it: the involvement of Constable Steve Tresidder and what happened to him later. This is how Hemi Hikawai saw Tresidder's involvement.

Hemi: If we talk about the kidnapping and the trial, the biggest insult from my perspective was when they got policemen up there who lied in order to support the prosecution case against us. They were willing to lie against their own. And some very blatant lies were told and blatant lies were told in particular about me.

It was said that I admitted involvement in the kidnapping. Steve Tresidder was the cop who lied. He lied about hearing my voice on the radio, directing the patrol to the old Reedy homestead where I lay in wait to grab Maxwell. He lied about the fact that I had admitted to him that I had done the kidnapping. Now ask yourself. I've been interviewed by experts in this job and I've never admitted nothing. Now I'm staring fourteen years in the face. And some fuckin' hairy-arsed constable straight out of the college is saying, "I got'm to admit it." And he got up in court and said that, which is total fuckin' bullshit. He also lied during the cross examination – and this is why the whole trial was so crooked - in that you had the same constable being asked at depositions under cross-examination whether or not he had a hearing problem. He said no he didn't. He was asked whether or not he had ever been referred by the police surgeon to have a hearing check and he said no. And then his medical records said he had. (The hearing issue is relevant because it was raining very heavily when Tresidder says he heard Hikawai on the radio).

Now knowing that, when the High Court trial came he was asked those questions again. The police prosecutor at the time was a guy John Laurenson, who is now a High Court judge. Laurenson was aware of what Tresidder had said at depositions. He was aware when Tresidder was cross-examined at the High Court of what his medical records indicated and he allowed him to lie. He did absolutely nothing. We were prevented from producing his medical certificate.

Steve Tresidder: On the day of the Dick Maxwell incident, I'm working. And I'm driving around. It was a pretty crappy sort of a day. And I actually saw Dickie in the car with them. Then I heard the Gisborne guys on the radio, late in the afternoon. I wasn't really paying much attention. The next minute I heard them say, "Aw yeah, we've just lost Dickie Maxwell."

And I was thinking to myself, "Typical CIB… think they're the big time. Heh heh heh."

The next minute they were talking about, he's run across here and we're gonna run across here and get him. And I didn't think much of it.

Then I buggered off down to police college for a course. I'd been there a couple of days and I get plucked out of a lecture there and sat in a little room with a Detective Superintendent and a Detective Senior Sergeant and asked a lot of questions.

I asked, "What's all this about?"

This was after the revelations on the Close Up programme. But I didn't even know that had been on. I basically didn't know what the *hell* was going on. I asked them and they said, "Nothing really. It's just a typical internal inquiry. We're just making a few inquiries."

They asked me a whole lot of questions like, Was I working on this day? What was the day like? Did I see anybody? What vehicles were they in? Who were they? Did they have anyone with them?

I just told them, whatever they asked me.

And of course I finished my course down in Wellington and I get back to Gisborne and the shit's really hit the fan then. Guys are getting charged with kidnapping. And I thought, "Shit, what the hell's going on here?" You've got to remember: I'd only been in the job just over a year at that stage.

So I shot up and saw Hemi Hikawai. And I told him. I said, "Hey, look I was down at my course. I got plucked out of the lecture by these cops asking questions."

He said, "What did you say?"

I told him what I'd said.

He said, "Na, na, that's all right." And that was it. It just escalated from there basically. At that stage, Hemi was okay with everything.

The problem *later* was that I wouldn't change my mind. It proved that the cops had Maxwell in the car with them and it tied in with what Maxwell had said. As the investigation went on, what I was saying became quite incriminating.

Once again, I reiterate, Hemi Hikawai maintains this conversation never happened.

*I think the whole dispute between Tresidder and Hikawai boils down to a misunderstanding. Tresidder was supposed to hear Laurie Naden on the radio – that was part of the plan - and it **was** Laurie Naden on the radio. But for some reason, Tresidder thought it was Hemi Hikawai's voice. That was disastrous for Hemi, because it tied him to the sequence of events involving Dick Maxwell. Hikawai was having the finger of blame pointed at him because of a mistake. The master plan was under threat because of a silly bloody mistake that no one could foresee! That would have riled Hemi as much as anything else.*

Of course, the next best thing for Hikawai and his defence counsel would be to prove that Tresidder couldn't hear very well, which they tried to do. But in the High Court trial, Tresidder admitted, under

*cross-examination from John Laurenson, that he'd been told he had a
condition known as surfer's ear. He went to a specialist about it. And
there was nothing wrong with his ear. The defence mentioned that his
four wheel drive vehicle would have been noisy and it was raining.
Whatever they said, Tresidder was adamant he'd heard Hikawai's voice.*

TRESIDDER'S HONEST MISTAKE

Sergeant John Robinson (retired): Steve Tresidder and I
were on duty the night that it happened. And we heard this call on the
car radio saying that there was an incident up on Ngarimu's Hill or
something.

And I remember saying to Steve, "Who the hell was that?" I
couldn't recognise the voice.

And he said, "That's Hemi Hikawai."

"No it's not."

"Yes it is."

"I think it's Laurie Naden."

"No, it's Hikawai."

I thought it was Naden. But it was a wet and windy night so it
was hard to tell.

But when I got interviewed I couldn't remember that incident
in the car. And it wasn't until about five years later, after I'd left the
police, that I remembered it.

At the time when I was interviewed I said I couldn't remember
anything about that call on the radio, because I was under a lot of stress
then. I was stuffed actually. I had a stress test and the police
psychologist rang me up and said, "God, John, you've gotta go. You're
stuffed. Your results are terrible." See, I couldn't remember things and I
was doing things that I would not normally do.

Anyway, I couldn't remember that so it went back to Tresidder
saying Hikawai made the call. And Naden said in court that he made
that call. So the police said, "These guys are telling lies so we'll charge
them with being accomplices." But if I'd remembered I would have said,
"I thought it was Naden." With Tresidder thinking it was Hikawai, they
couldn't have done anything about it. The doubt would have been there.

I woke up sweating one night in bed and I could remember that
incident as clear as day. And that was five years afterwards. And yet I

couldn't remember it when I got interviewed. I wasn't covering up. I was telling them what I knew.

Steve Tresidder: They gave me shit. A Gisborne Senior Sergeant came to me. He handed me a statement, told me to read it. I read it. He said, "Sign it."

I said, "I can't. It's not right. It's not what happened."

"Well that's what everyone else will be saying. If you stick to what you're saying, you're going to be the only one saying that. So sign it."

"No. I'm not signing it. It's not right." I walked out. I made a complaint to the inspector that year, the Gisborne Inspector, told him what had happened and nothing eventuated.

Look, if it happened now, having been in the job sixteen years, or even if it had happened two years later, I would have known what to do and I would've taken things further.

Shit, I'd only been in the fuckin' job just over a year. I didn't really know what was going on. These guys had got me involved in something I wanted *nothing* to do with. That's what I was angry about. They *knew* I was working on that day. They *knew* I was the only permanent relieving officer in Ruatoria. All they had to do was come to me and say, "Hey, look, we're doing something today. Take a drive to Te Araroa." Or: "Go and watch TV for the next hour." And then when I was spoken to, I could've honestly said, "I saw and heard nothing." But they didn't. They did it while I was working, told me nothing, basically dropped me in the shit.

And I got threatened and had all sorts of shit happen to me leading up to the court case.

By the time the court case had started it had virtually all stopped because as you know a few of them also got charged with other offences as well, basically for roughing up the Rastas. And I knew quite a bit about some of that shit that had happened. And when they were giving me a hard time and things of mine were going missing and my locker was getting broken into I made a threat that stopped the threats straight away.

Malcolm Thomas was the worst of the guys who were harassing me. He's still in Gisborne and he's still a prick to me, even now.

So what happened was I went to one of the guys, who prior to that I'd been really good friends with, Dave Neilson, and I said to him, "You tell your mates to lay off or I'm going to the inquiry team. And I'm gonna tell them," this, this, this, this and this. And I told him all the extra stuff that I knew and that no one else knew. Well, a couple of the cops involved knew that I knew because they'd seen me while they were doing what they weren't meant to be doing. And all the hassles just stopped.

Former Sergeant John Robinson: As a result of his evidence, Tresidder started getting all sorts of hassles, threats and abusive phone calls. Eventually, he just rang up one guy. And he said to this guy, "Tresidder here."
"Aw yeah. Whadda you want?"
Well, remember that time I went hunting on Horehore station? And you and such-and-such a guy were beating the shit out of that Rasta?
Silence.
"If I get one more phone call, one more hassle, I'll tell them about that. They've never asked me and I haven't told them."
You know, overnight the word went out: "Leave Tresidder alone."
See, he'd gone out hunting at Kevin Brown's station, Horehore, on his day off.
And he saw this CIB car parked up near this hut. And he walked in. And this Detective Sergeant and this other Detective were beating the shit out of this Rasta.

I interviewed Steve Tresidder in late June 2002, a few days before he started a nine-month jail sentence for perjury. He and a friend had been caught poaching game in a huge Hawke's Bay high country station. His mate was found guilty of illegal hunting but police dropped the case against Tresidder on the condition he pleaded guilty to the lesser charge of giving a false name and address. He was later charged with perjury because of his testimony during his mate's trial. Tresidder believed the conviction was a jack-up, the latest incident in a revenge campaign waged by police ever since he gave evidence against Hikawai and the others. I was interested to find out what he knew about the police's treatment of some of the Rastas. I told him that one of his old

*police mates had mentioned to me that he'd seen something in an
isolated hut. He knew what I was talking about. So I asked him to
recount the story.*

TRESIDDER MAKES A THREAT

Steve Tresidder: I was up at Waingakia, up at Wiri. There's a
little dirt road that goes through Waingakia Station that gives access to a
place called Horehore Station, where I used to hunt a lot. And there's a
little wee fencer's shack in there amongst this patch of bush.

Anyway, I was coming back from hunting on my motorbike
and I was coming up this road. The next minute Eric Newman pops out
of the bush right beside me.

So he stops me and I had a bit of a yak to him. He wanted to
know if I had a plaster. He said he'd been bitten on the hand.

I said, "Yeah, I have. It's in the bottom of my pack. I'll get it
for you if you want."

"Aw, na, it doesn't matter. I'll sort it out later."

So we had a bit of a yak and away I went. I got half-way up the
road and I thought, "What's he doing? I wonder what those buggers are
up to?" So, being a bit nosey, I stopped my motorbike up the top of the
hill and I parked up and I snuck back down through the bush to where I
knew this little hut was. And, yes, there was Eric and Dave Neilson in
there with one of the Rastas, Jonathan McClutchie from memory. He
was getting a slap around and a pistol whip, and they were sticking it up
his nose. From where I was standing I couldn't tell if they were pulling
the trigger or not. But that's what it looked like to me, like they were
playing the old scary game.

So when I later told Dave Neilson what I'd seen, mate, the look
on his face was incredible. I told him a few other things I knew about as
well. And he obviously went back and told the others. And the
harassment just stopped.

I'd been getting dog-shit put in my file tray and stuff like that.
A lot of my files were getting stolen. I'd have a file completed ready for
court. I'd go to get it and it would be gone. And I'd have to start all over
again. Stuff like that.

I used to get threats like, "You're gonna get yours," in written
notes and telephone calls. That went on for months. And basically it

turned most people against me. I could go into the meal room at the Gisborne Police Station and there'd be ten or twelve people in there and I'd walk in there and it would go dead silent… wouldn't speak… say nothing. Then I'd walk out and they'd all start talking again. It was just shit like that, you know.

One of the guys I'd been quite friendly with, they told him, "Stay friends with him, stay friends with Steve Tresidder and you'll never *ever* get into the CIB."

I had no family. So at least it didn't impact on anyone else. And violence against me; don't be stupid. They were too scared to do that. They're gutless… very much so. Throughout the whole ordeal not one single person ever said anything to my face, *ever*, and they still never have. And that's what pricks they are.

But I've been punished within the police throughout my career for testifying against those cops, just not so obviously. And I'm sure the stuff that's happened to me recently is just a continuation of that. You try and find another reason. You try and find another reason why I'm the only policeman *ever* to be charged with perjury in New Zealand and for an offence so minor no one else would even get looked at for it. But here they make a big deal out of it. Why else?

Some of those people who were tied up in all that Ruatoria stuff have now moved up the ladder. One of them, Brett Kane, is an inspector at headquarters in Wellington. It just makes you sick. And over the years it's all the other things they've tried.

They've tried to prosecute me for unlawfully converting police cars. They've accused me of being a drug dealer. Just crap stuff.

It's like, everyone else in the police force can do something but if I try to do it I'll get in trouble for it. Everyone else is allowed to do certain things but I wasn't allowed to do nothing. And the worst thing is that they've tried to get me for things I haven't even done.

The accusations of me being a drug dealer were ridiculous. They came and did a warrant on my house, a warrant on my bank accounts. And the only information that they had was a guy who I'd been pig hunting with a couple of times got caught with eight pounds of cannabis. And that was it. That was their grounds.

Email from David Neilson received by the author on November 29, 2008: Anyway, to the McClutchie trial. Yes it was no secret that we had a plan to isolate and interrogate the Rastas away from the influence of other Rastas in town.

We were dealing with real terrorists that were trying to burn every white farmer off the East Coast as well as believing that Ruatoria was the new Jerusalem and that Mount Hikurangi was Mount Zion.

The NZ Government would not acknowledge the fact that they were out of control terrorists so we had to try different approaches.

I think we were up to 32 arsons at this time and, yes, Stuart McEwen came to Gisborne/Ruatoria and had a meeting with police bosses.

Jonathan Stuart Shane McClutchie was one of the Rastas that Eric Newman and I interviewed, from memory we didn't obtain any startling information from him to help solve the arsons. He was a relatively minor player in the Rasta movement at the time.

I presume there may be a job sheet somewhere recording the details of the interview.

As for that information that Tresidder gave you about witnessing an assault on McClutchie, well, it is just bizarre.

You obviously realise that he is a convicted perjurer and has done time in jail for perjury.

He is an inveterate liar, cannot help himself. I would be very wary of printing anything that he has told you.

Former Sergeant Alex Hope: All Steve Tresidder did was answer the questions that were asked of him. They accused Tresidder of lying. But Steve was just naïve in the way he went about it. Others gave evidence as well and didn't get the same treatment that Tresidder got.

Steve was a big mouth and a loner. And if he'd just kept his head down he would have survived. But he took them head on and said, "Stuff ya, I'm telling the truth." And I have no doubt that stuck with him to the end. And I have no doubt that that coloured his career, and the end of it.

Retired Sergeant John Robinson: Another cop that got hassled was Api Rangihuna, who played rugby for Poverty Bay. He told the inquiry team that he saw this cop (Mike Wilkinson) slapping this guy and punching him in the face. He'd walked past the garage behind the police station when they were interviewing this guy. He told the inquiry team that.

But when it came to the trial he was hassled so much by the others that he changed his story and said that it was just a light slap.

And the cop admitted to that and said that he only slapped this Rasta because the guy asked him to. He said the guy wanted to be roughed up a bit so that he had an excuse for any information he gave.

So they got at Rangihuna and he toned his story right down.

EMBATTLED RATAHI LEAVES GISBORNE

Wednesday, December 24, 1987: It's announced that Chief Inspector Whiro Ratahi is leaving Gisborne. He's applied for a transfer to Wellington, where he has a house, one of his married children and grandchildren.

Wednesday, January 13, 1988: Ratahi talks about his decision. He admits that ill feeling generated by the Maxwell inquiry is a factor in his decision to leave. He originally planned on a three-year stint in Gisborne; despite his decision to leave after just two years, he maintains he's not sour or bitter.

"A lot of people have come up to me and said, 'Even though you have had a hard time in court and in the media we support you because you are you.'

"I've had a lot of anonymous phone calls about the inquiry and the case. That's not unique because other people in the community get that as well. The telephone calls were not the main reason for my decision to leave."

He rates the Maxwell inquiry as the most difficult task in his twenty-three year career, on a par with being in charge of a special policing squad for the 1981 Springbok rugby tour of New Zealand.

"What made the Maxwell inquiry so difficult was that I was investigating the actions of people I regarded as friends or for whom I had a high regard as individuals and police officers."

Whiro Ratahi, interviewed in 2008: *Do you feel that you were fairly treated by the police after that?*

No, I don't think so. No. Later on in the piece the Deputy Commissioner John Jamieson phoned Paul Wiseman and said they wanted to see us both in Wellington, both Paul and I. But Paul Wiseman said over the phone because they had a bit of a yelling match, "You're not going to transfer him because he's doing a good job. He's being faithful and honest."

And Jamieson said, "No, no. I just want to bring him down here and I want to talk to him." But it was a one-way conversation. He told me, "The administration is of the view that you should come back to Wellington." And he's the Deputy Commissioner, so…

You can't argue with that can you.

Well, he would have transferred you anyway.

What sort of stuff did they have you doing back in Wellington?

Well, the rank that I had it was awkward to place me because the quota was quite full and therefore they were quite meaningless jobs. Brian Dawes was the District Commander at the time in Wellington and he was really bloody good. And he looked after me and tried to give me some meaningful tasks. In fact when he went away he got me acting on his behalf, sitting in his chair. But there were tasks we were doing that normally an inspector would do. When I was posted out to Upper Hutt I was doing, of all things, the traffic fines. I'd get the speeding tickets delivered to me in bunches of a hundred and you'd just authorise prosecution.

It was quite amazing. You've got thirty years service and this is what you finish in. You'd think there were meatier things to do.

You're obviously out of the police now. Has it left a bitter taste?

No. I thoroughly enjoyed the job while I was there. I enjoyed working with most of the people who were there. The politics was testing at times because, whether you like it or not, politics did affect what we did at the time.

What about the guys that were on those different charges, have you ever seen any of them since?

No, I've only seen one of them, Hemi. Hemi is a typical Maori. He'll come and shake hands if he's seen me and that's normal. I haven't really interacted with the others since because our paths went different ways.

Do you have any regrets about the whole process?

No, because it occurred and regardless of the police hierarchy at that time we'd have still had to go down the same path. And it's not a thing that you can push under the carpet. It had to be dealt with openly and honestly and tested in the court.

Why do you think the court got it wrong?

No, I think the court got it right. I think with those charges being dealt with in the Gisborne arena, that was going to be the conclusion.

So you reckon if the case had been held in Auckland or Wellington, they might have had a different conclusion?

Might have. I'm not saying they would have because part of the evidence is the word of a Rastafarian who had several criminal convictions against serving police officers who are in big communities with the court and who have been in Gisborne for a long time and have a huge mana in that area. It would have been an uphill battle regardless.

So what are you doing these days?

These days I've got stretch limousines. We're called Champagne Limousines. I'm also a finder in security. I place people in Iraq and Iran and Afghanistan. And this year I just finished a diploma in adult education because I teach self-defence and I teach reiki, the Japanese massage. Cyclist Hayden Roulston used it to help him overcome a few health issues in the lead-up to the Beijing Olympics and since then a lot of people have become interested. It just calms down the body so that it can do what it's supposed to be doing.

But the main thing I'm doing is teaching self-defence. When I left the police I got a black belt in aikido and opened a club up in Lower Hutt and I teach in Upper Hutt, too.

Next year I'm going to go for a bachelor. I'll do that extramurally at Massey University. That's the next step.

Former Sergeant Alex Hope (now a lawyer): Whiro Ratahi was a dark man. He was known as The Wetsuit merely because of the colour of his skin. They were just derogatory and Whiro left Gisborne literally broken. I think he's out of the police now. But he never fully recovered from that and I know that personally. I spoke to him while he was still in the police *after* he had left Gisborne. The way he was belittled and obstructed unreasonably and unfairly and the racial slurs – that all destroyed Whiro. There was nothing overt; it was all done covertly. But when it came down to it, underneath it all when you lifted the skin, they just didn't like having a Maori as a boss, a Maori like Whiro Ratahi anyway.

Whiro Ratahi: One thing I'll say about the Rastas: they knew their Bible and they knew their Maori roots. They were refreshing to be around. They were on a different planet to what I was on. But by the same token they were entitled to their own beliefs and rights.

CHAPTER 7

THREE OTHER TRIALS INVOLVING COPS

Apart from the Dick Maxwell case, there are three other cases of police officers being charged with assaulting Rastafarians.

Detective Brett Kane, Detective Constable Malcolm Thomas and Constable Christopher Wallace are accused of assaulting Michael Paiti.

Detective Sergeant Eric Newman and David Neilson are accused of assaulting Jonathan McClutchie.

And Hastings Detective Constable Mike Wilkinson faces two charges of assaulting Tony Tuhou.

November 9, 1987: *Wilkinson's depositions hearing begins.*
This is Tuhou's version of events on March 20 this year.
Wilkinson and two constables arrive at Tuhou's home that morning. They tell him he's wanted for questioning about the burning of two churches. Tuhou refuses to accompany them.
The police grab him by the shoulders and tell him he's under arrest. Tuhou braces his arms against the doorway.
"Wilkinson grabbed my hair," says Tuhou. "He pulled me out of the doorway. It kinda happened so fast. I went to the ground outside the back door."
The three policemen drag him for about 4.5 metres.
"Wilkinson kinda stomped on my guts. He stomped once. It didn't hurt."
Wilkinson drags him by his hair along the driveway.
"I told him to let me go. I got up and walked to the car."

Tuhou is driven to Ruatoria and then to Te Araroa, where he's questioned for about one and a half hours by Detective Constable Brett Kane.

Later that day, Wilkinson takes Tuhou into a shed at the back of the police station in Ruatoria.

"Api (Constable Api Rangihuna) came too."

Wilkinson punches Tuhou in the face.

"He was trying to get me to fight," says Tuhou. "He kept saying, 'Come on, come on'. I said I did not want to fight and he punched me a couple more times in the face."

During the punching, Rangihuna is standing about two metres behind Wilkinson with his back to them.

Kane comes into the shed and Tuhou asks him if he can go home.

"He said I could but I had to walk back (about fourteen kilometres) because all the cars were busy. I wasn't charged with anything."

Rangihuna tells the court how, while in the shed, he had seen Wilkinson slap Tuhou's ear twice.

"Mr Tuhou became quite arrogant and smart towards Wilkinson. I saw Wilkinson slap him. Mr Tuhou kept apologising. I don't know what for. After the first slap, Mr Tuhou grabbed hold of Wilkinson's clothing and said something like 'stop hassling me'."

November 10, 1987: *Two more Gisborne police officers are committed for trial on assault charges after depositions.*

Detective Sergeant Eric Newman and David Neilson are charged with assaulting Jonathan McClutchie with intent to facilitate the crime of wilfully perverting the course of justice.

This is McClutchie's version of events on March 18 earlier this year.

In the morning, Newman and Neilson come to his house at Makarika, near Ruatoria, and tell him he's wanted for questioning.

Although they do not say where they're going, McClutchie agrees to go with them.

Instead of heading towards Ruatoria, they go the opposite way and, after about fifty minutes, arrive at a small shed at the back of Waingakia Station.

McClutchie's asked to go into the shed and take a seat. The two policemen question him about two church fires the previous Saturday night.

They handcuff his hands behind his back and put a pillowslip over his head. They hold a gun to his hands and ask him if he knows what it is.

"They took me into the room with the wooden floor and they pulled my arms right up behind my back and a few punches were put in."

The policemen punch him three or four times around his stomach area and then he falls over. While he's on the ground the pair kick him in the legs, stomach and backside.

The incident lasts about five to ten minutes. Then the pillowslip and handcuffs are taken off and they ask some more questions.

The three then have some lunch the policemen have brought with them. Afterwards the two policemen begin asking more questions about the fires.

One of them becomes frustrated, slaps McClutchie, then grabs him by the head and pulls it back and forth. He's also punched in the side three or four times.

Late in the afternoon they hear a jeep stop near the hut. The two detectives tell McClutchie to stay in the hut while they have a look.

"They both went outside, I could hear them talking but I didn't know what they were talking about."

When they come back in they tell McClutchie to go and wait by the car. The two detectives tidy the shed and take him home.

"DIG YOUR OWN GRAVE"

November 12: *Constables Brett Kane, Malcolm Thomas and Christopher James Wallace are each charged with assaulting Ruatoria Rastafarian Michael Paiti with intent to facilitate the crime of wilfully perverting the course of justice.*

This is Michael Paiti's version of events on March 19 this year.

Kane, Wallace and Thomas pick him up from a house in Makarika Road, near Ruatoria, for questioning about the two church fires.

They take him to the Ruatoria Police Station, then to a reserve about 16.5 kilometres away.

On the journey to the reserve, Kane holds Paiti's head down behind the car seat.

Thomas tells Paiti: "There's a hard way out of this and an easy way. Just give me a few answers, a few names."

Paiti tells the court: "They reckon just give us a few names and it'll all be between us. I told them I knew nothing, don't know who lit the fires, just don't know."

When they reach the reserve, he and Kane stay in the car while the other two constables go off down the road and then up the hill.

"Like they were looking for a spot or something," Paiti says.

Thomas tells him to strip. He's told to put his hands behind his back where they are secured with his belt.

His track pants are put over his head and face. He's taken across a creek and up a hill where threats are made to push him over the cliff. He hears them refer to a gun in the car.

"They reckoned, 'pull out the gun'. One chap reckoned, 'I don't want nothing to do with this, I'll let that other fulla do it'."

Someone kicks the backs of his legs and he falls to his knees. He's later told to lie down before walking back to the road.

Kane punches him, more than once. He's told he'd better start talking.

One of the constables says there's a shovel in the back of the car. They ask him if he's afraid to die and suggest he could dig his own grave.

"We were at this spot and they were saying something like: 'You haven't told us anything', going like that. I was still tied up and Kane was in front of me. He lashed out, ay, gave me a couple of blows to the chest."

He says Wallace, who was standing behind him, punched him in the head.

The questioning continues until the belt is removed and he's eventually taken back to Ruatoria where he's released.

Defence counsels Les Atkins and Tony Adeane cross-examine Detective Senior Sergeant Norm Cook, who says he's not surprised that Paiti was taken to the reserve.

A policy of isolating and pressurising suspects was being developed. This had been discussed with the Assistant Police

Commissioner during his visit to Gisborne and Ruatoria a week before the alleged incident.

There had been thirty-two suspicious fires reported to police in and around Ruatoria. They'd caused a marked change to the appearance of the township and hundreds of thousands of dollars in damage.

Anyway, this is just a depositions hearing. At the end, the judge decides the case should be heard in front of a jury. A High Court trial is set for next month. When it comes around, Paiti recounts his version of events. The cops say he's lying. They did take him to the reserve but didn't assault him. A few minor points are bandied about. Paiti said he wasn't stoned in one statement. In another he said he was stoned. He got some times mixed up. In his notebook, Detective Brett Kane recorded his plan as to how he was going to interview the young Rastafarian. "Was that the preparation of a detective planning a violent assault on a suspect?" It can't have been. The jury takes just twenty-eight minutes to find the three detectives not guilty.

Wednesday, February 2, 1988: *Jonathan McCluthie fails to show for the opening day of the trial of Detective Sergeant Eric Newman and Detective Constable David Neilson, who are accused of assaulting him. Instead, he appears in court in Ruatoria on a cannabis possession charge.*

In McClutchie's absence, prosecutor John Laurenson states the Crown's case.

He notes that Newman and Neilson told the investigating team that dealt with the complaint that McClutchie started the tussle.

Newman claimed he was flat on his back and Neilson pulled McClutchie from him. Laurenson points out that Neilson's version had him putting McClutchie on the ground to subdue him.

Thursday, February 3: *McClutchie turns up for court today and recounts his version of events on March 18. He also says he hadn't initially wanted to lay a complaint against the police officers but, after talking with Chief Inspector Whiro Ratahi, later reconsidered.*

During cross-examination, defence counsel Peter Kaye asks McClutchie if he told Ratahi about the gun when he made his complaint. He says he thought he did.

The witness is given the statement he made and is reminded he didn't mention anything about a gun. He first mentioned it during the depositions hearing of the Maxwell allegation.

"You made it up didn't you," says Kaye. "You did not see a gun."

"I saw a gun."

"You're lying to us. You're making it up as you go along."

"I'm telling the truth."

McClutchie denies that he lunged at Newman and that Neilson pulled him off.

"There was a lot of yelling and struggling," says Kaye. "You were biting at both men with your teeth."

"No."

McClutchie concedes they told him he was in trouble for assaulting a police officer, but denies making a deal with them in exchange for the recovery of cannabis from Joe Campbell's home. He gave them the information on Campbell but it was not a deal.

He's asked if he told Newman and Neilson that Dick Maxwell had lit some of the fires, and replies he can't remember.

Detective Senior Sergeant Norm Cook reads to the court the job sheet from the interview in the shed with McClutchie. In it, McClutchie alleges Dick Maxwell lit some of the fires and says he didn't know which church would be next – they were all targets.

In the interview record, McClutchie says that since he's been a Rastafarian, Tony Tuhou, Dick Maxwell, Barney Wharepapa and Hamana Brown have claimed they lit fires, while another Rasta told him the two church fires were Jah's doing, the Lord's work.

Friday, February 4, 1988: *Detective Sergeant Eric Newman takes the unusual step of taking the witness stand to give evidence in his own defence.*

This is how he remembers the incident inside the shed at Waingakia Station.

Newman and McClutchie are talking about the Bible. Newman hopes to "establish a link" by discussing McClutchie's "silly interpretations".

McClutchie refers to the Queen of England as "the harlot of Babylon" mentioned in the Bible (a common connection made by and believed by Rastafarians all over the world) and Newman laughs contemptuously. This, Newman says, is when McClutchie starts to "get wild".

McClutchie states that the seed Jacob cast in Genesis was cannabis seed.

Newman suggests it was fruit or vegetable seed or the seed of life.

Neilson says, "This is getting too heavy for me, I'm going to get some lunch," and leaves the hut.

After Neilson leaves, McClutchie jumps from his stool and lunges at Newman, grabbing him around the throat. The two men fall to the floor with McClutchie on top.

Neilson returns, picks up McClutchie in a headlock and handcuffs him.

"It was all over in a flash," says Newman.
He tells McClutchie, "You're in a power of shit now my friend."

Knowing he's in a corner over assaulting a police officer, McClutchie offers to do a deal. He says his friend Joe "Boots" Campbell has a lot of "herb", which police had missed in a recent raid.

Newman and Neilson agree not to press assault charges as long as McClutchie agrees not to warn Boots of a forthcoming raid.

They take off his handcuffs and the three of them eat lunch.

Being a vegetarian, McClutchie picks the meat out of his sandwiches and also refuses a can of drink because of artificial colourings and preservatives.

While eating, he admits Dick Maxwell had "lit a few fires", but doesn't know which ones. He names a few other names, but Neilson is having trouble recording the information while eating.

McClutchie sits in the hut for about twenty minutes, not handcuffed and with the door unlocked, while the two detectives chat outside with a hunting friend of Neilson's (Steve Tresidder).

Eventually he yells to McClutchie that they'll return him to his pad. Newman tidies up the hut and the three of them drive back.

He warns McClutchie to say nothing about their talk for his own sake. They'll be "doing Boots' place" the following day. If McClutchie warns him, the deal will be off and he'll be charged with assault.

At no time was McClutchie threatened. There was no pillow-slip and no gun.

McClutchie waves to the detectives as they drive off and they wave back.

***Monday, February 7, 1988:** After a lunch break and a half-hour deliberation, the jury acquits Newman and Neilson. The reaction in the public gallery is subdued compared with the conclusion of the trial of five detectives last year.*

There was an interesting post-script to this case. In January, 1995, Eric Newman was back in Ruatoria investigating the murder of Stuart James Te Wano, a 21-year-old Mongrel Mob prospect, who was shot twice, his body found in a paddock near a gang shelter in Hiruharama. (As of late 2000 the murder was still unsolved).
Newman was the detective sergeant in charge of the Mount Maunganui CIB by that stage, but, because of his experience in Ruatoria, he was asked by the officer in charge of the inquiry, Inspector Murray Lewis, to help out.

Eric Newman: I sought directions to a house to see a possible witness on Waiomatatini Road, Ruatoria. But I was either given the wrong directions or I misinterpreted the correct directions. Whatever the case I knocked on the front door of this house and Jonathan McClutchie answered.

When we saw each other we both took a step back in surprise. I think I broke the silence by telling him who I was looking for and he quite freely gave me the correct directions. I thanked him and asked him how he was. He said he was fine. Then I asked him, "And, so, have you been behaving yourself?"

He quickly replied, "Yes I have. What about you?"
We both burst out laughing, shook hands and I carried on.

DRAGGED BY THE HAIR

***Tuesday, February 8:** An arrest warrant is issued for Tony Tuhou, who fails to show for the opening day of the trial of Mike Wilkinson. The Hastings detective constable faces two charges of assaulting the twenty-year-old Rastafarian.*

Prosecutor John Laurenson says the case hangs on whether Wilkinson knew of a means test warrant for Tuhou's arrest at the time he was taken to the police station by force.

The existence of a means test warrant for Tuhou's non-payment of court fines wasn't generally known until later that day. Wilkinson couldn't have known about the warrant when he arrested Tuhou about 9am on March 20. And it's illegal for police officers to use force unless they have a warrant to arrest someone.

Crown witness Constable Peter Brown tells how he accompanied Wilkinson and Constable Rangihuna to the Makarika pad, where some of the Rastas stay.

They pick up Rastafarian Rangi Brown for questioning and, as they drive back to the station, a police radio message instructs them to return to the pad and collect Tuhou.

"We were not told about a means test warrant," says Brown. "I only learned about it later. If there had been a warrant we would have arrested Tuhou immediately."

Tuhou answers the door and refuses to accompany the officers to the station. After several minutes of talking, Wilkinson says, "You're under arrest for giving false particulars the other day."

Tuhou swears and tells them to leave "in no uncertain terms".

Wilkinson walks between the two constables and grabs Tuhou's arm. Tuhou's bracing himself in the doorway.

Pulling him by the hair, Wilkinson drags him through the door and out into the back yard.

"He was punching out at Wilkinson," says Brown. "I grabbed his arm from behind to restrain him. Tuhou and I fell to the ground struggling. He legged me in the thigh. People gathered around and Wilkinson still had hold of his hair."

Tuhou continues to struggle and plead with Wilkinson to let go of his hair. When he finally promises to come quietly, he's released and allowed to walk to the car.

Brown says he didn't see anyone stomp on Tuhou at any time.

Rangihuna also tells the court no mention was made of a means test warrant during the police radio message.

He says he was punched by Tuhou after Wilkinson grabbed the Rasta by the arm. "He hit me on the nose as Wilkinson and I pulled him through the doorway."

***Wednesday, February 9, 1988:** Tony Tuhou turns up for the trial of Mike Wilkinson today. He says he couldn't make it yesterday because he was at a beach up the coast and missed a ride into town.*

***Thursday, February 10:** In his opening address, defence counsel Les Atkins says the second alleged assault of Tuhou, in the garage at the back of Ruatoria Police Station, was a staged act prearranged between Tuhou and Wilkinson.*

After Wilkinson offered money for information about who was responsible for the church fires, Tuhou gave the name of one of his associates.

Wilkinson behaved aggressively because Tuhou didn't want fellow Rastafarians to know he was an informant.

Doors to the police house garage were deliberately left open, Constable Api Rangihuna was asked to come into the garage and a shouting match was arranged with Wilkinson agreeing to hit Tuhou several times.

Afterwards, Tuhou declined a ride home because it "would not look good to come back in a police car".

Giving evidence in his own defence, Wilkinson says the performance was staged to show other Rastafarians and police around the station that Tuhou hadn't been co-operative. The garage was left open for the audience of police and Rastafarians outside.

Wilkinson abused Tuhou in a raised voice and kicked a chair and Tuhou said, "Hit me, hit me".

"I did not intend going so far," says Wilkinson. "I slapped him. I think he got a bit of a shock it was so hard. I clipped him again and then thought it had gone far enough."

Wilkinson also gives evidence about the first alleged assault. This is his version of events.

He and the two constables are returning to Ruatoria from the Makarika pad with Rastafarian Rangi Brown. A radio message comes through from Detective Constable Brett Kane, who asks if Tuhou was at the pad.

They turn around and head back. The two constables start walking up the driveway, while Wilkinson tells Rangi Brown to wait in the car. That's when a second radio message comes through that there's a means test warrant out for Tuhou's arrest.

Wilkinson doesn't know Tuhou but recognises him at the door of the pad as a man who called himself Carl Tuhou several days beforehand.

Tuhou refuses to come with him, so Wilkinson tells him he's under arrest for giving false particulars (the wrong name for the offence).

Tuhou still refuses, so Wilkinson tells him again that he's under arrest and grabs him around the shoulders.

Tuhou braces himself against the door so Wilkinson catches him by the hair to pull him out of the doorway.

"He was throwing his arms around," says Wilkinson. "Constable Brown tried to restrain him from behind. They ended up in a heap about fifteen feet from the doorway. I still had hold of Tuhou's hair."

Holding Tuhou in a crouch position, Wilkinson starts walking him towards the car.

He denies pulling Tuhou along the ground by the hair, saying he's not strong enough, and denies stomping on Tuhou's stomach.

Back at the police station, Wilkinson tells Kane he's arrested Tuhou on a means test warrant, which Kane says he already knew about. Kane interviews Tuhou but learns nothing, so Wilkinson decides to interview him himself.

"Sometimes you need a change of interviewer, a different technique," he says. Wilkinson offers Tuhou a reward of $1000 for information. Within ten minutes Tuhou tells him that Rastafarian Hamana Brown is responsible for one of the church fires. "I was going to check it out with Hamana Brown before he got the money," says Wilkinson. "If it was bullshit he wouldn't get it." Wilkinson says he told Detective Sergeant Laurie Naden of the reward he offered, the information he received in return and of the stage acting that followed.

Wilkinson interviews Hamana Brown the following week. That's the same week Detective Chief Inspector Bruce Scott interviews Wilkinson about the Dick Maxwell case. Wilkinson doesn't mention the incident in the garage. He wants to protect Tuhou's confidentiality. "I thought I might still be able to use him in the arson investigation."

He also doesn't mention arresting Tuhou because he doesn't want to get in trouble for using a non-existent offence – giving false particulars - as a reason for arrest.

Detective Constable Kane and Constable Kevin Joblin also give evidence for the defence. Kane says he first heard of the means test warrant for Tuhou at about 10.30am on March 20 through broadcast on police radio.

Joblin says he also heard the broadcast from his office at Gisborne Police Station. Sergeant John Robinson made the broadcast from Ruatoria Police Station.

*But that doesn't mean a lot; earlier in the trial, Robinson told the court he examined Tuhou for a means test about **1pm** on March 20. Kane had phoned about ten minutes earlier to ask if there was a warrant out for Tuhou. Robinson phoned Gisborne and found there was a means test warrant for his arrest. (In other words, Kane had rung about the warrant **after** Wilkinson had dragged Tuhou out through the door).*

Friday, February 11, 1988: *Mike Wilkinson is found not guilty on both charges of assault on Tony Tuhou. It takes the jury just over an hour to come to a decision on both counts.*

The police who were on trial claim the accusations of assault against them by Rastafarians ground the arson investigations to a halt just as they were starting to make headway. But, while the investigations ground to a halt, the troubles in Ruatoria didn't. The fires and the stealing continued sporadically.

PART 6
A TERRORIST SITUATION

CHAPTER 1

RASTA INTIMIDATION

October 29, 1987: *There's a raging grass fire within 1.5 kilometres of Hikurangi State Forest. The fire on private land on*

Hikurangi Spur completely surrounds a radio hut containing thousands of dollars worth of equipment. The main source of radio communication on the East Coast is nearly destroyed as the fire burns to within twenty metres of the hut.

Lyn Hillock, former Gisborne Deputy Fire Chief: Over at (chopper pilot) Denis Hartley's place, because the helicopter's the key piece of equipment we've got, we have lots of security and alarms around it. Any time the security light goes on we're all leaping around. We're that wound up.

One time I'm staying up at Denis's over Christmas-New Year's. We're getting into it, having a few drinks, and this arsehole is down by the boundary fence. We can hear cattle moving across the road. But this prick is down at the fence on his horse. I'm thinking, "What an arsehole. What's he up to?"

I've got my shotgun. Denis grabs his. We grab a pocketful of shells. We decide if we see him, we'll let him have it. I take off down the side of the drive-way in the next door neighbour's property to cut the guy off one way. And Denis leaps over the fence and comes down the other side. I'm pretty sure by now that the guy's gone down to the next paddock where some 11kv lines are so I sneak down the bottom paddock and come up back towards the road. But there's no moon and it's bloody near pitch black. And I step off the frigging bank and fall onto the highway and break my bloody leg. And when I get up and go to run, "Aagh!" By this time I realise the guy's got off his horse and walked it further down the road away from us. He's lucky tonight. Because I reckon if we'd caught him he'd have been a goner.

So I'm wandering back up to the house and I'm thinking, "Shit this is bloody sore." Little do I know I've broken my fibula. So I hook into another couple of rums and see the party out. About four in the morning the effects of the alcohol are beginning to wear off and, "Aw, shit, this is hurting, Grasshopper." So I'm bundled off down to Te Puia Hospital and they chuck the leg in a plaster for me.

December 31, 1987: *After two days investigating the latest incident at Ruatoria, police say they're satisfied it's a burglary (a quantity of diesel was taken) and not arson.*

Detective Sergeant Gary Condon says the microwave repeater on Mount Hikurangi and another building on the site were entered on Monday night.

A fire was lit, but it was a safe distance from the buildings. Some suspects have been interviewed but no arrests have been made.

Lyn Hillock: John Heeney gets really serious because he used to be a technician for Telecom (actually it was for the P&T or Postal and Telegraph Service, when it was still a Government department). He breaks into the repeater, the police, fire and communications repeater, on Hikurangi Spur. It's just fortunate that it doesn't start a serious fire. But they sabotage some of the equipment there. They take the fire and point systems out. Really all he has to do is put a little dint in the microwave tube guide and he could take out all the toll services. But he doesn't.

John knows what he's looking for and where he's going and he goes for specific equipment.

The police and the fire service have already warned Telecom to increase their security around the communications system. But everybody in the rest of New Zealand just thinks we're on dope ourselves.

February 7, 1988: A storage shed at Manutahi Primary School in Ruatoria is set alight this morning.

The shed, which is used to store pre-school equipment and toys, is destroyed.

Police have no leads but say the shed door was unlocked and somebody got in and set the fire.

Monday, March 7, 1988: A regional state of emergency is called as Cyclone Bola batters Gisborne and the East Coast into submission. Three elderly people die when the car they are travelling in is swept away by the floodwaters. There would have been more deaths if not for the brave work of people like chopper pilots Bruce Kingan and Denis Hartley, who plucked several stranded families from their rooves. Yet a month from now, Denis Hartley's helicopter will be vandalised so badly it can't be flown. And once again the Rastas are top of the suspect list.

Lyn Hillock, Gisborne Deputy Fire Chief (retired): The wives are threatened. We're threatened here in Gisborne. Ian Clark, the fire safety officer, and his wife are also threatened. The threats are coming from the likes of Diesel Dick. Any time I ever meet any of the little arseholes I'm being threatened. So Ian and me have a talk between ourselves, and one night we go walk-about at 2 o'clock in the morning, typical cop time, between 2 and 4. We visit a few Rasta houses. In through the door . . . laying in bed . . . ram the barrel of the semi-automatic up their noses. "You wanna talk you arsehole? Any shit, you're gonna die, simple as that."

They don't have much to say. You don't really argue with a 762 barrel shoved up your nose.

Once you get a personal threat against you you've either got to do something about it or be stomped on. So you do something about it.

They're saying things like, "You've got a nice wife. You don't want her raped or mutilated do you."

In the fire station flat where we live in Gisborne, they often come into town and sit outside. One or two of them do occasionally, just to let us know they're there and things aren't safe.

You're always conscious of the threat of these guys. I don't like leaving my wife Laurel at home by herself. Her and Denise, Ian Clark's wife, move into the same flat if Ian and I are up the coast. They're pretty switched on. We've got an arrangement with the police and any problems, the girls just give them a ring and the cops will be there in about ten minutes to move them along.

But it's a tough time because you're not allowed to shoot them. If you could shoot them and get away with it, you would. But I guess it would look a bit obvious if you had a body slung under a helicopter going ten miles out to sea with a fuckin' concrete block hanging onto its feet.

Yeah, it's quite stressful. We carry an unlicensed number right through until 1998 so that these guys can't harass us on the phone.

Laurel Hillock, Lyn's wife: It gets a bit snaky there when we realise our place in Gisborne's being watched. I feel scared. It's a nightmare. We're living under siege.

It's late 1988. I've just finished doing quite a bit of Tupperware up at Rangatukia, near Tikitiki, and I've got another party organised with this contact of mine in Ruatoria.

The party's at the marae, where the Rastas hang out, and that's fine. Everything goes well and I go away and come back a second time to deliver all the stuff that was bought and to have another party. Well I arrive that second time and it's just pouring with rain. I'm thinking, "Oh my God. Will I get back?" Then the girl who makes the bookings comes down and says, "Sorry, you'll have to wait a bit." She's double-booked the marae for the Tupperware party and something else that's going on. So I have to sit in the car and wait in the rain. And these bloody Rastas come over. And they surround the car. I'm there by myself and they've found out who I am. This is about the time that our house is being watched. So I'm absolutely sweating.

Eventually, I think, "Bugger this," and I drive up closer to the marae. I'm thinking, "I'll just go up to the marae and deliver the stuff and get the money and go. Bugger the party. I've got to get out of here."

Lyn Hillock: Basically it's a terrorist situation and we can't do a thing about it. If we could shoot them we would. It's definitely getting to that stage. When we go up at night I always take my SLR, semi-automatic rifle, or my shotgun in the car. We're getting stopped at the Makarika turn-off. As soon as they stick their heads in through the car window, out goes the barrel. "If you've got something to say, talk to me. If not . . ."

During Cyclone Bola, they set fire to a woolshed down Whareponga Road that belongs to Tom Heeney's family. We fly in with Rex Harrison from the CIB. Since the arson of the courthouse a lot of firearms and ammunition have gone missing around town. So we go in with an armed member of the police with us.

Things have got to the stage where you need to be able to defend yourself because the Rastas are armed.

SERGEANT HOPE'S HOUSE IS BURNED DOWN

Saturday, April 2, 1988: Sergeant Alex Hope's police house in Ruatoria is burned down. The fire's noticed at about 9.50pm by two constables.

The head of Ruatoria police and his family are on holiday – Sergeant Hope is at the Flood Relief Concert in Te Araroa - when the home is gutted in what is thought to be an arson attack. Almost all their

Constable Chris Bunyan: There were thirty-plus arsons when I was up there. I remember the occasion where Alex Hope was the sergeant. It was the Easter Weekend after Cyclone Bola and they were having a concert up north to raise funds for Bola relief. And it just so happened that I was on days off. Kevin Weatherly had been brought up from Gisborne to relieve. And we were sitting on the couch watching the movie 10, with Dudley Moore and that female who was absolutely gorgeous at the time (Bo Derek). And I remember this thud of a sound and thinking, "What the hell's that." And I pulled back the curtains and the front room of the sergeant's home, which was very close to mine, was a ball of flame. And the hairs just went up on the back of my neck. It's just a horrible feeling.

The first thing I did was pick up the phone and dial 111. And then I went out with Kevin, set up the scene and got the fire guys in. The person had broken into the house using something that had been on the TV programme McIvor about a month earlier. They'd smeared golden syrup across the back window and then brown paper over it, smashed it, opened the window, got in and gone right through the house, kids' beds, everything, and poured petrol or some form of accelerant all through the house. And then got back out that window and probably lit a piece of paper and put it in. And it had gone VOOMFA, and blown up. The force of it blew the fire out actually. They didn't do a very good job at all. It smashed a few windows and the smoke damage was fairly extensive. I think they sold the house for a thousand dollars in the end. It was a write-off. And the bulk of their property had either fire damage or smoke damage.

Alex Hope was living at the house at the time. Fortunately, his family was away that weekend. The worst thing was I picked up a hand held radio to call Gisborne to let them know what had happened and I just said, "Look, I've just called the Fire Brigade. Alex Hope's house is on fire." And, unfortunately, I just didn't think, ay. Alex was up north at Te Araroa running the operation at the fund-raising concert. And he heard my message on his portable radio and it just blew him away big time.

I don't know if the Rastas did that one. Alex was a workaholic and, in a place like that, he upset a lot of people, just by doing his job.

He was very much by the book and pretty hyped-up. It wasn't until he left and Alex Bryant came along that you realised how stressed you were, how hyped up. Every time the fire alarm went off you basically got out of bed, put your uniform on and went to the police station because most of the time it was a suspicious fire to go to. And I always remember Alex Bryant going, "What the fuck are you doing?"

"Well this is what we do."

"Not any more. You wait for them to call you."

"Aw, okay." The reason for that was we didn't know the fire was an arson. So there was no need to rush out.

Alex Hope was very stressed and he did more than his due time there. But we'd had problems getting through to our District Commander at the time, Paul Wiseman, what we wanted. I had my wife, a two-year-old son and a brand new baby daughter. Welfare said, you're out of there, you just say the word and you're gone out of Ruatoria. But Wiseman said it was just a one-off thing, nothing to be concerned about. Well, I mean it was the second or third police property that had been burnt. Where the house that I was in was standing was where the courthouse had been previously. The fire station directly across the road was brand new because it had been burnt down. And there was a new police station sitting there beside us. So was it a one-off? Wake up.

As a result of some fire-bombings that had occurred in Masterton, they brought in some extra security measures. They had a special silicone product that they put on the windows. So that if someone threw a Molotov cocktail it would break the glass but it wouldn't come through into the kids' bedrooms. They put security lighting in the house and they put an alarm in. So that was the extent that they went to after a fair bit of pressure.

But I remember the day the commissioner, John Jamieson, was up in Ruatoria. And Alex saw that as his opportunity to say, "Look I've done my time. I wanna move on."

And I think he might have been looking at promotion at that stage. And they said, "Aw, look Alex, you've done a great job. We're gonna take you out to lunch."

So he went down to Te Puia with John Jamieson. Well, he came back a stunned mullet. He said, "The commissioner basically said to me, 'I hope you don't think this is your ticket out of Ruatoria. The only way you're gonna get out is either to be replaced,' – this is just a week after his arson – 'or to go on welfare grounds.'" And Alex was such a proud man he wouldn't do that.

They did replace Alex Hope in the end. But it took about another six months or so. That was when Alex Bryant came home.

Tuesday, April 5, 1988: The gathering of fingerprint evidence at Sergeant Hope's house begins today. DSIR scientists from Wellington are among many outsiders investigating the arson. CIB staff from Rotorua and Hamilton are also involved.

Officer in charge of the inquiry, Detective Senior Sergeant Steve Shortland, says the house was left securely locked but that entry was forced and fires were set at several places inside.

It's almost a year since the last serious fire in the town.

Wednesday, April 6: Police have no strong leads yet in their inquiry into the burning of Sergeant Hope's house, and say they're making no assumptions about its relationship to previous arsons in the town.

Friday, April 8: Police say they're following a number of promising leads in the investigation into the arson of Sergeant Hope's house. The public are assisting with these inquiries.

DSIR scientists and a fingerprint expert returned to Wellington yesterday to examine the evidence gathered and results should be known by next week.

Sunday, April 10: A woolshed at Waipiro Bay, near Ruatoria, burns down during the night. The two-storey building on Akuaku Station is completely destroyed by the time Ruatoria, Te Puia and Tikitiki fire brigades arrive.

For farmer Doug Gordon, the fire puts an end to a barely-begun holiday, which was a present from a daughter. He and his wife have just arrived in Auckland when they're called back to the East Coast with news of the fire.

Eighteen bales of wool - worth about $126,000 – are lost. The woolshed was part of a farm training scheme, recently axed by the Government.

"We were just getting it back on its feet," says the Gordons' daughter, Donna (who was in the author's class in school).

The fire's one more disaster on top of flood damage for the Gordon family, who live on Arero Station, Tolaga Bay. During Cyclone Bola last month, their fences were pushed over by silt and hills slipped away. Police are treating the fire as suspicious.

LAST STRAW FOR HOPE

Monday, April 11, 1988: *Sergeant Alex Hope is taking six weeks leave.*

"He's pretty stressed out," says Sergeant John Robinson, who's filling in while Hope's away.

Hope left for Waikato this morning and is hoping for a permanent transfer from Ruatoria.

I interview Alex Hope in late 2002. He says he felt hurt by the "Rastas'" arson of his house. He had a good working relationship with them and thought they might respect him because he didn't believe in beating them up or other criminal activity by cops to procure confessions. He also had empathy for the grievances of the Maori on the Coast. But what hurt him more than that was when he discovered the police had actually investigated him about the arson.

Alex Hope: Before my house burnt down, I'd made no secret I'd had enough of Ruatoria. It was too hard. I worked long, long, long hours for two years. And it was time to get out. I liked Ruatoria. I didn't dislike the coast. In fact, I loved living on the coast. But the job and the demands were really, really hard and I worked basically a six-day week. I was often doing two jobs because we had new cops up there and I'd be holding their hands. And they'd support me on that. Guys who were new cops like Chris Bunyan know the hours I put in helping him.

But to then be accused of burning my own house…
The police had what they call a back-inquiry into whether I burned down the police house. I had no idea when I was in Ruatoria that this was happening. I found out probably a year or so later, while I was stationed at Huntly. I seem to remember that I was on the phone to the Napier police about something. And I spoke to a cop there and he said, "Aw, *you're* the guy. Are you the guy who's house burnt down? Aw.

Did you know they had a back-inquiry on you? Yeah, they did and I was part of it."

What they do is sometimes the police will have a second inquiry going and they don't tell anyone about it. That's the back-inquiry. So they'll have the main inquiry going on and then they have another one behind it that's a secret one that's looking at a different angle they want to keep secret.

Tuesday, April 12, 1988: Police have narrowed down their investigations into the arson of Sergeant Hope's house to a list of suspects. Officer in charge, Steve Shortland, says they'd like to hear from a young person who bought a tin of golden syrup from the Sunrise Superette at about 2.30pm on the day of the fire.

Excerpt from an interview with Alex Hope in October, 2002: Did I burn my own house? No.

I was very hurt by my house fire. It was personal and I felt it was a personal attack on me. And I have no doubt it was in that I was the boss of the police there and I was identified as such and I was known as "The Down-presser Man". I never treated those guys unfairly but, yeah, I was the enemy and I knew that.

I didn't lock my house often although on that occasion it was locked. But often I would go out and not lock it. I didn't lock my garage. And I would comfortably go alone to deal with the Rastas in their homes.

I'm adamant John Heeney burnt my house down. He admitted it to police, he denied it, he admitted it, and then he denied it again. A detective inspector from Wellington called McFadgen ran the main inquiry. And McFadgen and Steve Shortland, who's now a high-flying cop in Auckland, discussed with me what happened with Heeney. They thought Heeney did it too, but they didn't think it would run. They didn't have enough hard evidence and Heeney kept retracting his admissions. He had a screw loose at that time. He was getting quite religious and he was really full of herb.

Not long after my fire we did the musterers' hut at Whakaahu. It's a couple of hours' walk up the hill. You go down the Whareponga Road and on to Koura Station and the hill's behind it. The Rastas used to stay up there. That's where the beheading of Lance Kupenga happened.

So we went up to the shed up there, looking for these guys. And there was no one there. But John Heeney's Bible was in there. And it was open. And it was open on a page of Revelations. And there was a passage highlighted in yellow. The words were: "After the floods the land was cleansed by fire." This was immediately after Cyclone Bola. I think John Heeney deliberately targeted me – as the head policeman – after the floods to fulfil what was said in The Bible.

That highlighted passage in his Bible, together with his retracted admissions, convince me that he did it.

CHAPTER 2

MAXWELL & HEENEY ESCAPE

Tuesday, April 19, 1988: The Police Association reveals that the total cost of defending officers accused in relation to the arson inquiries will be close to $1 million.

Meanwhile, Gisborne CIB staff arrest Dick Maxwell after a car chase around Ruatoria, during which it's alleged he smashed a police car windscreen. He ran off but was caught.

A warrant for his arrest was issued after an incident at Maxwell's house on March 11. He's been charged with aggravated assault of a policeman, and police have indicated he'll face more charges.

Wednesday, April 20: Dick Maxwell and John Heeney escape from custody as they're being taken to a police van with seven other men during a lunch break at Gisborne District Court. A policeman is knocked to the ground with a blow from behind by a gumboot. Two other men run off but are soon recaptured.

Police had been seeking Maxwell for about a month after a warrant was issued on a charge of aggravated assault of a police constable following an incident involving an axe. He appeared briefly on that charge in the morning and was to face further charges including another of aggravated assault and receiving stolen property.

Heeney had been arrested on a warrant for failing to appear on an arson charge.

Friday, April 22: *Three men appear in Gisborne District Court on charges relating to the escape of Maxwell and Heeney. They are Maurice Anderson, Edward Rameka and Gavin Smith.*

Sunday, April 24: *Police discover Maxwell and Heeney in a Ruatoria house with about twelve associates during a routine inquiry. But they manage to escape again.*

The Rastas run off in different directions and police pursue a small group to the other side of the Waiapu River. Two members of the group, Michael Heeney (John's brother) and Michael Paiti, are caught.

Monday, April 25: *Gavin Smith pleads guilty to helping Maxwell and Heeney escape from police custody. Maurice Anderson and Edward Rameka plead guilty to attempting to escape.*

Smith and Rameka also plead guilty to assaulting a police officer (along with Maxwell and Heeney) to facilitate a crime.

Sergeant Adrian Straayer tells the court how the men escaped.

In the courthouse cells a plan was hatched to create a distraction while the two Ruatoria men made their escape.

Anderson took off his gumboots in the cells and gave them to another man. When the prisoners were being taken out to the police van, Smith spoke to an escorting officer, distracting him, while another prisoner struck him on the back of the head with a gumboot.

Heeney, Maxwell, Rameka and Anderson ran off with Rameka and Anderson being found a short time later.

For trying to escape, Anderson is sent back to prison for a month.

Smith's remanded in custody until May 11 for a psychiatric report. He faces a total of eight charges, including arson of a schoolhouse at Te Araroa on March 8.

Meanwhile, Michael Paiti and Michael Heeney plead not guilty to assisting John Heeney to avoid arrest. They're remanded until May 20.

***Friday, May 13:** Edward Rameka is jailed for a month for escaping from police custody with Maxwell and Heeney.*

RADIO REPEATER, HELICOPTER ATTACKED

***Tuesday, April 26, 1988:** It's revealed that a radio repeater has been destroyed and a helicopter badly damaged in Ruatoria over the weekend. The Manutahi radio repeater station on a hill just outside Ruatoria was the first target on Saturday night. Civil Defence and the local Neighbourhood Watch Group used the station. The radio and control panels were removed and smashed, causing about $8000 damage to the repeater site.*

Denis Hartley was the next victim. His Bell Jet Ranger helicopter was broken into the following night. The intruders smashed all the instruments, control panels and controls, cut all interior cables and ripped out the lining, causing up to $50,000 damage. Hartley's been flying helicopters out of Ruatoria for seven years. He discovered his wrecked machine yesterday morning when he went to work.

"He was absolutely livid," says his wife Jackie. "The thing that upset him most was that they even broke a specially-made bone carving he had been given by two young Tolaga men. He always kept it in the helicopter."

***Thursday, April 28:** The Gisborne Herald cleverly mentions the destruction of the repeater station and the continued search for Maxwell and Heeney in the same story. It's a case of how to make a connection when you're not making a connection. Here's the story.*

"Police inquiries continued today into the Ruatoria police house arson and the destruction of a local repeater station and helicopter. Officer in charge of the inquiries, Steve Shortland, said police would welcome any assistance the public could give on the matters under investigation. Meanwhile inquiries are continuing into the whereabouts of courthouse escapers Dick Maxwell and John Heeney.

"Both men are known to be in the Ruatoria area and police are checking known addresses for the pair."

***Saturday, April 30:** A Gisborne Herald story today gives the connection a stronger nudge. It says: "The town can only guess at the* *motive for the attack. Police are not prepared to speculate on any possible connection with the hunt for two missing escapers. Both men are known to be in the area."*

Lyn Hillock, Deputy Fire Chief: Denis and me go walk-about one night. This is just after the Rastas smashed up Denis's helicopter. That's our only emergency helicopter, and they've pulled everything out and smashed up all the instruments. We've got our rifles and we visit every known Rasta house. We get to the last one, Hauhama Brown's place, and they're all there waiting for us. Hauhama's holding a pitch fork and John Heeney, Hamana Brown and Diesel are there, too. And I'm not sure whether I've got a bullet up the spout or not. Things are getting really tense and I'm thinking, "Gonna have to do something here brother." So I just rip back the slide. It ejects one round. The next one hooks on the approach of the magazine and the barrrel. So I've got a stuck fuckin' round. "This is fuckin' lovely," I'm thinking. "If this prick throws his pitch fork at me I'm in trouble. I guess I'll have to hit him over the head with the gun if I have to." It's quite terrifying actually. But nothing happens in the end. They don't realise my gun's knackered and we just say our piece and leave.

ANOTHER BLOW FOR JEREMY & JANE WILLIAMS

__Thursday, May 5, 1988:__ Arsonists burn down five unguarded farm buildings and destroy vehicles and equipment at Ruatoria's Matahiia Station early this morning.

It's a terrible blow for owners Jeremy and Jane Williams. They're now afraid to leave their new home, built just eighteen months ago after arsonists destroyed the original family homestead on their wedding night.

The woolshed, shearers' quarters, an accommodation block, kitchen, dining room, ablution block, hay rakes, tractor and other farm equipment are all lost in the attack.

Ruatoria firefighters manage to save a sixth building, where the tyres on a vehicle parked inside had already started to smoulder.

Jeremy and Jane Williams are still reeling from Cyclone Bola, during which Matahiia lost two thousand three hundred stock units of capacity, six hectares of top quality flats beside the river, sixty-one hectares were silted and seven kilometres of fencing was damaged.

Last night's attack has stunned the young couple, but comes as no surprise.

"It's always in the back of our minds," says Jeremy. "These guys seem to know all our movements. We had been busy cleaning out the woolshed yesterday afternoon to get it ready for shearing on Monday."

The woolshed will be rebuilt to handle the fourteen thousand ewes and lambs Jeremy Williams expects to shear this year.

Matahiia sheep are mustered on the hillside behind the smoking wreckage. Now they'll have to be shorn at a neighbour's shed.

The arsonists struck while shepherd Graeme Mathieson was away from the living quarters to attend a family funeral (the same tactic that had been employed against Bob Kaa). Mathieson and his fiancee lost all their possessions.

Former Sergeant John Robinson: I think the Rastas did the fire at Matahiia Station all right. There were two reasons. The Williams had sold the Taitai block to the Forest Service. And the Rastas weren't happy that the Williams had made all this money out of this land and that they were rich. Another reason is that Graeme Mathieson was living on the place. He was a shepherd there. And he was the one who had just burnt out John Heeney. Mathieson got acquitted, even though he admitted doing it. The jury still said not guilty.

Jeremy has no doubt as to who's responsible or that they knew the buildings were unguarded.

"What worries us is that one day they will make a mistake and burn a house with someone still in it."

There's been a lot of fence cutting in the area recently, including some just across the river from Matahiia Station.

"It's easy for them to get across the river on horses."

The woolshed had been the scene of a large black tie party just last year to celebrate its one hundred years. The idea was to raise the spirits of invited friends, former workers, shepherds from as far back as the 1940s. Now the farm looks like a war zone. "We will keep going," Jeremy says. "We can't stop."

Former Sergeant John Robinson: I was on the night Jeremy Williams lost his woolshed and his other buildings at Matahiia Station. I was just about to knock off and the phone rang. It was an old guy down at the end of Whakapaurangi Road. He said, "Aw, I just got up to go to the toilet and there's a big glow in the air. I think the Taitai Forest is on fire."

It was about midnight. I called the fire brigade and got them on their way. Then I rang Jeremy and said, "Look, we've got a report that there's a big fire down your way. Could you check if it's Taitai Forest."

We also got a call from Gisborne to say that Ian Smith, the carrier, had driven the truck down. And he said that when he came through over Ngarimu's Hill he saw a big glow in the sky over Matahiia. And he drove all the way to Gisborne, which took him well over an hour, before he reported it.

We received his call five minutes after the one from the old guy. Some of those buildings may have been saved if he'd called straight away. He wasn't very popular in Ruatoria for a while after that.

The fire engine headed out Whakapaurangi Road (now Puhunga Road). But then Mrs Williams rang back. "It's not the forest. All our buildings have been burnt."

So the fire service had to go back out Whakapaurangi Road, down the highway, up Makarika Road. That's quite a drive. And there was nothing they could do by the time they arrived.

Friday, May 6, 1988: The swathe of destruction at Matahiia Station extends over a hundred and fifty metres. The huge century-old woolshed and all the other buildings are reduced to smoking heaps of roofing iron.

When he sees the destruction retired Matahiia shepherd Syke Manuel weeps in disbelief. The sixty-five year old Ngati Porou elder raised and educated his family in the married men's quarters. And that's where his family always returned for Christmas.

When his thirty years of service came to an end recently, the Williams helped him to furnish his new home in Hiruharama as a gesture of appreciation.

Saturday, May 7, 1988, The Gisborne Herald: The lull is over. Ruatoria has had plenty of other troubles in the past year, loss of forestry jobs and the impact of a cyclone two of the biggest.

Now the crime spree thrusts the township back into an unwelcome spotlight. Ruatoria is unique in New Zealand's history – this reign of terrorism against the town's homes, farm buildings, businesses, churches, schools and symbols of authority, is unmatched by anything police have had to deal with in this country.

Whether Ruatoria likes it or not, the rest of the country is looking on in amazement.

__Sunday, May 8:__ The Sunday News claims that Dick Maxwell has been openly boasting that he was paid for his evidence in the trial of policemen accused of kidnapping and assaulting him. "$79,000 is the sum most frequently mentioned."

Assistant Police Commissioner Stuart McEwen says the suggestion is totally untrue. "I'd be most surprised if he received even $7.50. As a Crown witness Maxwell would have been entitled to standard witness expenses, nothing more."

__Saturday, May 14:__ The Eastland Sun, a weekly Gisborne paper (now defunct) runs a story quoting an anonymous policeman. The officer says the solution to arsons in Ruatoria is for "a number of people to go missing".

"Murder is serious but missing people are treated as fairly routine by us."

__Tuesday, May 24:__ Gisborne CIB Head Detective Senior Sergeant Steve Shortland says he's close to an arrest for the arson attack on Jeremy Williams' Matahiia Station.

"We have some suspects. We are now going through the evidence with a view to charging someone." But he concedes that much of the evidence is circumstancial.

NOT ENOUGH EVIDENCE

Jeremy Williams: Some of the suspects for the arsons on my property were already in jail for previous offences. And that chap Steve Shortland, the senior detective, came and saw me. He had a file this thick on the cases. He said, "We've had so many court cases and they've all got off on technicalities or lack of conclusive evidence. We

don't want to have another one and have them get off." You've virtually
got to catch them on a movie camera striking the match for evidence.
Arson burns the evidence a lot of times. Shortland said to me, If so-and-
so is convicted, he might get four years. He's already got three years to
serve on a previous conviction so we have the risk of losing the case and
if we win he only gets a few more months anyway.

So I said, "Well, if that's the way you feel, we'll let it slide.
Just drop it."

My parents in particular got some amazing letters from some of
the uncles, cousins, aunts of some of those guys who were reputedly
doing the arsons. They were never convicted for the two fires on my
property so I can't name names even though gossip knows who did it.
And some of them were very gracious letters where obviously a lot of
thought had been put into what had been said. And they gave us quite a
lot of strength that these older people knew the young were doing
wrong, but didn't know how to bring them back on track. You can put
up with quite a lot of problems if you know that there is support.

*Saturday, May 28, 1988: Police arrest John Heeney without
incident on the outskirts of Ruatoria at about 8.30am. He's taken into
custody and will appear in Gisborne District Court next week.*

*It's been five weeks since he and Dick Maxwell escaped from
police custody. Maxwell is still at large.*

Jeremy Williams: I was at home when the woolshed went up
in smoke. It was a lovely old Kauri wool shed. What they'd done is
they'd brought the logs down from Northland, chucked them off the ship
out in the bay at Port Awanui there. And they all floated ashore. And
they had these big saw-mill pits. And they hand-sawed all the logs. Then
they carted it all up the valley on horse and dray. We don't really know
how old the shed was, but in the order of a hundred and ten years old.
And the men's quarters and shearers quarters were still functional.

My great aunt, who was my grandfather's generation, while she
didn't live in that house, when the woolshed was burnt she said to me
then, as an old lady, "Now the last building of my childhood's gone."
And you tend to forget about the people who actually grew up around
the buildings.

At the time the woolshed went up in smoke I'd recently
purchased a small part of the family farm. And I couldn't easily just up

sticks and walk away unless I walked away from everything. Apart from that, who would want to buy a farm in Ruatoria in the middle of the Rastafarian upheaval. It was a buyer's market. And secondly, if somebody burnt one room off your house, do you walk away from the house? No. Well they'd burnt down my house and my wool shed but they were only parts of the farm, not the whole thing. And I had no money. Everything I had was tied up in the family business. Then I began to think, "Bugger it. Why should we run away anyway."

I never really felt all that threatened by them. Inconvenienced and annoyed, but not threatened. It was inconvenient that we had to get people to stay in our house when we went away so that it was always occupied. The fuel was put underground. A flash alarm system was put in. And we took precautions that made it hard for them to leave obscene or threatening messages on the phone.

GISBORNE POLICE CHIEF RETIRES

Gisborne District Commander Superintendent Paul Wiseman (announcing his retirement): The problem in Ruatoria is manifold. It can be attributed to a lack of work in the area, a racial problem, a religious problem with one particular sect, a land claim problem, persons who don't like others who hold positions of authority, a pyromaniac or maniacs operating in the area and drug growers and dealers.

There have been cannabis plots pulled out by police. The recent operation run by the police throughout the whole of the district where well over fifteen thousand plants were pulled out shows that this is a major cannabis growing area in New Zealand.

That causes us grave concern, especially when two helicopters, Andy Shaw's and Denis Hartley's, were wrecked without reason. The police deliberately do not use local helicopters for police operations other than for search and rescue purposes.

It is important they do not become the targets of vandals.

Until the problems that are causing the situation are solved, the arrest of offenders for specific crimes won't stop the arsons in Ruatoria.

I base that on the fact that one man is serving seven years in prison (Chris Campbell) and other members of a certain sect are doing lengthy prison sentences and the arsons are still continuing.

It needs unified action from a lot of people and a lot of organisations at high level to bandage the sore.

I have great sympathy for all the police staff who have been away from their homes for months at a time in the past three years trying to solve the problems in Ruatoria. I admire them for their efforts.

I have total admiration for the people living in Ruatoria and thank them for their perseverance and hope they will continue to support the police trying to eradicate the problem.

Taking the law into your own hands is not the answer.

Former Ruatoria police boss Alex Hope: Paul Wiseman was at the point of having a breakdown when he retired. He walked out the door with no farewell, a man with thirty odd years of police experience. He didn't like the staff in Gisborne and they didn't like him by the time he left. I think the man's done an injustice because I think he was very good at a lot of things.

He arrived at Gisborne at a difficult time and I don't think anyone had the answers. I certainly didn't. No one had the answers. Lots of people might have thought they did. But I mean Hemi Hikawai didn't have the answers. Hemi's way of doing things didn't work, nor did Alan Davidson's, nor did Chester Haar's.

Wiseman was a man to do it by the book. He demanded that people set up formal operations and all that sort of thing. From a planning perspective, in retrospect, I think things weren't organised well enough and he helped change that. So I think in some aspects Wiseman's way was the best.

Other people were gung-ho. The CIB were too slow. They had this laborious operation. They had a set way of doing things. They'd come up, they'd set up a base and they'd have briefings and everything was gone by the time they got round to doing anything.

Then you had tired people in Gisborne. Being a backwater, a lot of guys there were just filling in time. And in a small station there was probably a fairly high proportion of tired people who just did bugger all. And they were protected. And Wiseman was intolerant of them. See, Laurie Naden… I like Laurie. But Laurie was tired. They did the minimum. Hemi broke the law. Don't ask me to say any more. Hemi broke the law regularly in all sorts of ways.

Q: He was kinda like he'd been watching a few too many Clint Eastwood movies or something?

Alex: Um… it went a bit beyond that, too.

The management within the CIB was appalling.

Whiro Ratahi, who was the Deputy District Commander, was treated the worst of all. He was made a scapegoat and Wiseman had him go and do some very difficult jobs. He was honest, Whiro Ratahi, *very* honest, not a hugely experienced policeman but not incompetent either; yet he was painted as incompetent because of his lack of experience and because he wasn't an investigator. The picture that was painted of him being incompetent came from the Gisborne CIB, who were looking after themselves, particularly the ones who were themselves useless or incompetent. There were some very talented people in Gisborne as well, but they were out of control.

CHAPTER 3

MAXWELL, HEENEY ON TRIAL

Sunday, May 29: Dick Maxwell is recaptured near Te Araroa.

Monday, May 30, 1988: Dick Maxwell and John Heeney appear in the Gisborne District Court, handcuffed to police officers.

Maxwell makes no plea to charges of escaping from custody and assaulting a police officer with intent to facilitate an escape. Heeney pleads guilty to escaping from custody (and will be sentenced tomorrow) and not guilty to assault to facilitate escape. They're remanded in custody until June 15.

Tony Tuhou pleads guilty to comforting Heeney to enable him to avoid arrest and is remanded on bail until June 9.

Sergeant Graham Whyte says that during a search for Heeney at Joe Campbell's house, police discovered Heeney asleep on a bed with Tuhou lying next to him.

Joe Campbell pleads not guilty to receiving Heeney and assisting him to avoid arrest.

Nehe Reuben pleads not guilty to comforting Heeney to enable him to avoid capture.

During the search of Joe Campbell's house, Reuben was asleep in the living room and was found to be carrying a hundred and four cannabis seeds. He pleads guilty to possessing the cannabis and is fined $200.

Tuesday, May 31: *John Heeney's sentenced to a total of nine months jail after pleading guilty to two charges of escaping from police custody, two charges of cultivating cannabis and one charge of possessing a pipe for smoking cannabis.*

He pleads not guilty to assaulting a police officer to facilitate escape and is remanded until August 6.

Heeney tells the court he escaped because he wanted to see his family and get their support before standing trial on arson charges.

He says he came out of prison in February last year and went to Kawerau where he and his wife worked in a Salvation Army home for battered women.

They left the house because of a Salvation Army rule that no men were allowed there.

"I returned to Ruatoria to clean my own backyard up," says Heeney. "When I got back to Ruatoria, I was frequently visited by the police. They searched our house monthly and then started visiting at midnight with search warrants."

Heeney tells the court he had been waiting for over fourteen months on arson charges and had been remanded "more times than I have fingers on my hands".

The constant remands, visits by police and the fact that his wife had a baby due had all placed a huge burden on his shoulders.

When he escaped, he visited his family all around the North Island to discuss what had happened and his reasons for escaping.

July 28, 1988: *Dick Maxwell's committed for trial on twelve charges after a depositions hearing in Gisborne District Court. Charges include escaping from custody, assaulting a constable to facilitate escape and receiving "survival type" items.*

Other charges Maxwell faces are: three burglaries, assaulting two other police officers, wilfully damaging a police car windscreen, receiving a stereo, defrauding the Department of Social Welfare and possessing cannabis. He's remanded in custody until September 12 at

*which point he's found guilty of escaping from police custody and is
sentenced to three months' jail.*

But guess what.

October 20, 1988: *Dick Maxwell is acquitted in the Court of
Appeal of escaping from police custody. Mr Justice Barker says that at
Maxwell's trial in Napier the defence raised the issue of the lawfulness
of Maxwell's custody. The Crown had failed to provide evidence of what
had happened to Maxwell at the court appearance just before he
"allegedly" escaped. There should have been evidence of whether he'd
been remanded in custody or whether something else had happened.*

*The judge says that there were also shortcomings in the
directions the trial judge had given to the jury about inferences they
could draw from properly proven facts. Mr Justice Barker, delivering
the judgment of Mr Justice Richardson, Mr Justice Somers and himself,
says it wouldn't be appropriate to order a new trial for Maxwell. The
Crown could easily have called evidence of what had happened to
Maxwell in the court, so Maxwell should be acquitted.*

*Of course, any layperson who knows nothing about the law but
something about life could sum up that decision in one word.*

HEENEY, MATAIRA ON TRIAL FOR ARSON

Monday, August 22, 1988: *John Heeney and David Mataira
plead not guilty in the High Court in Gisborne to the arson of the
Ruatoria courthouse-cum-police station on November 19, 1985. Heeney
also pleads not guilty to three further arson charges (two haybarns on
Colin Williams' Kaharau Stud Farm in July 1985 and an unoccupied
police house on Mangakino Road, Ruatoria, on December 12, 1985).
Both men were arrested and charged with the offences in March 1987.*

Wednesday, August 24: *It's the third day of Heeney and
Mataira's trial. The first two days have been taken up by legal argument
over admissibility of evidence.*

*Detective Stuart Dever tells the court that in 1987 he took four
statements from Heeney in which the Rasta admitted his part in the four
arsons.*

Heeney told him the arson campaign began because the Williams family refused to return Maori land to locals when a hundred-year lease ran out in 1985. Mt Hikurangi was leased to the Williams family last century because they were missionaries who had brought the word of God. The lease was a gift to the Williams family and had been honoured for a hundred years by the Maori people, Heeney said. But the Williams sold part of the land to the Government for over a million dollars. The Government immediately began to plant the area in pines. This infuriated the Rastas, who cut down sixteen kilometres of fences on the block. But after a meeting at Hiruharama Marae, the Rastafarians had returned and fixed the fences.

Later, Heeney said, Colin Williams approached a Ruatoria Maori elder and offered to sell the land back to the local people, but wanted a large amount of money. "Money our people didn't have." The Rastafarians became "totally disgusted" with Williams' attitude because he wouldn't listen to their grievances unless large sums of money were involved.

"To plead our case we decided to burn down his bull sale venue," Heeney told Detective Dever.

Heeney described how he and others drove out to Colin Williams' farm, parked on the side of the main road and walked across a paddock to the building. Heeney put a match to some hay bales then they walked back to the car and stood and watched the building burn.

"That was the first fire the Rastafarians lit in Ruatoria. We did it to plead our case."

Heeney told the detective that Ruatoria people knew the Rastas had lit the fire. A Maori elder approached the Williams family to mediate "but they had hardened their hearts" and were not prepared to listen.

"A couple of weeks later we lit the second fire."

Heeney and an associate set fire to the second haybarn in the same way. It was totally destroyed in the blaze. Damage to both buildings was estimated at over $50,000.

Detective Dever tells the court that Heeney told him he set fire to the police house in February 1986, just after arriving back in Ruatoria. Other Rastafarians told him of how they were being harrassed by locals. On numerous occasions people had tried to run them over on the road. One Rastafarian had a rifle pointed at him and a group was shot at as it rode through a paddock. But the Ruatoria police said they could do nothing. Frightened for their lives, the Rastas took to living in the bush. Heeney decided to burn the police house to plead their case again. He and another person broke into the house and checked that it was empty. There were pieces of wood and boxes on the stove. He turned on all the elements and waited until they glowed red before leaving, knowing it would burn. Something had to be done so people would hear the Rastas' cry. Everyone was asking who lit the fires but no one asked why.

Heeney told the detective he was motivated to set fire to the courthouse after the Rastafarians had discussed killing one of the Ruatoria vigilante group. The group had discussed attempts on their lives and talked of killing someone. He had never heard that sort of talk before. But the group was upset and almost at breaking point. He and Mataira decided to burn the courthouse to "let some of the steam off and cool down the heat building up in Ruatoria".

Heeney told Detective Dever that he and Mataira prayed before the arson attempt to get enough courage to carry out their plan. Then they broke into the building, piled tyres, inner tubes and mats together, and poured petrol and some oil on them before turning on a heater next to the pile. Heeney lit some paper and threw it on to the pile and the pair left the building. The paper went out and they returned, lit it again and made sure the fire took hold.

Heeney told Detective Dever a meeting of all the "brethren" could sort out the Ruatoria problem. "I look at it this way," Heeney said. "We have been in a deep, dark hole and continued to fall for three years. There is no hope to stop us falling. If we can come forward in unison and admit to the wrongness of our ways, we are prepared for judgment, for a just punishment and we can look forward to the future."

Heeney insisted Chris Campbell be at the meeting. But Detective Dever said there was no way Campbell could be present because he was in prison.

The next day, Heeney flew to Auckland with Detective Dever and spent five hours talking to Chris Campbell at Paremoremo Prison. Afterwards, Heeney told the detective he was confident he could call a meeting of all the brethren and solve the problem. They flew back to Gisborne that night and the next morning Heeney made three statements about his involvement in the arsons. He was then taken down to the police station cells and charged with setting fire to the haybarns and the police house.

Thursday, August 25, 1988: *The High Court jury trial of Heeney and Mataira comes to an abrupt end when Mr Justice Thorp discharges the jury.*

He tells them he's received evidence of one of their members talking about the trial outside the jury room. It leaves him no option but to discharge them and make an order for a new trial.

We'll lose the chronology for a while and stick with Heeney and Mataira's trial, while it's still fresh in the mind. It's not like nothing was happening in Ruatoria between the failed trials. There was a murder and there were arsons. But we can deal with them later so we don't lose our thread.

Friday, February 21, 1989: *After one jury was discharged and another empanelled yesterday, the second trial of Heeney and Mataira finally gets underway in the High Court at Gisborne this afternoon.*

Crown prosecutor Phil Cooper says Heeney told police he lit the first haybarn fire because of dissatisfaction over land issues.

Cooper says that on March 22, 1987, a major breakthrough occurred in the investigations into the Ruatoria arsons. Mataira admitted, in an interview and written statement to police, burning down the Ruatoria Police Station and Courthouse. And he also implicated Heeney.

Heeney was subsequently interviewed and said he wanted time to think and pray. On March 24 he admitted he was also involved, later saying he would tell the police of other fires. These turned out to be the two haybarn fires at Colin Williams' Kaharau Stud farm.

The prosecution goes through Heeney and Mataira's admissions and written confessions for the arson of the police station and courthouse. Then it brings in the investigators' forensic findings at the scene. They all seem to fit together quite nicely.

HEENEY CHANGES HIS TUNE

Monday, February 24: *John Heeney says he signed a statement claiming responsibility for three arsons to protect his family and fellow Rastafarians. He says if he hadn't signed, it would only have been a matter of time before a Rastafarian was shot in Ruatoria. So,* *according to Heeney, the signing of the confession was not an admission of guilt but a selfless sacrifice to save others.*

In March 1987 he and his partner Donna and their children were living in Kawerau with his brother. He'd been living there since his release from jail three weeks earlier.

Heeney describes how he talked to a detective about a spiritual experience he had with other people from around the world up the mountain at Kawerau.

Later that evening, the detective returned with two other detectives.

Heeney was taken to Kawerau police station and was worried he'd have to go back to jail for a fourth time.

He says the police intimidated him; and that, coupled with the fears he had for his brethren back in Ruatoria, motivated him to sign the statement.

It's true that Heeney may have had noble motivations for making his confession. People say he went through a spiritual upheaval or awakening of sorts during his time in Kawerau. He was determined to unburden his heart and soul and start again. Donna was expecting another child and they were planning their marriage.

But while the confession may have had noble motivations, it was still a confession and would therefore end in jail time. And it is the author's opinion that the confessions were for real crimes that Heeney did commit. Why do I think this? One reason: Because it seems obvious. Another: New Zealand is a small country.

I used to get therapeutic massages from a woman who would travel from Rotorua to Auckland once a month to see her regular clients. This woman, knowing I was writing a series of books about Ruatoria, told me her sister-in-law was heavily involved with the Salvation Army in Kawerau and that, while he was there, John Heeney had spent a lot of time at her church. This woman's sister-in-law had in fact taken Heeney under her wing and become his confidante and confessor. He was at a very vulnerable point and had apparently broken down to her and admitted all his crimes. I later called John Heeney's confidante on the phone to see if I could get an interview. She knew who and what I was talking about all right. But she declined the interview. Heeney had trusted her and she wasn't prepared to break that trust.

Heeney's reasons for confessing may have been noble. But when it came to the crunch, he just didn't want to go back to jail and he tried to wriggle out of it.

Detective Hemi Hikawai is accused in court of threatening David Mataira with a beating if he didn't confess to the police station and courthouse arson and of pulling out some of his hair. Mataira says he felt intimidated by Hikawai after that. Hikawai denies the allegations.

Hikawai says that when Mataira was interviewed it was initially about other fires. But he went on to tell Hikawai that he burned down the police station, using a match to start the fire.

Reading from his notes, Hikawai quotes Mataira as saying, "It was a spur-of-the-moment thing for me. I want to say now I feel really good I've got it off my chest. I feel free."

He asked to be able to tell his mother, father and wife – to have the chance to hold each member of his family "before you fellas take me away".

Kawerau CIB detective Stuart Dever quotes Heeney talking about the first haybarn fire: "I was present once when we had a reasoning. Some of the brethren were steaming. You could feel the hatred and tension in the room. One said we should go and kill the vigilantes. Someone said instead we should do a burning. I thought this was better than a killing. It would let off the tension. Some of us drove to the barn that night and I put a match to haybales and walked back to the car. It was the first fire the Rastafarians lit in Ruatoria."

March 1: *After eight hours of deliberation, the jury in the trial of Heeney and Mataira is unable to reach a verdict. After discharging the jury, Mr Justice Hillyer orders a new trial at Gisborne High Court on May 15, remanding the pair in custody. It will be the third time Heeney and Mataira have gone to trial on these charges.*

May 19, 1989: *The third trial ends with Heeney and Mataira found guilty of burning down the building housing Ruatoria's police station and courthouse.*

Heeney's also found guilty on two charges of setting fire to barns on Kaharau Stud in January and July 1985. He's found not guilty of setting fire to a police house in Mangakino Road in February 1986.

June 14, 1989: Heeney is sentenced to five years in jail for burning down the police station/courthouse and the two haybarns.

In the High Court in Auckland, Mr Justice Gault says Heeney had embarked on a course of conduct, which might best be described as that of an outlaw.

"On one hand the picture can be painted as reflecting some misguided acts of despair motivated by a sense of grievance," the judge says. "On the other hand the series of fires can be regarded as what was, in effect, a reign of terror, in a small community."

Mataira, at the request of community leaders in Ruatoria, is sentenced to community care.

CHAPTER 4

"SECRET SERVICE TYPES"

A Gisborne tradesman related by marriage once told me about how he was doing work on some police houses in Ruatoria, not long after Jeremy Williams' woolshed was burnt down at Matahiia Station. He said he opened the door of a room and got the fright of his life.

Inside, a man was sitting in front of a wall of TV screens. The tradesman reckoned the cops must have had surveillance cameras set up in every Rasta house in Ruatoria.

I could tell it was out of his comfort zone, but I asked my distant in-law if he would allow me to interview him. He declined, worried that he might say something that would get his former boss in trouble.

Former Sergeant John Robinson: The police moved up a gear as a result of that fire at Jeremy Williams' woolshed and farm buildings.

Peter Tapsell was the MP for Eastern Maori at the time. He also had his farm next door to Jeremy Williams and across the river from the Campbells.

The police went and saw Tapsell and told him, "We can't handle these guys. They're now terrorists." And Tapsell went to the Prime Minister at the time, David Lange, and under the Terrorists Act got permission to bug the homes of all the Rastas who had phones. I would say this happened because Jeremy was a prominent person in the community. Had it happened at a Maori property, they wouldn't have cared.

All these boffins came up from Wellington. And they were supposed to be secret service types. But they were walking around Ruatoria, calling into the police station. You weren't supposed to know who they were. *Everyone* knew who they were. And they were absolutely useless.

First of all they never had the proper equipment. Now I don't know much about it but they had to have their receiving station fairly close to the bugs. Anyway they got into Joe Campbell's house near the start of Makarika Road and set up their bugs.

Joe found there was something wrong with his phone. He kept hearing a click when he picked it up. So he rang up Telecom. And the local Telecom man, he was Peter Bradley the cop's brother, goes there and has a look and says, "Your phone's bugged, Joe."

Now come on, they haven't even bothered to tell the Telecom man that they're bugging the phones. And they get caught out straight away.

Bradley tells the police he's found this bug in the telephone. So these secret service types decide they'd better get the gear out. These guys go in but Joe comes home unexpectedly. They couldn't have been watching the road.

These guys run out of the house with Joe in hot pursuit. They jump into the river out the back and come along the riverbed out to the highway. Of course, Joe's right behind them.

And Sergeant Hope arrives in a plain-clothes car and picks them up, because they're in radio contact, and they take off. Joe sees all this. Everyone knew what sort of car these guys were driving. A brand new plain-clothes car would come into town and everyone would know it was a police car immediately.

I think Joe Campbell made an official complaint through Russell Fairbrother, his lawyer. Now they got evidence from the Rastas talking among themselves on the phone that they had burnt down

Jeremy Williams' woolshed and farm buildings. But they didn't use it because it was such a balls-up.

These intelligence security boffins from Wellington were more technicians than cops.

Napier lawyer and long-time Labour MP Russell Fairbrother, interviewed at his home in November, 2000: Joe Campbell phoned me and he was quite distressed. He and his wife had arrived back from somewhere to find people in their kitchen. I think he caught one of them in a wardrobe. And they challenged them and these people took off over the back fence to a stream. Joe chased them up the stream until they scrambled into the paddocks and he lost them.

At some stage he heard them talking on radios and he was sure they were policemen. And he found signs that they'd been into a cupboard in his kitchen, I think it was. He was convinced that they were tapping his house.

There was a chase up the riverbank. He showed me the riverbank, which was right over the back of his house.

It was totally illegal because there was no legal base for tapping a house in those days.

The police at the time denied any knowledge of this tapping. I did make inquiries on behalf of Joe but they knew nothing and suggested he was just imagining it. But I know Joe and his wife were very upset. But it didn't go anywhere. You're faced by denials and you've got someone who's got no credibility in official quarters; it went nowhere.

No one even admitted they'd been in his house. It's only in the last twelve months it's been admitted to me by senior policemen that this incident did happen.

Joe actually went and complained to the police and said, "Well, come and take fingerprints." And they refused to take fingerprints in various parts of the house. They said, "Aw, you people have touched it. They'll be smudged." And they refused to investigate.

It just all seemed at the time to me so incredible that it couldn't be true. And yet, with what I know now, well, it's been confirmed to me since that what Joe was saying to me *was* true.

Former Ruatoria policeman Steve Tresidder: The police had a surveillance camera at one of the civilian houses that was tipped off to be burnt down. They just wanted to see who came and went. But the house wasn't burnt down until a couple of years later. That was the house up on the hill that Luke Donnelly was in at the end. That wasn't burnt down until after Luke shot Chris Campbell.

THE RASTA PAD BUGGING DEBACLE

Former Sergeant John Robinson: The technical boffins also put a listening device in the Rastas' Makarika pad.

What happened there was the guy actually got caught in the place taking it out. And they had him tied to a chair for about an hour or so. Steve Tresidder, the cop, was on duty and he must have got word from this guy's mates who were supposed to be watching this place that they'd got this guy. Steve Tresidder knew all the Rastas. And they had a bit of respect for him because he was firm but he was fair to them. And he went down there on his own and he just drove right in. And he said, "Look you guys… kidnapping. You've got him tied up. Kidnapping's a pretty serious charge. All sorts of things will happen if we have to charge you. Let'm go. And we'll forget all about it."

And they thought about it. And they weighed it all up. Eventually they let the guy go and there was nothing ever said about the incident.

Former Ruatoria policeman Steve Tresidder: I remember one time a tactical support unit from one of the big cities was trying to bug the Rasta pad at Makarika Road. What happened was the Rastas came back to the pad when these guys were trying to bug the place, and they managed to catch one of them and hold him prisoner. This is one Rasta kidnap that never made the papers.

The guy they caught was the only civilian in the group. He was actually the technical guy. How I got involved was I got a phone call at the Ruatoria Station late at night saying to go out to Makarika Road and drive up and someone would meet me on the road. I don't know if you've ever been up there. But it's just in the middle of nowhere. Now of course this is a time when there's shit coming down everywhere on me from within the force. So I'm driving along the road when this bloody guy jumps out of the long grass on the side of the road. He's in camouflage gear with his face all blackened out. He tells me he's senior sergeant someone. And I went, "Yeah, right." I was thinking, "This is a set-up. This is payback time from the Gisborne CIB boys."

This guy showed me his ID. Okay, he was whom he said. He told me what had happened: they were trying to get some bugs into the pad and their OB guys, their observation guys, didn't see the Rastas coming. These guys were from the city. They'd never been off the tar seal. They're watching the road. But the Rastas ride on horses. And they came in over the hills from the back. And the tactical support unit never saw them until they were virtually right there. But they all got away, bar this civilian, the technical guy who was doing the bugging.

They'd been told that if anything should go wrong or happen to them, to call me, because I had a pretty good relationship with the Rastas. I got on pretty God-damn well with them because they saw me as the guy who stood up for Dickie and, basically, someone who was prepared to tell the truth even though it was my own guys that I was telling it against. They trusted me. Shit, if I told them it was raining gold bars they'd all go running outside to have a look. They believed everything I said.

So I had a quick chat with this guy in camouflage and he told me what had happened.

I said, "So how can I help?"

"Well, we could rush in there guns blazing, but we don't want to cause a scene."

So we got our stories straight, what I was going to tell the Rastas, and then I just went in.

There were only about four or five Rastas there. But they were pretty fired up.

They were actually all outside the pad with the technical boffin. They hadn't beaten him up or anything. But he was petrified. He was absolutely terrified. The Rastas had axes and machetes and they were yipping and yahooing around this guy like maniac Red Indians. They were pretty well wound up.

But I can honestly say that I wasn't scared walking in there. I used to talk to the Rastas virtually every single day without fail. And I'd never had a single bit of bother with them. I'd had a few altercations with Dickie Maxwell that had ended up in fisticuffs. That's just the sort of person that he was. You'd say to him, "I'm locking you up," and he'd say, "No you're not." That was par for the course with Dick. Other than that, I didn't have a problem.

Jonathan McClutchie was there at the pad this night. He was the main one I was talking to. Now Jonathan's not the type of character you'd expect to get angry. He's usually very easy-going. But he's really wound up. The Rastas are actually pretty pissed off, because they think these guys have come to burn down their pad. The fact that these guys might be a tactical support group who'd come from the big city to bug their ramshackle hut never even enters their minds.

So I tell them, "Look, I've just got here. I don't know what's going on. But I guarantee you they haven't come to burn your pad down."

Jonathan says, "We've caught one of them. He's ours."

"You can't do that. You'll have helicopters and cops with guns swarming around before you know it. Give the guy back to me. Just get rid of him. I'll find out what's going on. And I'll come back tomorrow. And I'll tell you what's happening."

Of course, because they trusted me they gave me the guy back. So we went and had a debrief, got the story straight as to what I was going to tell them. The next day I went back and told them that the guys were there to do a warrant on the pad because accusations had been made that they were supplying cannabis to all the schools in Gisborne. And they were quite happy with that. Were they supplying cannabis to all the schools in Gisborne? Of course they weren't. But we had to tell them something to explain why these guys were there in the middle of the night.

Email from former Sergeant Nigel Hendrikse: Just had another funny memory... cops (secret squirrel types) from Wellington went into the Gisborne cells when the Rastas were in there and pretended to be Firemen doing maintenance on the fire alarms when they were in fact bugging the cells to listen to the Rastas in there... The Rastas asked why were those fucking cops pretending to be firemen... They weren't always stoned!!

CHAPTER 5

ARSON AND MURDER

We need to jump back in time a bit now to catch up on the other things that had been happening in Ruatoria, while all those trials and the spying on Joe Campbell were taking place.

October 9, 1988: *Nine people escape unhurt when a house is totally destroyed by fire at Tuparoa Beach near Ruatoria.*

Sergeant Alex Bryant of the Ruatoria police says there appears to be no reason why the house at Tuparoa Beach caught fire in the kitchen as the house had no power. That suggests it was an arson. Having said that in all the fires the Rastafarians were accused of starting, none of them were of buildings with people inside. This was probably in fact a retaliatory attack against the Rastas. They were staying in baches at Tuparoa Beach around that time. And locals did eventually use arson to drive out the Rastas. In 2006, I called Alex Bryant, the former sergeant in Ruatoria, and Alan Davidson, who's since retired from the Gisborne police, to confirm whose house it was. But neither could remember that particular fire. There were too many of them, too long ago.

You might think it strange that the local Volunteer Fire Brigade weren't able to race out to Tuparoa and stem the fire. This might help explain. Among Ruatoria Deputy Fire Chief Tom Heeney's papers is a photo of a blackboard in the Ruatoria fire station. Written on the board in white chalk: "Brigade is NOT to respond to fire calls at Tuparoa." There is more, including the word "Gisborne", but the photo isn't clear enough for it to be read. The caption, handwritten beside the photo, reads: "Notice in station after being stopped from attending fire by Gisborne."

Having said that, I'm not sure that this was the particular fire at Tuparoa that Gisborne stopped them from attending. As you read on you'll see there were a few fires at Tuparoa the Voluntary Fire Brigade never quite made it to in time.

Saturday, December 25, 1988: In the early hours of Christmas Day, there's a double murder at Tuparoa, near Ruatoria. It's worth pointing out straight away that this crime has nothing to do with the Rastafarians although the killer, forty-eight-year-old Robbie Grace, is an acquaintance of theirs.

Grace shoots his twenty-five-year-old nephew, Michael Joseph Junior Grace, and Michael's twenty-four-year-old wife, Mary Dale Grace.

Robbie also shoots Michael's brother, twenty-two-year-old Tunoa Grace, in the shoulder. Tunoa goes to Te Puia Hospital on Christmas Day and is then transferred to Gisborne Hospital. He undergoes an operation to remove the bullet and afterwards his condition is reported as satisfactory.

The bodies of Michael and Mary are found on the side of the road leading into Tuparoa, which is eight kilometres from Ruatoria.

Police surround Robbie Grace's house and eventually Grace and a twenty-five-year old man give themselves up.

On Monday, they appear in the Gisborne District Court: Grace charged with the double murder and the other man with helping him to avoid arrest.

They are remanded in custody to appear at a later date.

Detective Sergeant Gary Condon: Now I ran the Robbie Grace homicide inquiry. He killed two people and it was domestic-related. But the press just wouldn't leave us alone. And their angle was it's gotta be gang-related or Rasta-related.

It really was just a straight domestic. During the domestic there may have been things said to the two parties. But as for the Rasta part of it, there was no connection.

Saturday, January 1, 1989: Three men in their twenties visit Robbie Grace's house at Tuparoa Beach on New Year's Morning and ask the occupants to leave. Once the house is vacated, it is set alight with Molotov cocktails and destroyed in revenge for the double murder.

Gisborne police are called to the scene at about 11.45am. And, when it's alleged arms are involved, members of the armed offenders squad from Gisborne and Rotorua are also called in. Tuparoa is sealed off but the three men give themselves up without incident.

*They're arrested and appear before a Justice of the Peace at
Ruatoria later in the day and are remanded on bail until late February.*

March 11, 1989: *The East Coast Pest Destruction Board
announces it's pulling three of its staff out of the Ruatoria area. It says it
won't be returning until it's safe to work there.*

*Board supervisor Vaughan Neill says vandalism and
intimidation are too much of a problem during the summer months,
when a minority of locals are growing marijuana crops, "running
around armed" or just being unlawful.*

*The situation came to a head on February 14 when two of the
board staff were inspecting a property along the Whareponga Road.*

*A report read to the board members by Neill says they returned
to their vehicle to find it had been vandalised. All the side windows and
windscreen had been smashed in with a steel ramp used for loading
motorcycles on to the truck's deck.*

*The ramp was also used to smash the vehicle's deck and radio.
The poison locker box was broken into and a set of keys removed from
the glove box.*

*The only evidence of anyone being near the truck was the
hoofmarks of horses around the vehicle and the steel loading ramp,
which was left lying across the bonnet.*

*When inspecting in the field earlier, staff heard whistles from
what they thought were people on horses some distance away.*

Thursday, March 23: *Six people are arrested and charged
with drug-related offences after a two-day operation around Ruatoria,
Tokomaru Bay and the surrounding hill country.*

*Detective Wynn Van der Velde says about three hundred two
metre high plants were found.*

Friday, June 2, 1989: *Three men charged with arson are
committed for trial to the High Court on July 3 after a depositions trial
in Gisborne.*

*Darryl Whitu White, Thomas George Ryan and Maku Jim
Turei, plead not guilty to a charge of wilfully setting fire to Robbie
Grace's house at Tuparoa Beach. They're granted bail but are told they
have to live at Tuparoa Beach, report once a week to the Ruatoria
Police and not communicate with any witnesses.*

***Thursday, March 1, 1990:** Robbie Grace is sentenced to life in prison after being found guilty of the murder of his nephew Joe Grace and his nephew's wife, Mary-Dale.*

The forty-nine year old beneficiary is convicted on two counts of murder by Mr Justice Thorp after a trial by jury in the High Court at Gisborne.

The jury takes just over an hour to reach its verdict, which is delivered before a packed public gallery, with many more people waiting outside.

One of the main issues behind the killings was that Joe Grace belonged to the Mongrel Mob and his uncle, Robbie Grace, didn't want the Mongrel Mob moving into Ruatoria.

HIDDEN FACTOR BEHIND THE RASTAS

Former Sergeant John Robinson: Robbie Grace was one of the hidden factors behind the Rastas. He supplied them with a lot of dope. He had a tonne of it up there.

When he shot these two people dead and wounded another one, he tried to get up in court and say his eleven-year-old daughter shot them. Of course, she was under the age of accountability. But they didn't wear it.

Then after Robbie was found guilty he needed some new evidence for the appeal. So his daughter and Quinton Takarangi said that Detective Sergeant Hemi Hikawai had *planted* some bullets on the scene. They even produced this plastic bag with some bullets in and said they saw Hikawai hiding around the house. And that was used as evidence against him.

Anyway that allegation was fully investigated. The DSIR tested the bag. And it was one of those bags you buy your bread in. And they were able to prove that the bag wasn't even manufactured until after the murder trial. They'd obviously planted the evidence themselves.

They charged the mother and Takarangi with perjury. They got convicted but the penalties were pathetic. Hemi Hikawai's job was on the line and he was accused of planting evidence in a murder trial. And it's proved false and the offenders walk away with suspended sentences. No wonder the cops get annoyed.

***Monday, March 26, 1990:** Turei, Ryan and White plead guilty to a joint charge of arson when they appear in the High Court at Gisborne.*

They also plead guilty to a second charge of having a firearm with them with intent to commit the crime of arson.
Mr Justice Wylie remands all three in custody to appear for sentence at Auckland on April 11.

***Wednesday, April 11, 1990:** Turei, Ryan and White are each sentenced to three years in prison.*

Earlier, counsel for the trio, Tony Adeane, tells the court the incident arose after Robbie Grace murdered two people at his home on Christmas Eve, 1988.

The murdered man, Joe Grace, was a cousin of Turei and the murdered woman, Mary Dale Grace, was the sister of Ryan's wife.

The three men attended the funeral and tangi of the deceased at Matamata where they decided on a course of retribution.

"Their intention," Adeane says, "was to extract a measure of utu and, more than that, to expunge Mr Grace from the Tuparoa community in a way to ensure he wouldn't return there."

On December 31 the three men took an old rifle, which was unloaded, and went to Grace's house. There they asked Grace's estranged wife and other friends to leave the home before setting fire to the buildings.

"The purpose was the destruction of the kauta (meeting and socialising point) where the killings had occurred a few days earlier.

"Having burned the building, the three then sawed down surrounding trees, walked back to their own home, drank some tea and waited for police to arrive.

"When the police arrived they made a full and completely unreserved confession about what they had done and why they had done it.

"These men acted together with two motives – first, to cleanse the place where these killings had taken place, and secondly, revenge.

"From a distance, the court would be aware of the notorious situation at Ruatoria where arson has become all too common, and it's my strong submission that what happened on this occasion was an entirely different thing from the numerous offences of arson for political or anti-law and order motives."

Mr Justice Wylie sentences each of the three to three years in jail on the charge of arson and one year on the firearm count, the terms to be served concurrently.

MAXWELL'S HOUSE IS BURNED

__Tuesday, June 13, 1989:__ The trial of Dick Maxwell on one receiving and two burglary charges is unable to proceed because Maxwell fails to show up two days running.
A bench warrant is issued for his arrest.
The jury was called back again this morning. But Judge Richard Kearney of Tauranga discharged the jury and extended the court's apologies for the inconvenience and delay.

__Friday, August 25, 1989:__ There's another spate of suspected arsons in Ruatoria. Dick Maxwell's house was burnt down last night. It's a four-bedroom Housing Corporation rental home in the township and, despite the efforts of the Ruatoria Fire Brigade, it is extensively damaged.
There was a party in the house earlier in the night but it was unoccupied when the fire broke out.
While investigations begin into that fire, two more fires are reported at about 9.10 this morning at Tuparoa Beach.
More than an hour later they are both still well alight.
The Ruatoria Voluntary Fire Brigade reportedly has difficulties getting its appliance over a river ford to get to the scene because the river is still in flood. These houses are owned by members of the Grace family. Mereana Grace lives in one of them. Maku Turei, also known as Jimbo Grace, who at this time is one of three men awaiting trial for burning down Robbie Grace's house, lives in the other. Neither house is occupied at the time of the fires. Both houses and their contents are destroyed.
The suspicious fires end a period of relative calm in the community, which has already suffered more than thirty suspicious fires.

About this time, three stories start developing simultaneously. They are about Dick Maxwell and his run-ins with the law, a fight between police and Rastafarians at Tuparoa Beach and the arson of a marae. For clarity's sake, I'll deal with them one by one.

Friday, September 8, 1989: *Dick Maxwell appears in the Gisborne District Court facing charges of wilfully setting fire to two houses at Tuparoa Beach last month.*

He also faces charges of driving while disqualified, no warrant of fitness, two of assaulting a constable, possession of an offensive weapon, escaping from custody, unlawful assembly, assault and theft.

No pleas are taken and he's remanded in custody.

After a depositions hearing, Dick Maxwell is sent to trial in the High Court in Gisborne. Gleaning points from both hearings, here is the Crown case, which is based almost entirely on circumstantial evidence.

On Thursday, August 24, 1989, Maku Turei (also known as Jimbo Grace) goes into Ruatoria with some friends. He leaves his 650cc motorbike outside his house, taking his chestnut horse instead.

Turei is angry that a man who borrowed one of his horses, fell off and didn't return it. He and his friends jump in a car and go looking for the horse and the man, Turei saying, "I'm going to kill some bastard."

They find the man and Turei punches him, knocking him to the ground.

While Turei's at the pub that night, someone steals his chestnut horse and saddle from outside.

Turei and his friends head around to Dick Maxwell's in the car. Turei agrees in court that he's in the car as it goes through the gate to Maxwell's home. They go inside but there's no one there. A short time later, the house is burning. Turei denies he lit the fire but agrees he heard someone breaking glass.

It's worth noting that police spoke to Turei and his friends about the fires but they weren't charged. In court, Turei denies he told another man he burned down the house (he says he saw it burning as he walked home from the pub). He also denies telling the same man that his house and another man's house would also be burned.

Asked by defence lawyer Grant Vosseler if he's ever set fire to a house, Turei exercises his right not to answer (he burnt down Robbie Grace's house).

In one of the hearings, Detective Sergeant Mark Templeman reads from his notes of an interview with Maxwell in which he admitted having trouble with Jimbo Grace (also known as Maku Turei). He claimed the old people wanted him to sort out people like Grace.

At 10pm on August 24, Sergeant Alex Bryant is called to a house fire at Dick Maxwell's. When he arrives, there are about thirty people gathering, lights flashing and a house burning. There's noise from pumps and fire appliances. It's Thursday, dole-day, the big night at the pub, and most people have left the pub and are congregating at the fire.

Sergeant Bryant knows Dick Maxwell and his wife have been living in the house recently.

While Bryant's there Maxwell rides past on a horse. He wears a balaclava and is carrying a white stick as a horsewhip.

Bryant approaches Maxwell and tells him he wants to speak with him.

Maxwell says: "Who did this? Who did this? I know who did it. I'll get them."

Bryant says: "I heard you did it."

"It wasn't me."

Bryant tells him again that he's heard that he burned down his own house.

"Bullshit, man. I didn't do it."

According to Maxwell, there's utu between him and Jimbo Grace.

When a large green car goes by, Maxwell says, "Look. There are the bastards. I know who you are. I'll get you."

After telling Bryant that he stole Grace's horse from the hotel that night, he says: "Why don't you catch them? You're not doing your job properly."

When asked to tell who did it, Maxwell says he knows and that he'll get them and rides off.

Later that evening, Maxwell has a fight with Maku Turei. Maxwell accuses Turei (Jimbo Grace) of burning down his house. A drunk Turei tries to punch Maxwell but comes off second best. He ends up needing hospital treatment for injuries he suffers in the fight and Maxwell is later charged with assault.

The next morning Turei's house (the Shady Rest, located next to the river) and his mother Mereana Grace's house are burned down.

The remains of Turei's 650cc motorbike, which he left outside his house, are found among the ashes. Whoever burned down the house put the motorbike inside first.

Farm worker Maui Whangapirita is driving a tractor at his father's farm at Tuparoa when he sees smoke from Mereana Grace's house.

Before leaving to use the phone to get help, he sees a lean man on the other side of the river in a dark green hooded cape behind a truck belonging to Maku Turei. As the man walks away, Whangaparita sees a rifle – probably a .303 - in his hand. (Maku Turei claims such a rifle went missing from his house when it was burned down.) The man's heading towards a horse tied up to a poplar tree. It looks like Turei's horse: Fairly tall with a white sock on one of its hind legs and a white mark on its head.

Whangaparita uses the phone at another property and returns to where he saw "Girlie" (Mereana) Grace's house on fire. Now he sees that Maku Turei's house is also engulfed in flames.

He goes and looks around the houses and notices fresh horse tracks and gumboot marks in the ground.

Peter Te Purei also sees Mereana Grace's house on fire.

After noticing the smoke he goes to look and sees someone in the vicinity of the house, "walking towards Jimbo's bach".

Like Whangaparita, Te Purei leaves the scene for a short time and when he arrives back he sees Jimbo's house is also on fire.

Melsen Turei sees someone acting suspiciously around the time the fires started. He sees smoke at Mereana Grace's house and a person walking from there to Maku Turei's house.

The next day, Phil Kitchen, then a reporter for The Dominion, is being driven to Ruatoria by Detective Hemi Hikawai.

They see Dick Maxwell riding a chestnut coloured horse, on which he uses a white whip or rod, from a paddock onto the road.

Detectives locate the horse in a paddock the next day. They also find the white riding whip and a green hooded raincoat, which, it's said in court, Maxwell was seen wearing the night his own house burnt down.

When Maxwell is finally apprehended by police, they find Turei's chestnut-coloured horse and saddle and, in a canvas bag next to where Maxwell's been sleeping, a bone carving and a silver-coloured metal container used for keeping cannabis. Maku Turei says the bone pendant had been hanging on a nail on a wall in his house when he left it and the oval metal container had been sitting on the mantel piece.

In court, Brown Turei identifies the bone pendant as one he carved for his brother Maku. The carving is to his own design and no two are the same. He's adamant that he did the carving and it was that particular pendant that he gave his brother.

When originally found with the pendant, Maxwell denies involvement in the fires and claims he found the carved pendant on a table at a Rastafarian house.

Maxwell's interviewed by Detective Sergeant Mark Templeman. Maxwell says he wouldn't have burnt down his own house because it was a ticket to his wife coming back to make it into a home, a place of reunion.

Templeman asks him: "Did you burn Jimbo's house for utu?"

Maxwell says he didn't burn the house because he wanted to burn Jimbo.

"You had reason to burn those houses."

Maxwell replies that his revenge is to go for the person, the heart of the matter, not the property.

The Gisborne Herald, Thursday, March 22, 1990: Late News: Maxwell Discharged: Dick Maxwell discharged by judge during High Court trial on two charges of arson involving houses near Ruatoria. Judge found Crown case insufficient for trial to proceed and said onus not on Maxwell to prove innocence. Evidence of identification nowhere near sufficient.

Here's an interesting little footnote on this case from an unexpected source. It's a quote from Witi Ihimaera's novel The Dream Swimmer. "They stole horses to reach their remote plantations of marijuana... Sometimes, returning from their crops, their breadbags were full of high-quality marijuana ready for smoking. They said it was essential for practising their religion.

"Black Power couriers provided the supply routes to Auckland and Wellington. And if anybody objected, they took swift reprisals. Their Black Power tactics had taught them that the best way to control the situation was to scare opponents into submission by beating the shit out of them.

CHAPTER 6

MAXWELL ON TRIAL FOR AXE ATTACK ON COP

Wednesday, September 20, 1989: Dick Maxwell lists his occupation as peacemaker when he appears in the Gisborne District Court. He's on trial for attacking a police constable with an axe.

Basically, the police wanted to catch Dick Maxwell offguard so they went to his house very late to search it. Maxwell got angry and intimidated Constable Chris Bunyan with an axe and the police retreated. The police charged Maxwell with assaulting a constable. But it was later shown that the police search warrant was invalid so Maxwell got off.

Instead of going into the details of the trial, I'll quote Bunyan and former Sergeant John Robinson's memories of the incident from interviews I did with them.

Chris Bunyan: I remember one time Dickie Maxwell attacked me with an axe. It got to court but it ended up getting ordered for a retrial. Because of the circumstances the judge dismissed the trial. We could have relaid the charges and tried to prosecute again but the Crown told us not to.

During Cyclone Bola the power went off and the alarm back-ups in most of the businesses were good for about twenty-four hours. And I think we were without power for two or three days. And I was up to about a thirty-six-hour stretch, working non-stop. Then a looting had taken place at the Wrightsons Building and a lot of gear had been stolen.

I actually spotted a young girl who'd gone into Carlyle's Drapery shop and stolen jeans. She just admitted it. And I said, "Why did you do it?"

"Aw, I saw Dickie and John and Cody walking out of Wrightsons with bags full of stuff and I thought I'd go and get some gear for me."

Anyway we went back to the station and it's about eleven o'clock at night. We had relief staff from Gisborne on and John Robinson was the boss during Cyclone Bola. As the probationary cop, I typed up the search warrants. And we went to Dickie's place first. And it's our policy when you do a search warrant, if you've got a target person you don't let them out of your sight. And he brushed past us and just started ranting and raving and went out to his garage. So I followed him out to the garage. And in the garage on a couch lying down was Hamana Brown. And he started ranting. And they worked themselves up with all this Jah and Rastafari and baldhead stuff. And they froth at the mouth, just get lathered up. And we're in the confines of this Skyline-type single garage. The front door was open and there's a little side door about the width of this office (three metres) from the house.

And I'm just keeping an eye on him. I've got a PR24 and I'm thinking, "Well we've gotta deal to this and then go and search the house." His mum and some kids and I think his partner were in the house. The next thing he just turned and there was an axe hanging on one of the 4x2s between two nails. And he grabbed it and he just came at me with the axe over his head. And if he'd come through with the blow he would have cut my head in half. So he's like this, all lathered up. And I just, boom, out that side door. And I was looking for space and it was out on the front lawn between the house and the shed and as I came out of the gap at the end towards the front lawn, he came out the front of the shed and just went BOOM with a big mad swipe and it missed my stomach by inches.

And I got out on to the lawn and the others at the address by that stage were getting over the fence and putting a good distance between them and Dickie. And he just chopped into the concrete and there were sparks flying. By this time it's after midnight. All the lights in the neighbourhood are coming on. He's at the top of his voice yelling, "Utu," and all this carry-on. So, yeah, that was the experience with Dickie Maxwell on that occasion.

I heard stories of Dickie assaulting women. On one occasion I was told a few of the riff-raff sideline type guys had got him up at

Tikitiki and beaten the living daylights out of him. They had a knife to his throat and they were gonna take him out. But they didn't have the balls to do it. But it didn't stop him. That episode was for assaulting a woman. No complaints, as I recall, to the police.

Former Detective Sergeant Laurie Naden: Dickie Maxwell sort of floated in and out of the Rastafarians. He was disliked. There were all sorts of allegations made about his conduct towards some of their wives. But you never got complaints about it. But at some stages Dick would be a member and at others he wouldn't.

PRAYER SESSION TURNS UGLY

Former Sergeant John Robinson: Then Cyclone Bola came along. I was up there when Bola happened. And Dalgety's got broken into and so did Carlyle's clothing store. There were only two of us on duty, me and Chris Bunyan. But they'd sent up a sergeant and another three men from Gisborne. And these guys caught the kids who did the Carlyle's robbery.

The next night we got word that there was a vacant house and a lot of stolen stuff was inside it. One of John Heeney's brothers lived beside this house and he rang up and said, "I think a lot of that stuff you're looking for is in this house."

The house actually belonged to one of the Rastas, Charles Oliver Turnbull, better known as Charlie Cheese. But he hadn't moved into it yet.

Anyway, what happened was it was midnight and we got all this stuff. And these guys who'd come up from Gisborne said, "Dickie Maxwell's behind this." And they wanted to go round and do his house over straight away.

I was against that. I'd worked all day and I wanted to go to the hotel to sleep. I wanted to go and see Dickie at a reasonable hour in the morning.

But they said, "No, we'll go now. If we go in the morning all the property he has in his house will be gone."

"All right."

So Chris Bunyan typed out the search warrants and they went down to Bob Kaa's and got them signed. And then they went round to Maxwell's.

Maxwell comes to the door. He'd been having a prayer session with his mother. This is about one o'clock in the morning. We said, "We've got a warrant to search your house."

He goes mad. He rushes into the garage. He picks up an axe. And he starts smashing it onto the concrete. He says, "I'll take any of you with me." And all these cops are shitting themselves.

I'm standing on the porch with my arms folded. "Aw, come on, Dickie." I knew him well because we were up there all the time, the uniformed cops. We got on well with these guys. We didn't punch them up and hassle them. They knew: if they did something wrong we'd do 'em and they were quite happy with that.

Anyway these cops were hiding behind fences with their long batons out. I just walked past Dickie and I said, "Come on, we'll go. We're not gonna have a bloody massacre here."

And all these gung-ho cops were so bloody happy to get away from the place.

Dickie Maxwell left home for a while and we never saw him for ages. Someone said he took a whole lot of property with him. But I think he only had a backpack with a few horse-shoes that had been stolen from Dalgety's in it.

Eventually we got Dickie Maxwell to court over this incident with the axe. We charged him with having an offensive weapon and threatening the police. And the bloody warrants were all wrong. They said, "Who signed the warrants?"

"Bob Kaa."

"Bob Kaa? He's prejudiced. He's had his garage burnt down. He'll sign anything against the Rastas. Where are the duplicate copies?"

"They're kept in the Ruatoria Police Station."

"Why are they kept there?"

"Because the sergeant at Ruatoria is the deputy registrar of the court. And they're kept there."

"You can't have that. It's a police station and these are all court warrants. They should be kept in the court."

Then they started going through the warrant and Chris Bunyan had put wrong dates and wrong addresses on the warrants. The warrant was invalid therefore the whole police operation was invalid and they just dismissed the charge.

I was responsible in the end because I was in charge of the station. It falls back on to me. But you'd think your men would type up the warrants properly.

That guy Maxwell had a mental problem though. He wasn't the full quid. His brother's almost a vegetable because Dickie whacked him over. He cut his wife's finger off with a knife. Yeah. A domestic argument, held her hand down, hhhhhwwk.

(Former Rastafarian Cody Haua and Sonny Brown said this last bit about the finger wasn't true. They weren't sure where John had heard that or what he was referring to, although it's worth noting that in Watene Wanoa's trial for the murder of Dick Maxwell the defence mentioned that Maxwell had once chopped someone's hand off. Then again, I don't think that means it's necessarily true. The defence could have just thrown that into the mix to further discredit Maxwell and help get Wanoa off on self-defence, which they did.)

MAXWELL FOUND NOT GUILTY (AGAIN)

Thursday, March 15, 1990: Dickie Maxwell's found not guilty of assaulting constable Murray Maxwell with a knife. On another charge of assaulting constable Solomon Jale with a knife, the jury can't reach a verdict and Maxwell's remanded on bail.

Following a ruling by Judge Richard Kearney of Tauranga, a charge of escaping custody is withdrawn.

Maxwell defends himself for part of the trial, before re-instating his lawyer, Grant Vosseler.

Here's the Crown case, as put to the court by prosecutor William McCartney.

On August 9, 1989, a number of police officers go to Dickie Maxwell's house to execute warrants for his arrest. Constable Murray Maxwell and Sergeant John Robinson are the first to arrive. They see Dickie leave the door of his home and run to the rear of his house. Constable Maxwell chases him to Holland Place. Dickie stops, faces the policeman and produces a large knife. "Come on cop," he says, "you and me," and runs towards him, holding the knife. When Dickie gets close, Constable Maxwell pulls out a revolver.

They head back towards Dickie's property. When they get there, Dickie jumps on his horse. Constable Solomon Jale arrives and tries to pull him down from it. But Dickie makes attempts to stab him and then escapes on horseback.

Constable Maxwell says that when he pulled out his revolver in Holland Place, Dickie told him to "put it right there". "I was concerned for my life," says the constable. He says when Constable Jale tried to pull the accused from his horse he warned him, "Watch out for the knife." He says: "The accused raised the knife above his head and brought it down his side in a stabbing motion, down and around behind him. It appeared he was deliberately trying to stab Constable Jale."

Dick Maxwell, defending himself, asks the constable if he tried to find any way, other than drawing his long baton or police revolver, to procure an arrest.

Constable Maxwell: "Because of your history I didn't consider any less preparation would have been sufficient to effect that arrest."

Dick Maxwell then shows the court his previous criminal history sheet. He asks Constable Maxwell to count the number of times he's been convicted on assault charges. Only two occasions are evident, in 1977 and in 1979. At that point Vosseler is re-instated.

Vosseler asks the constable if he pulled out his pistol because he thought it would be a sufficient bluff.

"I pulled it out because I thought my life was in grave danger. The accused stopped running at me with his knife."

Constable Maxwell admits he didn't get on with Dickie Maxwell and also agrees that he's drawn a picture in court of a Hulk-like man with the words "Rasta Slayer" written at the top.

Constable Jale tells the court that when he arrived, Dick Maxwell was on his horse, yelling abuse and threats at policemen who were already there. He tried to pull Maxwell off the horse and Constable Maxwell yelled at him to watch out because Dickie had a knife. The knife narrowly missed his face. "I swung my baton and hit Maxwell on his back."

Dick Maxwell says that as far as he's concerned the police did not observe the law that day. He was concerned for his safety because of the time he was kidnapped and had his dreadlocks cut off. He thought Constable Maxwell was coming to do him "violent harm" and he felt that if he didn't pull out his knife he might be injured. "When I pulled my knife out it stopped him."

"You hate police don't you," says McCartney.

"No, I don't hate the police. I hate the bullshit they do. I feel sorry for them." Dick Maxwell claims the conduct of the police that day was worse than the Mongrel Mob's. He says the police are meant to uphold the laws which are constructed from the Ten Commandments in the Bible. "I know the police act outside the law because they kidnapped me. They reconstruct their cases, not on truth but on a lot of bullshit to imprison us because they can't trap us using their mentality."

PART 7
A MARAE BURNS

CHAPTER 1

RASTAS SCRAP WITH POLICE

Wednesday, August 30, 1989: *Police arrested eight people in Ruatoria early this morning.*

At this time the Rastas are all living in baches at Tuparoa Beach and the locals, who consider them to be squatters, want them out.

District Superintendent Rana Waitai (who will later become part of the New Zealand First Party's "tight five" Maori MPs) says a team of Gisborne uniformed police and detectives were sent to the Coast to carry out the operation.

"Search warrants were executed on a number of addresses and as a result eight people were arrested."

Jonathan McClutchie, Charles Turnbull, Nehe Reuben, Cody Haua, Tuck Morice and Hata Thompson are charged with unlawful assembly and assault using a shotgun as a weapon.

McClutchie and Michael Paiti face a joint charge of assaulting a police constable with intent to obstruct. And Tony Tuhou faces a separate charge of assaulting a police constable with intent to obstruct.

Former Sergeant John Robinson: Half the problems with the CIB were among themselves. They hated going up there and getting called out to another fire in the middle of the night, then staying up there for two weeks and getting no results.

Now Rex Harrison was one of the detectives and his father owned the hotel and, of course, the police were saying that, "While we all stay here, *he's* getting rich out of this." So the police started rumours themselves that the Rastas were gonna burn the pub. They did that because they were jealous of the Harrison family getting rich.

Anyway, they put an armed guard on the hotel. He had to walk around the hotel and patrol around it at night. And every time there was a noise, a possum in a tree or an owl hooting, the guard was yelling and screaming.

The guy who was doing the night patrol in the car, he was getting sick of getting called down to the pub every time there was a noise. In the end he told the guard, "You drive the bloody car and I'll stay here."

But this guard who was posted at the pub got sent back to Gisborne. He was too frightened. He was a uniformed cop but the CIB had really psyched him up. "We're sleeping in here. Don't you let anything happen to this pub."

Of course, the uniformed branch did all the cordons and extra work. The CIB just did there nine to five and then they'd knock off and go back and go on the booze. That caused a bit of friction between the departments.

Anyway CIB ended up in Te Puia. They got their way. The uniformed branch stayed in the Ruatoria pub, quite happy.

As it turned out there was an arson attempt on the Manutahi Pub by a Rasta, but this one could hardly be called a Ruatoria Rasta.

About the same time as Mawell's run-ins with the law and the Rastas' scrap with police, Ngati Porou Marae was burned down and an attempt was made to burn down the pub, which was filled with guests. The arson of the marae was the final insult to many Maori. The main culprit was Dion Hutana, who wasn't even from Ruatoria or the Coast. He had grown up in a Mongrel Mob family in Waipukurau and Flaxmere. He had come under Chris Campbell's spell in Hawke's Bay's Mangaroa Prison and Wanganui's Kaitoke Prison and basically committed the arsons to impress Campbell. To tell the story of the marae's arson, I feel I first have to tell the story of Dion Hutana and Chris Campbell or, rather, allow Dion to tell the story.

Before I do that, I'll tell you how I got to interview him. I was in the H.B. Williams Library in Gisborne (yes, donated by the same family the Rastas were at war with) looking through a coffee table book on Maori moko or facial tattoo. The photos and text were by a visiting German and he had done a chapter on the Ruatoria Rastafarians.

I also noticed in another chapter of the book, a man with a tidy short haircut in a black suit with a full moko. His name was Dion Hutana.

I thought, "Isn't that the guy who burned down the marae?" I recognised his name from the newspaper clippings I'd read. He was working for a Government department.

I needed to go to Napier, in Hawke's Bay, to interview the lawyer and Labour MP Russell Fairbrother for this series of books. So when I was with him I asked him if he knew Dion Hutana. He did. Was he the same Dion Hutana who burned down the marae? He was. And he'd left the Rastas and become a bureaucrat? That's right, he'd wanted to get in a position where he could actually help his people. So where was he now? Mangaroa Prison: On remand for assault. He'd been dragged into some feud involving family.

Russell knew Dion Hutana well and asked him if he'd talk to me, which he agreed to do.

So one sunny morning I drove from Gisborne to Hawke's Bay with my dad, Iain, in the passenger seat. He was on holiday and was really enjoying travelling around with me while I did my interviews.

We met Dion with his lovely partner – a young Maori woman - and their two cute kids in a special cell where prisoners could meet their guests.

Dion impressed Dad and I immediately. He was good looking, he was big and strong and he had presence. He also had an easy, honest way about him and eyes that seemed to want to communicate. He'd had his Rastafarian moko tattooed over. He'd always been in competition with John Heeney and believed that Heeney, who did all the Rasta moko, had deliberately defaced his face.

Dion later told us he'd done a previous stretch for sexual assault, so he obviously had a dark side. But I couldn't help thinking that there was a very strong positive side to him, too.

The more Dion spoke, the more obvious it became that this guy was highly intelligent. And as his life story unfolded it also became obvious what a waste and a tragedy it was.

Before we left, Dad gave Dion's partner a hundred bucks to spend on the kids. It was nearly Christmas. And the gratitude in the couple's faces was genuine, which meant more than their thanks.

As we drove home Dad and I couldn't help feeling sad. Here was a guy who had all the natural gifts and talents you can hope to get from nature. His people were screaming out for charismatic leaders and visionaries. And this obvious leader had been kept behind bars most of his adult life. He was a walking, talking example of the Maori tragedy.

Here's his story, for the most part, in his own words.

CAMPBELL RECRUITS A WARRIOR IN PRISON

Dion Hutana, interviewed by the author and the author's father, Iain, at Mangaroa Prison, November, 2000: I first seen Chris, I think it was in '86 up in the Napier Prison. It was round by the bluff. They don't use it now. It was the one that we all used to go to before this prison was here.

First of all I wasn't always with the Rastas and the dread. I come from The Mob background. I grew up in The Mob as a little kid. My family was all in it.

I'd heard a lot about Chris on the TV when he kidnapped Laurie Naden. And I thought, "Wow, this is awesome! I'll have to meet this man one day." I mean, the police couldn't find him and he was on TV. And it just so happened that a guy that used to live with us in the shearing sheds used to live with Chris himself. And he was telling me, "Aw na, they'll never find him in the bush."

And I said, "Why?"

"He's an expert bushman."

And I thought, "Wow, that makes it even better." I was quite intrigued. So in '86 I was up the hill and I seen him for the first time in my life. I thought he was about seven foot myself just from the stories I had heard. But when I seen him I saw he was shorter than me. I thought, "Aw, what?" But he still had a way about him.

They used to keep them all together in one yard and they'd keep the Mob all together in the other yard even though there was no animosity between us. Chris had a Mob background himself. I didn't know that 'til later, 'til I'd met him.

I used to look through one of the windows because I could see into their yard and I'd watch him. I watched the way he carried himself and the way he spoke. I was just automatically drawn to him.

He could speak with authority. But what struck me the most was that I found him to be really humble. But also it was the way he walked: with the head up high. It was very charismatic. And I think that's the right word to use.

But eventually I was sentenced. I was still involved with the Mob at this stage. And I got five years for sexual violation.

Then I got to Kaitoke in Whanganui. And I heard that Chris Campbell was coming down from Paremoremo. We all heard about it. And then I heard that he was mokoed up (he had his face tattooed).

Now I was drawn to Chris. But at first I had my doubts about him and the moko. I knew that he was right into his Maoritanga. And I could relate to that with my background because one thing I've always held to is my Maoritanga. And one thing I knew while I was in the Mob – I don't know if you've heard the expression Mongrelism; it's something like a creed or code of ethics for the Mob – well I knew deep inside myself that you couldn't put Mongrelism and Maoritanga together. That's just my own opinion. I'm not speaking for any of the others. My mother could korero Maori all her life. And even though I was in this background my mother always made sure to give me a good understanding of my Maoritanga, all my life. So I knew that never the two could meet.

Well I saw Chris one time while I was walking around in the yard. I saw him up at the window. He was in a room looking down. And I looked up and I saw his moko and I was devastatedly blown away. He was fully covered and it was well done.

Most mokos you saw in jail were either Mob ones or Black Power ones. And you saw fullas that had Maori mokos that weren't really very well done. But his one was awesome. There again I was attracted (clicks his fingers), straight away, like that.

When he came off remand he was in West 2, I was in East Wing. And I seen him. I wasn't apprehensive. But I kept my distance. And I had a co-offender, who was already talking to him. And my co-offender kept coming back and telling me, "Aw, bro, that fulla's awesome."

But I had a problem straight away because Chris had a moko but he had this thing on the top of his head and it was Jah Rastafari. He had it written across his forehead. And I had a problem with that.

We had a culture group going every Friday at Kaitoke, where we used to do waiata and haka. So I wasn't sure what angle Chris was coming from, and how his Rastafarian beliefs fitted in with his Maoritanga.

Eventually, he came up to me and introduced himself. And he says, "Kia ora, dread."

My thoughts were, "Hey, hey, hey, hey. I'm not a dread. I'm a dog." But I didn't say that. And I always wondered why I didn't say that. I looked down and I said, "Kia ora, bro. I gotta tell you something, bro."

And he goes, "Aw, what's that?"

"I always wanted to meet you."

And he goes, "Yeah, I know. I know that."

"How do you know that?"

"I just know."

"Well, okay then." I didn't say too much. But every now and then we'd have quiet words together, whenever we bumped into each other. Eventually I figured out he knew exactly what my problem was with him. I could relate to him on the Maoritanga side of things or the Ringatu Church stuff he talked about. But he came up to me one day and started talking and then we sat down and we spoke for hours. And I let him have it, ay. "Why are you all mokoed up? What's that Jah Rastafari got to do with our Maoritanga?"

And he says, "Well, you know, it's not that difficult, dread."

And I'm thinking, "Wow," you know, "stop calling me dread."

But he explained to me why he wore his moko from a Biblical point of view and a Maori point of view and even from his own point of view. The result of the conversation was that I thought I owed it to him to check this guy out.

I thought, "I'm gonna check this dude out. Either he's onto something. Or he's just full of shit."

So I went back to the wing and I did something that I had never done since I was a little kid. I grabbed The Bible. And I started reading it, cos he used to quote a lot from The Bible. I had just turned twenty-one at that time. Now I'm thirty-four, just about to turn thirty-five.

I started reading a few passages and what was blowing me away was it wasn't that I was searching for the scripture that he had given me, it just sort of seemed that when I opened it up the first one I read was one of the ones he'd given me out in the yard. And I was thinking, "Aw wow! This is getting a bit mind-blowing. Here I am, I've just opened it up and boom."

So I'm checking through The Bible and I'm coming to all these scriptures that he's just finished quoting to me out in the yard.

So I was checking everything he told me. And I was studying my Bible. And I was challenging everything he said. I wasn't just taking it for granted. If I wasn't happy with his reasoning, I'd say, "You gotta do better than that."

But then he gives me some more and I go back and check it out and, hello, I'm finding what he told me again. So from the Biblical point of view he already had me hooked. Then I needed to check it from the Maori point of view. But he was able to speak Maori. And I have a huge respect for my culture, so that meant a lot to me. No matter what organisation I belong to I will always respect my culture. That takes a bit longer, explaining things from the Maori perspective, but he simplifies it down to a point where I think, "Sheez."

He got me when he explained about the moko. Then again I can only say that he explained it from his own perspective, through his own searching and understanding of his culture. I can't say what he told me was true and therefore true and applicable to every Maori who's got a moko because I believe every Maori who's got a moko will have their own interpretation and their own perception of what it means to them. And I now have that same understanding for myself. He basically put it down to me that our ancestors were such a humble people that they thought: who were they to have a face like God.

And I thought, "Whadyu mean?"

"Well, you know, they believed that they were sinners. And to hide their sins they covered their face with the moko. It was a symbol of their feeling that they didn't have the right to carry the image of God."

And I was devastated by that because that was the first time I'd ever heard something like that. Then again I've got to make sure to tell you that that was just where *he* was coming from. But I agreed. I can't be exact why I agreed. But I went away and I thought about that and I was so blown away by his interpretation that I thought, "Wow!" Because I remember when I went away to boarding school at Te Aute

College. And I had a Maori teacher there. And he explained to me that when you see all the Maori carvings in the meeting house and the heads don't look human, the reason that they carved them in such a nature was because they thought that they never had the right to carve the face of God onto wood. And I remembered my teacher telling me that as I went to sleep that night. And I was blown away cos I thought, "Wow, Chris has basically just told me the same thing but with the carving on a person, on a human, in the form of a moko," (clicks his fingers) so I was hooked.

Then I asked to get moved out of East Wing so I could go to West 2 where he was, cos what was happening was the two wings weren't allowed to work together. And I used to sneak around there into his cell. And the screws used to keep kicking me out.

I was taking heaps of risks to go round and see Chris. Whenever they caught me I'd have to go down to the pound and do seven days pound. You get locked up for twenty-three hours at a time. The only contact you have with anything outside your cell is a little hole in your door. But I didn't care. I thought it was worth it because I was learning something.

The other thing that was happening was that inside myself I felt myself pulling away from the Mob. That was a big huge risk. My life was on the line.

A lot of the Mob members were seeing me and Chris together all the time, every day. And they were wondering what we were up to. Some of them would ask and I'd say, "It's simple, bro. He's teaching me a lot about myself, a lot about my culture." I didn't tell them that I was reading The Bible. Cos what I was doing was I was reading The Bible and I was hiding it away under my pillow. I didn't want them to know that I was reading The Bible cos that was a big no-no with the Mob, ay. You couldn't do that. They always knew that that was the beginning of one of the members pulling away from the ranks. Most guys that got into The Bible became Christians. There's an old scripture that you cannot serve two gods. And that's true. You cannot serve God and the Mob. You cannot sit at the tables of angels and partake and you cannot sit at the tables of devils and partake. Somewhere along the line you have to make a decision, your own decision which table you want to sit at. Eventually I chose to sit at the table of my brother, Chris.

I had a good friend in the Mob who I believed would understand. I called him into the room and I said, "Aw, bro, I've got something to tell you."

He said, "Aw, what's that?"

I said, "Bro, I'm pulling out of the Mob today."

This guy's name was Maru Ratima. Now he's become a Rastafarian. He lives in Napier. He had a huge amount of respect for Chris. When he came out of prison he still stood with the Mob. But all of a sudden he pulled out and became a Rasta. I was blown away by that.

But when I told Maru I was pulling out, he just said, "Kia ora, bro, I knew that was gonna happen."

So that was okay. Then I went and seen another guy who was more or less running us, a fulla Bonz Manahi. He was involved with the Auckland Notorious group. He was sort of like the leader of us while we were in Kaitoke Prison. I went and seen him on a one-on-one. I was a bit worried because he was staunch, tough, whatever you like. But I knew I could handle it, ay. And I went and seen him and I says, "Aw, bro, I wanna have a word with you."

And he says, "Aw, well, what's up?"

And I says, "I'm pulling out of the Mob today."

And he just looked at me. I thought we were gonna have to fight it out. But he turned around and he looked at me and he says, "Good on you, bro. I'm really happy for you."

And I was really blown away. I thought, "Wow, that's not the reaction I expected." I thought we were gonna have a hard-out rumble. But he did say to me, "You might have to go back to the wing and go into a cell full of other Mobsters, bro, and maybe take a beating."

And I says, "No, I'm not taking it. I'm not taking no beating from no one."

And he just says, "Well, anyway, bro, I wish you all the best. I really do. I wish I could-a done that a long time ago. But I been here too long."

And I says, "Yeah, I think I can understand that."

So eventually I did pull out and my journey with Chris and with the movement really got going.

CHAPTER 2

DION HUTANA ESCAPES FROM PRISON

Dion Hutana: Chris was quite authoritative in his way. He didn't acknowledge authority in prison, like the officers and all this. He let them know sharply that even though we were into The Bible and all that we were the sort of crew that if we got hit on the cheek we didn't turn the other one for you to hit, too.

That's when Chris converted me to the Ringatu Church and I became involved in the Ringatu prayers. But having said all that, I'm not there now.

From all that crew of Rastas there, I'm the only one that's pulled away from it. While we were at Kaitoke, there was a fulla Edward Kotuhi, from Wairoa, and John Heeney was there, too.

I'm gonna tell you now, when we were in Kaitoke I looked after Chris. I looked after him as a friend, as back-up if there was ever any confrontation. And it was always just me and Chris, just two of us. And I don't mind telling you this part if it's not gonna be put out of context or get me into trouble and that is, you know, that we smoked marijuana as part of our Rasta thing, and I looked after him in that sense. And I used to get a lot of it. I had good contacts on the outside world to get it brought in. Now I don't mind telling you that but I don't want it to get me into trouble while I'm in here.

But what I will tell you now is that I have given up smoking marijuana. It has been hard for me the last four years. But something inside of me all of a sudden gave me the strength and discipline to give it up and now it's not so hard.

But yes I used to get us a good healthy supply all the time because he never had too many of his family visiting because they were too far away.

Up in Paremoremo Chris was put into the wing with the Headhunters. The screws were trying to get him wasted. But I think it turned on them.

See, they thought that if they stuck Chris in A Block the Headhunters would take him out. I don't know what their motive behind that really was. I think they saw him as a threat because he was quite intelligent, ay. If you *are* intelligent in a place like this, they can't handle that, ay. They shut you down. They start setting you up. I've been through that. They set you up with gang members. The prison authorities do that. I don't care if you don't believe me. But I know it's true cos I've lived that experience. I've lived it so many times it's not funny.

When you say Chris went through a baptism of fire, well so did I. I've been through that baptism of fire where I've had to go into the yard with five gang members. And it's, "Well here I am. Let's go." And I'm not worried that I'm outnumbered cos I'm ready to go, cos the message to them all was, "Well, I don't mind. But if you want to beat me you have to kill me cos I'll be fighting to kill. I won't be fighting to win."

Chris had verbal confrontations and spiritual confrontations in Paremoremo. But it never became physical. In the end Wayne Doyle, who was running the Headhunters in there, became very good friends with Chris. Chris became like a little brother to Wayne. Wayne looked after him, which was new, because even the other Headhunters were jealous of his relationship with Wayne. That's what I could gather from what Chris had told me.

Chris could handle himself with his mouth as well as his fists. He would never back away from a fight because he knew he could handle himself. I knew that too, from experience. We often used to have a few spars so to speak, in the cell, no one else used to see. Sometimes it was bare-knuckle, sometimes we might wrap a towel around our fists. He was an ex-boxer while I used to do kick-boxing. So we used to share a bit of our knowledge. We'd train together, pump weights, we did everything together.

Tape recorded note to myself after a conversation with Cody Haua: Cody said the prison officials kept trying to put Chris Campbell in dangerous wings in the prison. They'd put him in with the Black Power and then the Mongrel Mob, trying to put him in situations where he'd either get killed or severely beaten.

Apparently on one occasion, Chris knew these guys were coming to waste him. And he got down on his knees and said a karakia and he felt his arm getting stronger. And he got up and these guys were there, coming into his cell. And there was a guy with an iron bar. And he went up and punched this guy so hard that he dropped the iron bar. As soon as that happened Chris just started off with his mouth, talking and talking to these guys. He was a good fighter. But he was a better talker. And before long he had sorted out the situation.

Then he was stuck in with the Mongrel Mob. Two of the guys high up in the Mob came to talk to him. They'd organised to have a hit done on Chris. It turned out these guys were related to Chris and he pointed out what their relationship was and talked them around to his side.

Then the two Mob guys who were supposed to waste Chris came down the corridor and they saw Chris standing waiting for them with the two guys who had ordered the hit. And then Chris started talking to these guys and the situation was diffused and he was okay.

Dion Hutana: I think Chris got to Kaitoke in mid '88 and he left about mid '89. It was after nine o'clock lock-up one night when they came and got him and took him away to Paremoremo. I called it kidnapping. I believe they kidnapped him. They couldn't handle him. He had too many people following him and they didn't like the way he used to talk to the authorities. They became afraid of him. I was the first one in prison to follow him. Then there was old Ed Kotuhi. Me and Ed Kotuhi were really close.

The expression Chris used to use about himself was that he was a fisher of men… like Jesus.

After they kicked Chris out, well I was devastated. So I turned rebellious. I got a job back in the kitchen. And I ended up escaping.

It took me three months to suss it out, ay. I used to run the yard every day. And as I did that I planned the routine I was gonna use. There was only one part of it that I needed to be sure about and that was whether I'd be caught on camera when I was on the roof. So I'd run around the compound every night and as I'd run past the guard house I'd glance through the window at all the security TV screens. I couldn't just stop there and look in at all the screens to find the one that showed the roof and to check out just how much it showed. I didn't want to look too suspicious. I just had to keep running. Until one day I got a glimpse. I ran past. I looked in the window and I saw exactly what I needed to see, just like that. And I just carried on running. I knew the camera had only half the view of the roof. So I planned to escape on the 12th of September, '89.

I got hold of a hacksaw blade and I cut my way through the bars in the window the night before. I filled the gap up with soap cos it went with the same colour as the white paint on the bars. Then I got these little pebbles from the yard cos there was two doorways I had to block cos I knew once I got out they'd chase me and they could still catch me on the premises. And I realised if I block these two doorways they have to go the long way around. So that's what the little pebbles were for, so I could stick them in the keyholes. So they couldn't get their keys in to open them.

And I timed it so it was five to nine when we left, just before lock-up, cos I also knew that if someone had escaped they gotta lock the prison down first before they come and get me, which gave me at least a good twenty minutes headstart. And that's all I needed.

So when I was ready I pulled the bar off, went through. It was me and Ed Kotuhi. We went through, ran along the fence line, up on the roof, walked the edge so we're out of the camera's sight, got down, cut my way through the fence, pulled Ed through then I went through. Then I pulled out a big bag of pepper that I'd taken from the kitchen. And I doused that whole area in pepper so that when they brought the dogs down to chase us the pepper would block our scent and the dogs wouldn't be able to find us. I was told later that the officer broke down and cried his eyeballs out cos his dog died on him. And we ran into the forest. And up until this point we did everything we were meant to do. But this is where it turned right against me in the end.

All I meant to do was go to Ruatoria, pick up some herb, go to Auckland and go to the U2 concert – I used to really like U2 – and hand myself back in at Paremoremo, because that's where Chris was.

I bumped into one of the dread, Hurae Wairau, from Flaxmere. He'd been up in Paremoremo with Chris. And I ended up getting another seven years on my five. It ended up I was doing twelve and a half in the end. And that was because I attempted to burn the Ruatoria pub down. And the reason why I did that was because I was told that that's where the police and the CIB used to put boot polish on their faces and go and kidnap all the dread and beat them up. Now we'd been made to look like we'd told lies about all that sort of stuff. But in actual fact it was all true. But, you know, who would believe us. We haven't got any credibility. But because the police are the police they've got all the credibility. And that's why I wanted to burn the pub down cos it was like a central point where they all gathered. But we couldn't get it started because it was a bit damp. And we ended up burning down the Ngati Porou Marae. In retrospect I would rather the pub had burnt down.

We were just driving along after trying to burn down the pub. It was after midnight some time. And Hurae goes, "Aw that's the marae, dread."

"What marae's that one, bro?"

"That's where the police were camping when they were hunting the dread down."

I said, "Stop the car."

I got out of the car, ran over there. But I just didn't blatantly go and burn it down. I stood in front of it and I had a korero to it. And I told that marae I was gonna burn it down. I had a word with the ancestors and told them. I talked to that marae. I said, "You've got the mana. You can stop me. Just give me any little sign and I'm outa here." But I didn't feel that. Even if I had-a just felt the hair on the back of my head stand up I would-a been outa there. But I didn't.

I'm not gonna get in trouble saying this, am I?

I used a box of matches, just a box of matches. I started it around the back. I don't know. Maybe I should step inside myself and decide it's okay to be told cos I've never really told anyone before.

But, yeah, that's what I did. And we got away. We went up to Whareponga and we camped up at a place called the Pangi which is just below Whakaahu Hill.

A MARAE IS BURNED DOWN

Wednesday, September 20, 1989: Police and fire investigators are back in Ruatoria this morning after two more arsons.

One was at Ngati Porou Marae, where the meeting house was destroyed and the dining room was damaged. The other was at the Manutahi Hotel, where there was minimal damage to a toilet.

Te Aranga Church, which is situated on the marae, was undamaged. It was opened only last June. The previous church, which was over a hundred years old, was burned to the ground on March 15, 1987.

Earlier in the night, the marae caretaker, who lives in a caravan at the rear of the site, had checked the building when his dog began barking furiously. He noticed the fire because his dog began to bark again.

Ruatoria Chief Fire Officer Ken McKinnon says that by the time they arrived there were flames shooting out the window of the dining room.

The fire was contained fairly quickly and the dining room is expected to be repairable.

Police and fire officers have sealed off the marae and started to dismantle part of the roof to allow light into the gutted building.

Thursday, September 21: *In Ruatoria, the shock over the arson of the marae is giving way to sadness and frustration.*

"I never thought this would happen," says Erana Harrison, who has cared for Ngati Porou's meeting house and church at Kariaka Marae for over sixty years. "How could they do a thing like this to a meeting house?"

When Erana saw the flames, she thought the newly-rebuilt church had been attacked by arsonists again.

But this time it's a century-old meeting house, which, even after nearly forty arsons is a shock, because most assumed their marae was too sacred a place for the firelighters.

"It is as if all our work over the years has been for nothing," Erana says. "It makes you think about all the old people, the photos of tipuna and those who died in the war... they're all gone."

Erana Harrison is probably the closest person to Kariaka Marae, where Ngati Porou stood for about a century.

"It makes me wonder if they are attacking me or whether it is some sort of vendetta against the family."

The other target of Tuesday night's arson attacks, the Manutahi Hotel, is run by members of the Harrison family.
Some people are wondering if the fact that police personnel had stayed at the hotel and the marae during earlier operations, such as the hunt for Chris Campbell, Hata Thompson and Cody Haua following the kidnapping of Laurie Naden, had given cause for someone to hold a grudge.

Bob Kaa speaks for almost everyone in Ruatoria when he says: "As a citizen of this town I deplore what has happened. I am bloody angry.

The Gisborne Herald, Saturday, September 23, 1989: It was like a recurring bad dream for Ruatoria this week. The lull in the burnings is over. The attacks on the Ngati Porou meeting house and Manutahi Hotel were clearly designed to evoke maximum shock and anger.

The hand that set the fires showed a new level of callousness towards the feelings of elders. In the destruction of Ngati Porou's meeting house it is apparent that absolutely nothing remains sacred to the arsonists.

The senseless, random torchings of Ruatoria's public buildings, homes and woolsheds have touched everyone and some many times over.

People of the marae again found themselves shedding their tears for the history wrapped up in their marae, for the photographs of their tipuna and for the warped wisdom that appears to motivate such violation.

They are tears of rage at the affront to the mana of a marae, the contempt and hate expressed towards something so totally Maori.

It was not just Ngati Porou that burned on Wednesday. The fire was lit under all Maoridom. As one of the many victims put it, "the hurt goes too deep to describe".

Dion Hutana: We virtually got caught by the Armed Offenders Squad, which was quite scary at the time but also a relief. Had the vigilantes got hold of us before them I don't believe I'd be alive today. So I was quite pleased to be caught by the police. But even then they weren't much help because it was almost like they wanted to throw me out on the street with all the vigilantes. All the vigilantes were outside the police station with their guns. It wasn't even very nice in the cop shop because the police were threatening to kill me.

So I got to the Gisborne cells and this is the funny thing about it. What I didn't know when I had done this was that John Heeney, Dick Maxwell and Chris were at the Gisborne cop shop. They had been subpoenaed to give evidence in Robbie Grace's murder trial.

Anyway, I got arrested. I represented myself. They kept it a closed court.

Sunday, December 3, 1989: *Hurae Wairau becomes the first inmate to escape from Mangaroa Prison. The twenty-million-dollar prison began accepting inmates only a month ago.*

Wairau's returning from the prison chapel with other inmates at about 11am when he makes his escape. He has an injured leg but manages to scale a three-metre fence (the fencing hasn't been completed yet) and hobble away to freedom under the cover of a forest.

Wairau already faces charges of arson and assisting two escaped prisoners. He was on bail when he was arrested on a host of additional charges at 2am on Friday, when police were investigating several burglaries at Stortford Lodge.

During the arrest, Wairau bit police dog handler Barry Skjottrup on the cheek, and was himself bitten on the leg by the constable's dog.

Wairau's facial tattoos ensure he stands out in any crowd. The Lion of Judah, framed by a 12-point star is on his forehead. He has a page of the Bible on each cheek, as well as the name of Rastafarian icon, Haile Selassie, the late Emperor of Ethiopia. And he has the number 13 tattooed on his chin.

*****Tuesday, January 2, 1990:*** *The Armed Offenders Squad arrest Hurae Wairau at a Flaxmere house at 11am today. Police go to the house in Montrose Street after receiving a tip-off from a member of the public. Wairau has been on the run from police for almost a month.*

Friday, May 4, 1990: *Hurae Wairau, facing charges of escaping from Mangaroa Prison, continually disrupts his own trial in the Napier District Court.*

The twenty-four year old refuses to plead, claiming the trial is unjust, interrupts counsel and, while one witness is in the dock, he lets out a scream that silences the stunned judge, jurors and public for one minute. He's sent to a holding cell because of his disruptive behaviour then, when he's called back to court, refuses to leave the cell.

The jury takes twenty minutes to find him guilty and Judge J.D. Tucker sentences him to nine months in prison.

CHAPTER 3

TRIO IN COURT FOR MARAE ARSON

Tuesday, March 13, 1990: *Dion Hutana, Eddie Kotuhi and Hurae Wairau appear in the Gisborne District Court for a depositions hearing into the arson of the Ngati Porou meeting house and the attempted arson of the Manutahi Hotel. Hutana and Kotuhi are also charged with escaping from prison and Wairau with being an accessory after the escape.*

Hutana tells the court that he had only been in the Ruatoria area to visit Mount Zion. Mount Hikurangi is the holy mountain and he was going there to build a tabernacle for the Lord.

But the court hears that in a statement to Detective Sergeant Gary Condon, Hutana admitted lighting both the fires, saying he had done so because of a revealing prophecy.

"I was prophesised," he said in a signed statement taken two days after the fires, in September last year.

All three are acting for themselves.

Erana Harrison and thirteen police and fire service witnesses give evidence. Each witness is asked if they believe in God. Maori witnesses are questioned about kawa mate, according to which, Wairau contends, a person guilty of setting fire to a meeting house would be struck dead or porangi (demented) or suffer some other ill fate.

Most acknowledge this belief but decline to comment, although one witness says it might yet happen.

The three accused say they want a marae hearing, outside Pakeha jurisdiction.

Wairau says, "Our tipuna (ancestors) did not sign the Treaty of Waitangi which gives power to the law of the Pakeha."

But Erana Harrison responds: "A real Maori would not do that sort of thing, because to a real Maori a meeting house is more taboo than the church." As a person with both Pakeha and Maori ancestry, she says, she accepts the Queen's sovereignty. And as an elder of Ngati Porou she knows her tikanga Maori but also accepts the Pakeha laws.

Wairau says the three accused don't acknowledge the court system. It's a Maori issue that should be taken back to the marae. "It's a known fact that any Rastafarian cannot have a fair trial on a charge of arson in New Zealand."

"You should have thought about that before you lit the fire," says Mrs Harrison.

She tells the accused she knows they're guilty because their elders had come from Kahungunu to tangi at Ngati Porou and apologise for the actions of their mokopuna.

The old people knew who did it because their mokopuna told them that "Jah had told them to".

On September 19, Wairau approached his next door neighbour in Hastings, Alo Faalele, seeking a ride to Ruatoria. Faalele tells the court he gave Hutana, Wairau and Kotuhi a ride, arriving at Ruatoria about 1am on September 20, and stopping in Ruatoria's main street.

Hutana and Wairau got out of the car and went somewhere, returning about fifteen minutes later, seeking to go to the marae.

The Crown contends that during this fifteen minutes the pair set fire to the nearby Manutahi Hotel by setting alight a rubbish bin with beer crates piled on it in a toilet block.

Faalele tells the court that on arriving at Ngati Porou Marae, the pair again got out of the car and went to the back of the meeting house. He heard glass breaking and then saw flames coming from the building before seeing Hutana and Wairau sprinting back to the car demanding to be taken away. From there they had gone to Whareponga Beach, where they spent the night in an unused shearers quarters.

The following morning Faalele had taken Wairau back to Ruatoria, where he obtained groceries to take to Hutana and Kotuhi at the quarters, before returning to Hawke's Bay.

Much later, when Wairau sought help while running from the police, Faalele had asked him why he burned the meeting house. Wairau said it was because he didn't like the man who owned it, who was a Pakeha. Faalele had only been in New Zealand a short time. He hadn't known the building was a meeting house until Wairau told him.

Notes taken by the late Dr Harold Turner, an expert on tribal religions, after visiting the Rastas in Mangaroa Prison, Hawkes Bay, in September 1990: Sister Maureen re chapel services (which are voluntary): R's and "fundamentalists" attend chapel – latter see former as in grip of the Devil. Neither side can communicate with other. R's used to be a problem all round – disruptive conduct.

Shouting "Jah" endlessly at any time. Other prisoners annoyed.

Disruptive in chapel – heads down reading own Bibles and ignoring the service, or wanting to speak at great length on their beliefs and not easily controlled.

Less so now.

She sees rehab. And discipline potential in R community.

HAKA PERFORMED IN COURT

Monday, October 29, 1990: The trial of Dion Hutana and Hurae Wairau is set to begin in the High Court in Gisborne.

When they're brought into the courtroom, the pair perform a haka then yell "Jah!" They're taken back down to the cells and Mr Justice Wylie says they can return provided they behave themselves.

Later, they request to have their trial held on a marae. Mr Justice Wylie tells them this is just an ordinary criminal trial, which can only be held in a court.

"The Crown has brought the charges, not individual Maori people, the tribe whose meeting house was burned or the owners of the hotel. I cannot accede to the requests of the accused."

Hutana asks for the trial to be adjourned so that Chris Campbell can appear as a McKenzie friend (a person appointed to represent their interests in court). The judge grants the adjournment. The trial will proceed with Campbell present.

Former Senior Sergeant Alan Davidson: Chris Campbell was far more cleverer than me. He would spit in your face and then apologise. And I'd think, "You… fuck, you've outwitted me again. Fuck you."

No wonder he had Ruatoria eating out of the palm of his hand.

He was quite a charismatic sort of character. I was never frightened physically by him but I knew that he was a lot more cleverer than me, and that rather scared me. You know how you sum people up? And you do it automatically. And sometimes you can be way off beam. But this guy, he was clever. He could sum you up.

And he could play to the crowd. I'll tell you a *minor* example of Chris Campbell: The activist Tame Iti. I don't know how clever Tame Iti is, but the media seem attracted to him and he *seems* to be able to control the media and he appears very sincere. But at the same time he can suddenly go on attack, like when he smacked that cameraman with the spear. Now Chris Campbell could switch from good to aggressive five or six times faster than that and he was five or six times cleverer, too.

I remember Chris came down from Pare one time to give evidence. And he was saying to me, "Aaaay, they don't bring ordinary wardens down for me, brother. This man here, this man is 2IC of Pare. That's me. I'm no ordinary bloody prisoner." And it was true. The guy was the 2IC of Pare.

Tuesday, October 30: The trial begins with Campbell, Hutana and Wairau present. Shortly before noon, Hutana and Wairau again decide to remain in the court cells during the trial.

Mr Justice Wylie tells the court both men will be given the notes of evidence so they have the chance to cross-examine if they wish. "At present the indications are that they will be taking no further part in the proceedings."

The accused then ask to make an appearance in chambers and as a result Hutana and Wairau change their pleas to guilty to the arson of the marae and the attempted arson of the hotel. Hutana also pleads guilty to escaping from prison, while Wairau pleads guilty to assisting Hutana and Ed Kotuhi to avoid arrest, knowing that they'd escaped.

Friday, November 2, 1990: *Before being sentenced, Hutana and Wairau are allowed to address the court. Wairau says the reason* *the meeting house was burned was because "the Ngati Porou people were traitors to Te Kooti's movement".*

Hutana says the people were not only traitors to Te Kooti but to the Maori people and God. "I have no remorse for that meeting house being burned. The only remorse I have is that it was not totally destroyed."

HUTANA LEAVES THE RASTAS

Dion Hutana: We got seven years. We did our lag. And we all ended up here in Mangaroa in a wing together. And we all mokoed our mokos together. Chris already had his done. John Heeney had part of his done. I only had my top thing done.

But I've gone over mine because my heart wasn't with Rastafari any more. I had Atua Kaharau, which is Maori for Almighty God written on top of my head. And I had Haile Selassie written over here. I'm not saying I regretted being a Rastafari cos I loved it. I loved Chris. My journey at that stage of my life was like any other journey: It was a learning experience.

But what happened was – and I'll be honest with you – I was in a real bad state of mind psychologically. This would have been about '92. It was after Chris had died. And I was in a bad way. Psychologically, I was suicidal. But I didn't show it because it was too dangerous. If you show that, before you know it, they've put you in a mental institution. So I kept it hidden but inside myself I knew I was suicidal, ay. It was sort-a like the path or journey I was on no longer had *heart* for me. I felt like I was going nowhere, fast. I ended up being down the pound for something. I can't remember what it was. But for three days and three nights I cried. I couldn't stop crying.

And I realised that my time with the dread and with Rastafari had come to an end. And I was disappointed in myself that I never had the, I don't know, the strength, the intelligence to walk that path and to carry on walking it. But I believe if your heart is not in it, there's no point in continuing that way. So I took another decision to pull away from a group. And I did.

This friend of mine knew I wasn't happy with my moko. And he said, "Bro, this guy I know can do a new one over the top. He can redesign it and give you one exactly as you want it."

I looked at him and said, "Yeah? How much is it gonna cost?" Cos that was the burning question.

And he said, "Na, he said he would do it for nothing."

"Let's go and see him now."

So we went around there. And it just so happens I've got a mate in Wellington who owns his own hair-dressing place. And I walks in there to see if he's seen this guy, Shane, who's going to do the moko. And who's getting his hair cut? Shane. And I walk up to him and I look him in the eye, and I said, "Are you fair dinkum?" And I looked at him and I saw the strength in his eyes.

And he said, "Yeah."

I said, "Yeah, I know this man can do it." And him being an Irishman, you know, made it more intriguing for me.

He said, "When do you wanna do it?"

I said, "Well, when are you free next?"

He says, "I'll have to go through my appointment book." And then he says, "In a month's time. That'll give you time to prepare. The only other time I'm free is in three days time."

"Three days time."

"Yeah?"

"Yeah."

"Aw, wow."

I says, "Don't you worry about the pain. You leave that up to me. I'll deal with that."

And he did it and, aw, I loved it, ay. It took him seven and a half hours the first day. But what I liked about him was he was honest enough to say, "Aw, bro, my wrist is sore."

And I said, "Well, that's enough. I'll come back in two weeks time and you can finish it off."

So I'm really happy with this. And I told him afterwards, "You've really honoured me."

And he said, "No the honour was mine."

ARSON A "SPUR OF THE MOMENT THING"

Burning the marae was a spur of the moment thing. I didn't plan the marae. It was just when we drove past a guy mentioned it. And right there and then without even thinking, I did it… without even thinking. But the police made it sound like it was all Chris's fault. It may have looked like Chris was behind it. But I can give you my word it wasn't that way because I didn't really know much about it. I know Chris had told me about this marae once. But I had forgotten all about that. And it wasn't until when we drove past and the dread that was in the car with me said, "That's the marae."

And, like I said, it was the spur of the moment. I didn't think. In hindsight I wish I had-a thought about it. I most probably would not have done it. But I was really rebellious, ay. I suppose I was looking for some way of making my own name. But I could be honest enough to say that it was a silly thing to do because it cost me dearly, cos I had to do another seven years of my life. But then again it may have been a blessing in itself too cos I pulled away from the dread.

But the story that it was Chris that told me to burn the marae down is absolutely rubbish. I am aware that the people in Ruatoria and the police all say that Chris was behind the marae being burnt down and that I came specially on his orders to burn it down. But that's not how it was.

I don't know if I should tell you this. But I do know that Chris was really rapt with me when I did it… because if I hadn't-a done it, he would've.

Detective Sergeant Gary Condon: I locked up Dion Hutana. He was from Waipukurau in the central Hawke's Bay originally.

Now I interviewed him for about four to five hours. He was a strange guy: very deep. But he finally admitted trying to set fire to the pub. And he'd *really* tried to set fire to it judging by the scorch marks. If it had caught it would have gone down in ten minutes. He eventually said, "Yeah, I lit the fires."

The point I'm making is that we knew that Hutana had been in prison with Campbell – who'd moved from Pare to Kaitoke prior to his release - and he'd been instructed by Campbell to light the fires.

I remember saying to Hutana at one stage in the interview, "Did Campbell put you up to this?" He didn't say yes but he acknowledged that he knew Campbell and that they'd had communication with each other. I'm quite satisfied in my own mind that Campbell got him to escape and go up there and burn those buildings. Hutana came up to Ruatoria with two other guys.

And it would surprise me if Campbell wasn't controlling the Rastafarians' operations the whole time he was in prison because in my book they were a headless bunch without him. We thought that John Heeney might be able to do something with them but he got locked up himself for four years for arson.

Dion Hutana: There was talk about various reasons why I burnt the Ngati Porou marae down. And they all came into it, ay. But to me, I'm telling you that the bottom line was it was a spur of the moment. It had nothing to do with the marae facing the wrong way or because the cops were living on it when they were hunting the dread down or that the place was built and commemorated to Te Kooti. Those were all part of the reasons. But as the guy that burnt it down I'm telling you it was just a spur of the moment. As for the people saying he told me to do it, that's just a load of rubbish. That's why I think I broke down, ay, cos I sort of blamed myself for when he got killed. I don't think I have a right to have felt that way. But I did cos I was so close to this guy and I was so looking forward to getting out of prison and going to live with him up there cos he said, "When you get out I'll give you a little bit of land." I don't even know if he was going to own land. But he reckoned he was gonna give me some. And then again I'm not even sure that I would-a gone up there to live. But I would've gone up there regularly just to visit, have a cup of tea, maybe smoke a joint with him. But I think I would've been more prepared to live here, where I'm really from. And when he died I felt ripped off, ay. Cos he was only a young man.

Former Detective Rex Harrison: Everyone who represented the establishment was a baldhead. And the Williams families were considered baldheads. And I think the churches were burnt because the Williams families built them.

But in saying that my great, great, great grandfather was one of the early Church of England ministers on the coast. He was a Maori guy. Rangi a Kawhia, Eruera Kawhia: They were all Maori ministers. I don't think they called it Church of England at the time. They called it Hahi

Mihinari, or Missionary Church. But they were ministers who would have been trained by the Williamses.

But there was also a strong passing down of the Maori beliefs as well. See, what happened in my family, there was one great, great, great grandfather who was in the church. Then his son was within the church and so on until they got to my grandfather, Dan Kawhia, who although he was associated with the church, was not a minister. He was a farmer. But he still remained connected to the church, taking choir practises and things like that. And if you look back into the history of each of these ancestors, on the male side, they all had only one son.

And it's still going on today. In my family there's a brother and a sister and mum is our connection to the Kawhia family.

We actually lived on that Ngati Porou Marae. I lived in there as a kid. My grandparents brought me up. I'm not sure what was happening at the other maraes. But that specific marae was like a house to us as kids. We had little baches under the pine trees behind the marae. And when my grandfather died in the early fifties we stayed on at that marae. And actually the marae proper was facing directly to Ruatoria.

There was a reconstruction done on it at one stage and it was actually turned sideways so it faced the road.

Then it was burnt some years later, of course, and I'm not too sure if it's been built on the same site. There was a slight variation I think.

But there was a lot of heartache over what happened at that marae. It's like anything. Although it might have been the last straw for our people, whadya do? How can you improve it? I know for a fact that certain forms of compensation were offered by members of the offender's family. But we're still waiting for that. The sad part of it was the old marae was not insured.

But we're fortunate that we're in a position to have a good bank balance from fund-raising and also with the amalgamation with the kohanga reo, there was a subsidy involved which certainly helped in rebuilding the new marae.

Former Sergeant John Robinson: There was another incident before Luke Donnelly came on the scene. There was a murder in Hawke's Bay. The guy who did it was called Shortland. And the word was that he was hiding on the East Coast.

They described the guy who brought Shortland up the coast. And I spotted this guy in Ruatoria one day and rang up and said, "He's up here. He's in Ruatoria."

We shot down to Whareponga later on and we saw his car parked on the track that leads up to where Lance Kupenga was beheaded.

So the armed offenders went up there early one morning and caught this guy.

The Rastas had given him permission to hide in their hut on Whakaahu Hill.

Chris Campbell had made a lot of friends and connections in jail and even though he was still inside, he put the word out, "If you want to hide out, the Rastas will help you."

Lawyer Denis Kohn: If Chris kept off this Rastafari and all this rubbishy stuff that he used to quote from The Bible, which was a bit of Chris and a bit of The Bible, he was really quite a clever guy. I don't know whether it was the protracted consumption of dope or what, but he was just tunnel-visioned or tunnel-minded about the Rastafari, the movement and coupled with getting their own land back it was a real obsession.

He never seemed to be high when I was in his presence. From the socio-economic group that he belonged to, and I'm not being smart or anything like that, he had a better vocabulary than most of his peers. He was a funny sort of a mixture. He'd be talking about something for three or four minutes and you'd be right on track. And all of a sudden some phrase or something would come in, which had nothing to do with anything that had preceded it, some of this Rastafarian bullshit would come in or he would make some comment that really cut across the thrust of what he'd been saying and you'd think, "Where the hell did you get that from? What's that got to do with what we're talking about?" He'd just go boing. Then a couple of seconds later he'd be right back on track again. I don't know what you call that. But he was a curious guy to talk to. Man he could talk. Not ranting, because he never got hyped up or started shouting, and not a ramble either because he was very sincere. He really meant what he was saying, which is probably why he had all these, I suppose you could say, disciples. Because that fellow Eddie Kotuhi from Wairoa, he was just a boy in comparison. And I'm not surprised… you get locked up with Campbell for a couple of months, as Eddie was, and he says, "That meeting house is facing the wrong way. When you get out boy, you burn it down." That's what he did.

While they were inside, Chris convinced Eddie and Dion Hutana that this particular meeting house was facing the wrong way and that it would have to go. It was like that TV programme: "Your mission, Jim, if you should choose to accept it." And Campbell said, "When you get out, that meeting house has to come down."

For Chris to be able to convince those guys that this is what they must do - and in fact they did it after they got out and weren't under his physical control - is quite surprising.